# FISHING SECRETS
# OF THE EXPERTS

# FISHING SECRETS OF THE EXPERTS

Edited by Vlad Evanoff

Drawings by the Editor

DOUBLEDAY & COMPANY, INC.

GARDEN CITY, NEW YORK

# ACKNOWLEDGMENTS

The editor wishes to thank the following for supplying photos which were used in this book: The Canadian Government Travel Bureau; Florida State News Bureau; Kiekhaefer Corporation; Milwaukee *Journal;* Minnesota Division of Publicity; Ohio Department of Natural Resources; Ontario Department of Travel and Publicity, and the Oregon State Highway Commission. Also Pete Barrett, Dave Edwardes, and Dick Matt for use of their photos. Photographs otherwise unidentified are from the authors of the various chapters.

# FOREWORD

THERE are so many game fish found in both fresh and salt water that it is almost impossible for any one angler to have an intimate and extensive knowledge about each one of these fish. The best any angler can do in his lifetime is to choose a single fish and spend as much time as he can fishing for that species, studying its habits, and perfecting methods and techniques for catching it.

The same thing applies to the different methods or types of fishing. Not many anglers are equally skilled in fly fishing, spinning, still fishing, bottom fishing, trolling, surf fishing, or offshore fishing. Usually a fisherman concentrates on one or two methods and becomes expert in that particular field.

So when the idea for this book was conceived, some of the top anglers in the country were approached. Men who were outstanding or expert at catching a certain species of fish or skilled in a specific method of fresh- or salt-water fishing. Many of these anglers are well known in the fishing world and have national reputations. Others are better known locally or in certain areas. But they all have one thing in common. They are highly skilled at catching the fish they write about.

Most of the angler-contributors to this book have spent many years seeking a certain species of fish. Others have concentrated on a certain type of fishing and are considered authorities on that method. For example, when a fisherman hears the name Lee Wulff he immediately thinks of Atlantic salmon. Joe Brooks is closely associated with fly fishing in salt water. Frank Woolner is linked with striped bass. Think of Emmett Gowen and you immediately visualize catfishing on the big, broad rivers of the South. Joseph Bates, Jr., is Mr. Spinning since he was one of the first to introduce and write about spinning in this country. You'll find all these anglers in this book and many others equally renowned in the sport of fishing.

These fishing experts were asked to distill their experiences and knowledge and put down on paper the most important tips, hints, gimmicks, or "secrets" used in catching their favorite fish. They were asked to concentrate mainly on the most effective methods and techniques used in catching the fish. The result is a "how-to-do-it" book which by-passes the trivial and concentrates on the important, vital details of tackle, fish habits, and the deadliest methods of lure presentation and manipulation.

This book is not an anthology of previously published articles. All of the chapters for this book are specially written and are original and up-to-date. You'll find many new tips and hints about both fresh- and salt-water fishing which are used and known by that small group of highly skilled anglers who catch most of the fish.

VLAD EVANOFF

# CONTENTS

*Contents*

8

# ILLUSTRATIONS

*Illustrations*

# FISHING SECRETS
# OF THE EXPERTS

Don Shiner

## Chapter One

# TROUT ON NATURAL BAIT

### *by* DON SHINER

DON SHINER hails from Nescopeck, Pennsylvania, where he spends his time writing, fly-tying, and taking photos—when it doesn't interfere with his fishing. He has fished for a wide variety of species, but admits that he enjoys most the trout and bass fishing found in his home state. Having served with the Air Force in the South Pacific as an aerial photographer, he ranks as one of the country's top outdoor photographers. His photos and writing appear regularly in national magazines. He contributes two chapters to this book—on live-bait fishing for trout and bass.

BIG, hook-jawed brown trout, the kind that require measuring with yardsticks rather than the usual 12-inch rules, inhabit many streams in the northern latitudes of this continent. Most anglers will attest to the fact that these cagey browns have gained wisdom with age and do not succumb readily to just any lure. One group of fishermen, however, racks up these lunker trout—trophies that range from 20 to a whopping 28 or 30 inches in length—with amazing consistency. These are the minnow-men, schooled and skilled in the techniques of swimming a minnow effectively in the deep holes, the undercut banks, the log jams where the lunkers locate. In some cases the successful angler may also have earned a high degree in the art of using garden worms or one of several other varieties of natural bait.

The reason for the marked success by these anglers is simply that they present these headliner trout with exactly what they prefer in the form of a mouth-size meal. When the majority of trout attain the size of a man's arm, more energy is consumed pursuing a hatching May fly or nymph burrowing in the gravel, than the trout actually derives from the insect. Hence the husky finsters insist on food in mouth-filling proportions. This usually

consists of two or three minnows with one or two crayfish or salamanders thrown into the day's bargain. These fill the hollow cavity in a hurry. Should one of the minnows darting playfully past
the trout's lair be manipulated skillfully by a minnow fisherman,
the big fellow will grab the bait with little hesitation. Providing
the tackle has no weak link in the line, leader, and rod, and the
trout does not tangle the line in some underwater debris, the trout
is landed and destined for headlines in the local newspaper.

A great deal of water flowed over the dam before I became
fully conscious of these facts of life. I spent years following the
trout trail, armed with a fly rod and a box of wet and dry flies
and nymphs. The outing was a total failure if several trout were
not kicking about in the fern-lined creel after an hour or two of
fishing. But rarely would these trout measure beyond the 14- or
15-inch mark. Most would range from the usual 7 to 12 inches in
length. Occasionally one of the larger sized trout would nail a
streamer or bucktail fly. But for the most part, for years I caught
trout that measured on the small to medium size. Then, an incident took place one day, on one of my favorite streams that
changed my fly habit.

This day I waited for the late afternoon hatch to appear when
another fisherman stepped into view on this picturesque pool.
Casting what appeared to be a minnow, he guided the bait
through the riffles against the bank, which had been undercut by
savage currents the previous spring. Suddenly, as I watched, his
rod bent almost double and he struck hard. The fish did not
break water. It thrashed around in the pool, then sailed through
the low riffles into the pool some 75 feet below. The fisherman
followed, skillfully playing the husky heavyweight. I followed
too, out of curiosity, for it was quite obvious the fish was of ex-
traordinary size. When the angler was finally able to scoop the
spent fish into his net, it proved to be a 26-inch brown trout, as
beautiful a trout as I ever dreamed existed in this stream.

This particular pool and I were no strangers. Frequently during the preceding weeks we had renewed acquaintances. Not
once did I receive any indication of the size of the trout lurking
beneath that bank. Trout that I hooked with flies in this pool
measured from 10 to 14 inches in length, small in comparison to
this angler's handsome trophy.

I expressed my interest in this angler's trout and his particular fishing technique. He quickly noticed that I had a brace of wet flies leadered, and commented, "The way I have it figured, big trout rarely show interest in small flies, aside from the time when the big Green Drake May fly is on the water. They prefer minnows, the redfins, dace, riffle chubs, or the other variety found in the run of trout streams. Chuck one of these baits in front of an old hooked-nosed brown, like this one in the net, tease it somewhat and wham! It will slam the steel like a bull slamming a barn door."

It made sense. So I resolved from that day forward, I would learn the art of minnow fishing and take a share of these trophy browns. I did not part company with my favorite rod and flies, but if it required bait to catch a few real lunker trout, it would be worth the effort and time involved mastering the technique.

That was quite a number of years ago. Since that eventful day nothing occurred to change my mind about natural bait and big trout. On the contrary, now trophy browns, brooks, and rainbows were beginning to come my way. A few hit fat dew worms immediately following an evening thunder shower that rolled through the hills. Some hit a locust or cricket. Yet the majority succumbed to the minnow. The process of learning the technique was slow and sometimes frustrating, until I realized that just any haphazard manner of flipping a minnow into the stream would simply not do. Success depends on how the minnow is fitted to steel and how it is manipulated in the stream.

Let's discuss minnow fishing and taking trout on natural bait in some detail. First, the minnow must be fresh, though it is killed prior to being sewed to the line. The swimming action depends entirely on the maneuvering which the angler imparts to the minnow as it is retrieved across stream. Methods of sewing a minnow vary between minnow-men. Five methods are shown in the illustration. Study each system carefully. There are some anglers who prefer to insert the hook through the mouth, out the gill, then spirally wind the leader material around the body and reinsert the hook near the tail. Some insist on working in the reverse manner, from tail to head. There is no objection to either style.

The skilled minnow-man whom I met this day, Kenneth Sands,

Five methods of sewing a minnow bait to the hook. All of these systems have merit.

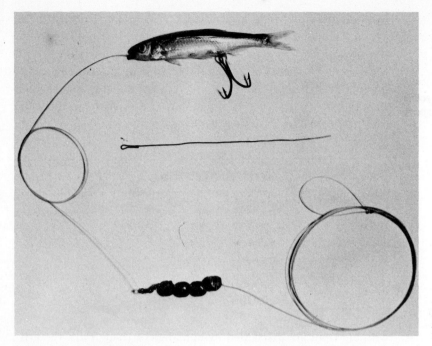

This minnow rig is especially productive of big trout. Note wire in center of photo which is used to thread leader through body of bait.

who became a close and dear friend and is to this day, developed a special rig for the bait. He employs a large darning needle, which has the eye partially cut away, to sew or thread a heavy 6-pound leader through the minnow's body. A double hook is then looped on the line in such a manner that the hooks cradle the tail. (See illustration.) About 18 inches in front of the bait, three or four big, split shot are fastened. Depending on the current of the stream on a particular day, the number of shot may vary.

Cast the bait directly across stream. The heavy weight will instantly carry the bait to the bottom. Then, with a series of short pulls sideways with the rod, the minnow is retrieved to the angler's side of the stream. It is important to permit the bait to pause and sink back toward the bottom between rod motions. Using this technique here's how the bait appears to big trout:

When the bait drops into the pool, the minnow sinks quickly

19

to the bottom and may be washed a yard or more downstream. When the angler begins the retrieve, the taut line pulls the minnow upward. A short pause then permits the heavy shot to pull the minnow down again to the bottom, in most cases with a twisting motion that represents a crippled or wounded minnow. Each time the action is executed, the minnow darts about in this slow roll. Big, hook-jawed trout visualize an easily caught meal. Few can resist the challenge!

The instant a trout strikes, set the hooks immediately for the fish will quickly expel the bait when it tastes steel. So, one must remain alert. This, with the constant casting and retrieving, is exhausting work. An hour of this exercise and your arm becomes tired.

Fly casting, including all those false casts to dry a high floater, is a very gentle art in comparison. Fortunately, the developing of the spinning rod and reel has made minnow fishing far less fatiguing and most rewarding.

One group of anglers that gives the minnow-men competition with big trout are the skilled nymph anglers, though like the artificial fly, the natural nymph is not always the best bait for the trophy-size trout. Nonetheless, it really takes trout! I met one such angler a few years ago who carried, as part of his trout tackle, a small sieve, similar to the net used by entomologists to catch butterflies. This tiny sieve was placed in the riffles below a flat stone. By overturning or partially lifting the stone, caddis larva, May fly nymphs, stone fly nymphs, waterworms, and other aquatic creatures are caught. These natural baits, for the most part tiny in size, are fitted to a No. 20 or 22 fly hook. Trout rarely resist tasting these naturals as they drift and swirl around the stones in the currents. The angler who used this method rarely experienced difficulty in catching a dozen nice trout most any hour of the day.

Meal worms fall into this category. Every gristmill or flour mill is overrun with these pesty worms. They congregate beneath damp sacks of grain or beneath stacks of moist burlap bags. The worms are roughly an inch in length, resembling very closely a caddis worm that has crawled free of its glued stick or gravel case. These meal worms are extremely fine baits for all three

The meal worm is an excellent substitute for a caddis worm. Use a small hook, preferably a size No. 12 or 14 with this bait.

species of trout, and are sold commercially under the name "golden grubs." They are also highly effective for ice fishing in the dead of winter for pan fish. For pure stream fun and excitement, try this worm on a small No. 16 or No. 18 fly hook.

Of course, with hooks and baits of this size, the leader tippet should be scaled down to the lightest possible size. A 2X tippet will work satisfactorily; better yet is a 3X size. With this light gear, drop the meal worm into the riffles, guide it around the rocks and the small whirlpools, and keep a firm grip on your hat. The action is quick and most exciting!

The centipede and millipede also work surprisingly well as baits for trout. These are the "thousand-legged" creatures found beneath rotted logs and damp leaves. In spite of their aggressive

21

appearance, these baits are perfectly harmless, so can be carried in an empty shirt pocket if nothing more suitable is available. Use a small fly hook, perhaps a size 12 or 14 with these baits. They are somewhat fragile, so cast gently and be ready when the frontal attack matures.

Recently, salmon eggs have become important in the bait line for trout. Of more recent vintage are the new "cheese eggs" or

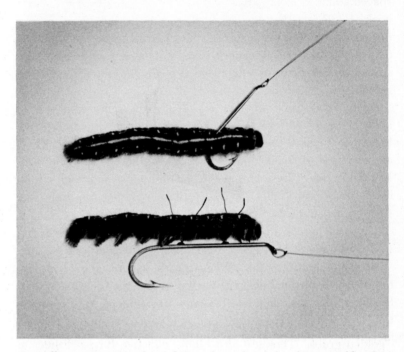

Caterpillars are top trout baits during the early weeks of June. Solder thin wires to hook shank to hold the bait in place.

tiny, pea-size cheese balls. These are used with outstanding success during the early spring months. In most cases only one egg is impaled on a small No. 12 or 14, short shank hook. Numerous fishermen claim that a gold hook has merit with this bait. There is no denying that the flash of gold adds color and sparkle to the otherwise pale white or pink bait ball.

This early spring bait should be kept rolling along the bottom stones and gravel, for trout, still numbed by the cold, icy water will rarely rise or move to any appreciable extent to intercept a passing bait. One or two split shot, attached to the leader, will keep the bait at a low level. And this added weight makes the salmon egg bait suitable for handling with a light spin-rod. This light gear can place the egg into each pocket in the stream with pin-point accuracy.

One trout angling acquaintance uses a setup of two hooks, spaced about 24 inches apart, with a salmon egg attached to each hook. He insists that he has hooked and landed many brook, brown, and rainbow trout which had both eggs in their mouth, and in some cases has caught two trout on a single cast. This speaks well of the eggs' effectiveness in the high, and sometimes roiled, spring streams.

Along about June, another excellent bait comes into prominence. This is the tent caterpillar. Trout gorge themselves on these hairy worms as they drop from overhead branches. They are somewhat difficult to attach to a hook, but the problem may be readily solved by soldering several thin wires to a long shank hook. The worm is then "wired in place" without requiring the steel to penetrate its thin skin.

Those who prefer this bait, and there are many anglers who do, solder a supply of hooks well in advance of the caterpillar season.

Drop this bait into the water beneath willow or wild cherry tree limbs that extend over the stream to give the impression that the caterpillar has fallen into the pool. Conditioned to this sort of thing for several weeks, trout will readily accept one that is attached to the angler's hook. From then on, it is the familiar and exciting story.

The last bait discussed here and one almost on a par with the minnow, at least in racking up trophy-size trout, is the common earthworm. Actually, more trout are caught each year with this soil building worm than with all other baits and lures combined.

In the early spring angry currents chew at banks and erode many worms into the stream and into the waiting jaws of nearby trout. Again, in midsummer, following a hard shower, worms find their way into the trout streams. Trout of all three species feed heavily upon this natural food and readily strike one that is offered by the angler.

The successful trophy trout angler is selective of worms and is even more exacting as to the method of fitting this bait to the hook. During the spring, and again after a summer shower, large dew worms are used for big browns that prowl the roiled water. However, during periods of drought, when streams are low and clear, large dew worms are entirely out of place. Best by far at this time is a very small worm about 1½ or 2 inches long at most. Such a tiny worm could easily have fallen from a rotted tree limb, or it could be mistaken for a caddis worm that has crawled from its case. Here too there is a need for fine tackle such as 3X or 4X tippets and fine-wire, size 14 or 16 hooks.

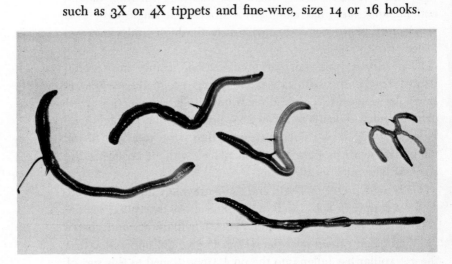

Various methods of hooking earthworms. Most preferred methods are with gang hook or single hook inserted through collar of worm.

In most cases the worm is hooked only once through the collar to permit it to stretch to its full length as the worm washes about in the currents. Few trout, even of lunker size, will resist the temptations of the passing worm. (It is universally agreed that, when a trout clips short the end of the worm, it is best to remove the remaining portion and substitute a fresh bait.)

The gang hook is also a popular method of presenting a worm to trout. This is simply a short snell to which two or three hooks have been positioned. The hooks are inserted into the worm at various intervals. This enables the angler to strike immediately when feeling or observing a trout taking the bait, for regardless of what position the trout might have struck the worm, one or more of the hooks is already in its mouth.

The stream level has a direct bearing on the success of worm fishing. When bank-full, with deep, swift currents, the worm must be kept near the bottom, and guided carefully into each little pocket behind or below rocks, undercut banks, and log jams which offer shelter against the full force of the water. Split shot or strips of wrap-around lead are a must at this time to keep the bait next to the bottom. Fishermen who experience little success

Natural baits handled with spinning equipment will creel beautiful catches of trout.

during the spring season can generally attribute the cause to that of having the bait skim over the heads of trout. Place the bait at a deeper level and the story changes almost immediately.

The next point to practice is to work slowly, covering not distance but every part of the stream thoroughly. In our haste to reach the challenging pool around the bend, we miss many potential "hot spots" that would yield nice trout. It is advisable to cast repeatedly across stream at the same location so that the currents can carry the bait through every tiny waterfall, foamy suds that have collected against log jams, beside rocks that break the flow of current, and into little backwaters and eddies away from the main flow of water. Here are the so-called "hot spots" where trout reside.

Grasshoppers or locusts, crickets, honeybees, butterflies, inchworms, crayfish, and many other natural baits will also lure trout into the creel. These baits are discussed in some detail in the chapter on Live Bait for Black Bass. Refer to this section of this book, bearing in mind, that what has been said in regard to bait fishing for smallmouthed bass also applies to trout—including those of trophy size.

Tackle for bait fishing for trout in no way differs from that used in other forms of fresh-water bait fishing. The spin-rod and lightweight monofilament line is by far the most popular bait outfit in use today, judging by the number of anglers using this gear on the trout streams. Small and lightweight baits can be handled beautifully with this rod and reel combination, and the lines, in most cases 3- or 4-pound test, are practically invisible in the water. A medium-action fly rod is also perfectly satisfactory for taking trout on natural bait. The value of one kind of tackle over another is of a relative nature. Far more important is the bait and the technique of presenting these natural baits to the trout.

*Chapter Two*

# CATCHING TROUT ON FLIES

## *by* RAY OVINGTON

RAY OVINGTON works hard to popularize the sport of fishing through radio, TV, newspapers, national sportsmen's magazines, fishing guides, and books. He is outdoor editor of the New York *World Telegram & Sun* with a daily column, "Hooks and Bullets." Ray has fished all over the western hemisphere for many species of fresh- and salt-water fish, but favors trout fishing, especially with the fly rod. He is currently working on five of an extensive series of Young Sportsmen's Guides, for Thomas Nelson & Sons, publishers.

THERE are standard procedures for the presentation of the various types of flies: wet, dry, nymph, streamer, and bucktail. If the angler were to follow these and fish enough he would come home with trout in the creel, for they work when trout are feeding, or at least in the mood to strike.

About 10 per cent of the fishermen on today's trout streams catch 60 per cent of the fish. This small group is successful because they have, through trial and error, developed techniques which work for them when usual methods fail. In order to develop these, knowledge of the stream, stream life including the basic insects and food life and their relation to the trout must have been seen, and then the facts utilized by the angler in the devising of presentations.

General fly delivery and simple approach and presentation must be known and practiced for on this base are added the refined techniques.

*Streamer flies,* and they include the bucktails, are basically imitations of the minnows, herring, smelt, or other small fish upon which the trout feed in locations where these baits exist. The object is to present these flies in as lifelike a way as possible under the conditions of the moment.

Stream fly fishing in the early spring calls for the delivery of these flies on or near the bottom, a pesky problem in broken water such as is found in most broad or heavy rivers. The reason why they are to be fished deep is that the temperature of the water renders the trout and minnows more or less inactive. The speed and power of the heavy water keeps the fish down under behind the protection of a rock or ledge. There has been no fly life to speak of which would draw them up from the depths. Taking the cue from the live-bait fishermen, the angler must sink these flies and at the same time make them act lifelike if a trout of any size is to be bothered to take hold.

To this end, streamers have been weighted under the body dressing. Split shot or wrap-around lead strips have also been added to the leader. Weight will tend to kill the action of the fly, so a compromise between weight and applied rod tip action is needed.

In experiments with weighted flies versus weighted leaders, the action of the rig was watched from a bridge overlooking a broad pool. It was noted that the addition of two split shot about a foot and a half apart from the fly worked best, for the rod tip action moved the split shot which in turn transmitted the action to the fly. The weighted fly hardly moved when the same amount of action was applied.

In extremely deep water, weighted flies and weighted leaders will work but this becomes a heavy rig to cast with the fly rod, so the use of light spinning tackle was called for. If the angler is going to be forced to the spinning rig, he might just as well use legitimate spinning lures.

The general approach to the presentation in fast water is to cast the fly on a 45° angle upstream, allow the fly to sink in the current, and when it is about opposite the angler, the retrieve is started by jerking the rod tip and stripping in line, causing the fly to dart across the current. If the stream has a number of underwater rocks and snags, the fly is allowed to drift down as retrieved to cover as many of these hot spots as possible.

Watching a successful minnow fisherman is one way to learn the tricks of casting and manipulating the streamer fly. One angler I know, who has probably taken more trout over the 3-pound mark on Eastern trout streams than anyone else, casts his lure

Ray Ovington

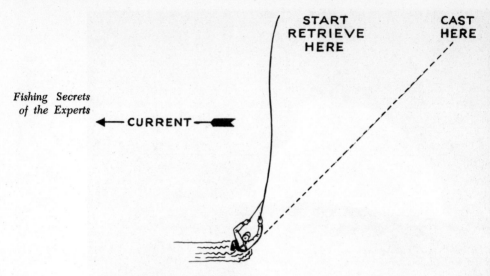

Using streamers and bucktails

slightly upstream, allows it to sink for a few yards, and then begins the fast jerky retrieve across the stream. The fly rarely goes below him. If he wishes to work the lower water he wades down to it. Another of his tricks is that of casting well above a hot spot so that the fly will be low in the water when it comes to a particular area. When it reaches this spot he then begins the enticing retrieve, not trying to fish the whole river on one cast. "Action where action counts" is his thesis, and it is mighty successful. Most anglers cast all over the stream, fishing as much of it as they can, and this is where they make their mistake when it comes to taking the larger trout. When you get to know that big fish inhabit certain parts of the stream at various times of the year, you work those spots and forget the rest of the water.

Later in the season when the waters become lower and clearer, smaller flies can be used with less weight, but the same general rules must be followed. Quite often two or three flies on a leader form the killing combination. Two small flies on the tippets, almost resembling wet flies, are followed by a bigger streamer on the end, a rig not generally used in orthodox fly fishing.

During the summer months when the trout begin to feed after the twilight shadows have fallen on the river, sparsely dressed

In fly fishing for trout a quiet, careful approach and delicate presentation of the lure is essential. (*Minn. Div. of Publicity*)

streamers, fished right on the surface, can be the most killing. The trout are keyed to the surface for drifting and hatching fly life. It is no longer necessary to go deep for them. The darting minnow imitation on the surface will attract smashing strikes from big trout.

Where most anglers make their mistake is in using too light leaders and much too light a rod. A flimsy rod action will *seem* to be manipulating the fly way out there in the pool. But it can't. A stiffer rod must be used for streamer fishing. The leader must also be heavier than that used for wet and dry fly fishing. The stiffer nylon carries the impact of the rod action more directly to the fly. Also, when a big trout hits a fast moving streamer he means business, and that is why nothing less than 2X test should be used.

Finally remember that a fly viewed from the fish's upstream position as it crosses in front of him will be seen. The fly which is dragged, no matter how enticingly alongside of him, directly upstream will hardly be noticed. Work the fly across at all times except when you are drifting it for the sink. Work only specified areas at a time. Covering the entire water is largely a waste of time unless you like to merely chuck and chance it, hoping that some fish may see your offering.

When working the minnow imitation, hold your rod high so that the action of the darter is up and down as well as forward. Use a stout rod to do the job.

*Wet flies* offer the broadest possible use of the above techniques as well as those designed to imitate the insects upon which the trout feed. These smaller wet flies are tied to resemble dead drift insects which have been blown into the stream, those which are water-bred but which have also been "drowned"—small minnows, hatching insects, and nymphs.

There are basically two types of delivery, which can be modified to suit conditions. One is the dead-drift method where the fly is allowed to drift dead in the current. In the spring, drifted down deep, these flies resemble the various types of nymphal forms of the caddis fly, stone fly, and May fly nymphs, which are continuously being torn loose from their footings in the mud, debris, or rocks of the stream. Trout feed on them as they drift down. Later the dead drift is used on or near the surface film where the fly imitation now attempts to duplicate the drifting hatching nymph as it is about to emerge into the winged form.

Mastering the dead drift is a tough project. Cast too much line to let the fly drift naturally and the slack therefrom will never let you know if a trout has hit the lure. Certainly too much slack is hard to pick up on the strike if a trout is seen to flash at the lure during its underwater drift. Cast too little slack and your fly will not drift dead or naturally. The trick is to compromise on both and learn to guide the fly during its course over the water. As in streamer fly fishing, don't make the mistake of trying to fish the entire river in one cast. Pick out your hot spots and work on them exclusively. Sink the flies with one or two split shot as described in the streamer section. Here again, weighted flies are dead in the water unless three are used and the water is exceptionally fast as in a big, fast, broad, deep river.

In mastering the dead drift, cast up and slightly across the stream at least 20 feet above the area to be "worked." When the fly approaches this area, false-cast a loop of line upstream so that the fly and leader will drift naturally across the hot spot. When the big moment arrives, gently work in the belly of the line so that at the right moment your line is taut and the flies "come alive" by moving up from the deep. Another way is to wade to a position directly above the hot spot, drift the flies down by dropping them at your feet. Pay out the line as the rig drifts down and gradually tighten as the flies reach their destination. This is the time to make the last tightening so that they rise up right in front of the trout's nose.

Quite often you will see trout rising freely to insects that seem to be riding the surface. This, to the beginner, seems to be the time to use the dry fly, but it is not. On close examination you will find that these trout are feeding on drifting nymphs that have worked their way to the surface and are in the act of hatching into mature flies. The trout action you see is generally the feeding under the surface film. Their tails, dorsals, and snouts will be seen breaking the water as they follow through during their rush at the insects. Use dry flies? No. Use wets, fished on a greased line and leader so that the fly will drift just in or under the surface film. Again this is the dead-drift technique. When you see these feeding rises, cast well above so as not to scare

33

A good fly fisherman learns how to use dry flies, wet flies, nymphs, and streamers so that he can fish all kinds of waters under varying conditions. This scene is on the Maligne River in Jasper National Park. *(Canadian Gov. Travel Bureau)*

them, and as the rig drifts below gather in the slack to ensure the strike being felt.

From spring into early fall this is one of the best tricks in wet fly fishing. The mastering of the dead drift is a must.

The other type of wet fly delivery is that of the "hunting method" over broken water stretches. Here, the angler is searching out the small runs, eddies, and holes between the rocks and gravel beds. Spot casting is called for and the fly is again cast just above and allowed to swim in these places. Keep it moving with rod held high and the rod tip moving rapidly to cause the

34

fly to dart. Best patterns for this type of work are those with white or bright wings.

This is the common and killing method to be used on small streams where a veritable dunking method is used. Drop the flies in the deep holes, behind the rocks and breaks in the stream, and swim them over the wide glides. This is essentially short-line fishing and is a delightful way to angle while casting and walking the stream or bank.

The use of two or three wet flies is recommended. The big reason for this is that three flies of diverse patterns will help you to arrive at the killing pattern and also the attraction of numbers is of much benefit. Casting the three flies is not easy. They will tangle if you throw too tight a bow in the cast or attempt to get too much distance in a wind. Wet fly fishing does not necessarily demand distance work. The most effective range is within 40 feet.

*Nymph* fishing is an art that started generally in this country only within the past twenty years. A few beginners became nymphing addicts and from those few a whole new field of trouting has opened.

Nymph fishing is really astute wet fly fishing with the use of nymphal imitations which resemble the underwater aquatic forms of the stream insects. Many wet fly patterns do this very well, but closer imitations such as actual nymph patterns are often needed.

In order to be a good nymph fisherman, the angler must have at least a smattering of information about the nymphal cycle of the insects and its relation to the trout at various seasons and under varied conditions. This information is hard to come by even in detailed books, for it must be learned in action.

Many of the same general wet fly presentation techniques are used with variations developed along the way. Quite often it is interesting to mix a nymph pattern in with the wet flies just to check on the killing qualities of the tie.

The nymphs of the May flies, caddis flies, and stone flies have very defined patterns of existence in relation to the trout's feeding habits. We don't have space here to even begin to describe it. We discovered these things for ourselves so the secrets are available to any trouter interested in the search. While nymphs might not be any more killing than wet flies, the study of these insects and the trout's behavior during hatching periods will put fish in the creel if what is seen is employed in defined techniques.

As to pattern, some of the best nymph patterns are wet flies with all but the stubs of the wings burned or cut off. From there on it is up to your creative abilities.

Presentation, as we said, is a modification of the general wet fly techniques described here earlier.

*Dry flies* constitute the theoretical high point in trout fishing. For generations we have been taught that dry fly fishing was the epitome of the fly fisher's art. This is not necessarily so. True, the dry fly presentation can be a tough proposition, but the subtleties of the other methods often outstrip the dry fly. Dry fly fishing in the classical sense requires that the fly be dropped on the water as daintily as possible and allowed to drift, drag free, with no waves or motion from the leader or line. On the quiet, glassy, chalk streams of England, where this delivery is a must, it is a pretty problem. But on our streams of America, where there is much broken and fast water interspersed by pools and riffles, the delivery of the fly takes on less importance, except in the glassy water sections.

Actually dry fly fishing is the easiest type of fishing once the cast has been mastered, the tackle is perfectly balanced, and the fly tied to a gossamer-thin leader. It is mainly upstream casting, allowing the fly to drift down on the currents while the angler gathers in the slack line, enabling him to strike if a fish comes up and hits the fly during its course of drift. The heads of pools are the hot spots most of the time and the feed lanes where the streamers, bucktails, and wets are used are also possibles at various times of the year.

The dry fly is obviously either the imitation of a floating insect which has been blown into the stream or the imitation of a freshly hatched insect that is riding the current preparatory to taking off. It is also the imitation of one of the return flight of insects as they return to the stream to lay their eggs.

The most killing time for the dry fly is when the fish are actually seen taking insects off the surface during a hatch, or when a great amount of blow-ins are riding the surface. It takes hardly any talent to kill fish that are avidly feeding on surface insects. Many times I have started a fisherman out on dry flies during a hatch and his success at that moment has made him a confirmed fly man from then on. It is generally much harder to take trout on bucktails and streamers when one never knows if they are even faintly interested in feeding at all.

Upstream fishing with the controlled downstream drift is the common method with dry flies. Across and downstream drift is also called for when specific spots must be reached in no other way. Another killing way to deliver the fly is the use of the stop-cast as you face downstream. Drop the fly almost beneath the rod tip and let out line as it drifts over the hot spot.

Many tricks are discovered in the presentation, however. One is the quiet and splash-free exit of the fly when another cast is to be made. Very few anglers can extract the fly from the water with hardly a ripple. The technique is to gather in the slack line and start the forward roll cast, lifting the fly almost vertically out of the water followed by the leader and end of the line. At that moment, the pull of the regular backward part of the conventional cast is started. In this way the entire rig is out of the water with a minimum of fuss. Retrieving it any other way will cause the line and leader to suck on the surface, thereby making a commotion to put down even the boldest of the little trout.

Good dry fly fishing demands several casting techniques, such as throwing a right- or left-hand curve in order to put the fly under an overhang or to bend the leader around a rock or mid-stream snag. This is done on the forward cast by a twist of the wrist. The leader curls in a gentle arc to the right or left depending on the desired direction and wrist action. The fly then drifts down to the trout with no leader preceding it.

The roll cast is also needed when there is little or no backcast room. A good roll caster can throw a tiny fly as far as he can with the conventional fore and aft cast.

The mend cast enables the angler to throw a loop of slack line up-current from the fly, thus enabling it to drift farther and longer before being pulled under by a tight line or action from the current.

All these are necessary general techniques for varied dry fly fishing. They are also quite important for nymphing and wet fly work as well.

Wet flies often account for big trout, like the 22-inch rainbow shown here.

The best bet is to use smaller flies than those seen on the water and always use the lightest leader possible. It is amazing how light a leader can be used even on big trout if the angler is sensitive and does not try to jab the hook into the fish or horse it in quickly to the net. When the water is clear and low, small flies and the thinnest leaders are musts.

Regardless of the method or fly type, the presentation of flies to trout depend on some very defined rules of stream conduct. Few anglers realize how very scary trout are—particularly the big ones. Most anglers approach the stream with a fast walk, enter the pool, or run without any idea of the timidity of their quarry. Most anglers wade too much. Staying under the cover of the brush or back from the bank or gravel beach would put more trout in the creel. Most anglers wade where they should be fishing and fish where they should be wading. A study of the water may take two or three minutes from a vantage point well back from the water. That study will cut down on a lot of water wasted and time spent over barren stretches. No matter how good the casting and presentation, a stream where the fish have been put down is a bare stream for an hour after the fright takes place.

Study the water before entering. Enter very slowly and wade very quietly and slowly. If you are heronlike, you can have fish feeding on the surface within 10 feet of you. Don't rush. Fishing is a relaxing sport. That is why you are there on the water. Forget the tensions of the everyday world. Take it easy. Keep your eyes open. If you want exercise, go for a hike up the mountain. If you want speed go water skiing. Trout fishing demands an Indianlike attack—calculated with no waste motions.

Keep your casting powder-dry. Don't make a cast over clear water unless it is first studied. "Chuck and chance it" angling is an aimless sport. Call your shots like the billiard player and you'll put many more big fish in the creel.

Joseph D. Bates, Jr.

*Chapter Three*

# SPINNING FOR BIG TROUT

## *by* JOSEPH D. BATES, JR.

JOSEPH D. BATES, JR., is credited with having done more to popularize spinning than any man in America. His *Spinning For American Game Fish,* the first and best-selling book on the subject, was followed by two works on fresh-water and on salt-water spinning, plus numerous magazine articles. In addition, he has designed tackle for the sport and has authored classics on trout fishing and on angling with streamer flies. Writing about fishing is an avocation for Colonel Bates. He is a vice-president and director of Reilly, Brown & Tapply, Inc., a prominent Boston advertising agency. He also is a sought-after consultant for large manufacturers on the development, marketing, and promotion of outdoor products.

SEVERAL years ago I was writing a book about how to catch big trout. At the time, Joe Brooks and I were on a fishing trip to the West Coast, where Joe wanted to catch a record striped bass on a fly rod, and where I hoped to land a big Kamloops rainbow trout on spinning gear.

As it turned out, both of us got our fish and both the fish were record breakers—which goes to show what can happen when Lady Luck smiles upon anglers. At Idaho's Lake Pend Oreille (where the world's record 37-pound rainbow had been taken by deep trolling), I fished for two days without catching anything very big.

On the evening of the second day, Joe Brooks quizzically observed that I was writing a book about how to catch big trout— but that the book couldn't be much good, because evidently I didn't seem able to catch one.

This timely remark set me to pondering during the night on what I had learned about the habits of big trout, as adapted to the geography of this particular lake. Between periods of fitful

41

sleep, I worked out my strategy for this third and last day. I went by boat to the place I had decided to fish, put on the lure I had decided to use—and shortly caught a 31-pound, 12-ounce rainbow, which was the largest ever taken on relatively light spinning tackle.

On another occasion, I was with a party of anglers fishing for big brook trout in Canada. The lake had produced several winners in the *Field & Stream* magazine's fishing contest, but we had caught nothing of trophy size. After considering where big brook trout should be at that time of year, I canoed to a selected location and, along about sundown, caught three beautiful male brook trout, each weighing exactly 6¼ pounds. Herbie Welch mounted the first one for me and I released the other two with the hope that they would give someone else the thrills they had given to me.

These two instances may indicate that knowledge is a very valuable partner to Lady Luck in catching big fish. We may not always be lucky, but the element of knowledge certainly improves our chances.

Two things stand out in this element of knowledge: One is to obtain suitable and properly balanced spinning tackle and to learn how to use it. Especially, we should learn how to select spinning lures for various conditions and know how each type of lure should be fished for best results.

Secondly, it is important to learn the habits of the species of fish being sought. It is valuable to know where they should be under specific temperature and seasonal conditions.

Comments here about tackle and how to use it will be brief because this information is readily available in other books. It is important to buy one of the best reels one can afford, preferably an open-faced reel of the true spinning type. For trout fishing, the reel should be of a small size, with a spool which will hold about 200 yards of 4-pound test monofilament line. Extra reel spools with lines of 6 pounds, and with 3-pound test (or less) also may be needed.

If one does not wish to go to the expense of a truly fine split-bamboo rod, it then is sensible to choose one made of glass fiber. This rod usually should be selected to flex properly with a ¼-ounce lure. When the lure is reeled in near the rod tip, the lure's weight should depress the rod tip ever so slightly. The rod's action should extend all the way down into the butt.

This combination of 4-pound test line and ¼-ounce lures—with a rod and reel to suit them—should be ideal for average conditions. On occasion, it may be advisable to use tackle somewhat heavier, and frequently, experienced anglers will want it a bit lighter.

For trout fishing with artificial lures, we'll usually stick to wobbling spoons and spinners. Sometimes a few of the smaller plugs may prove even better for certain species of trout. For example, I've had good luck with lake trout and Dolly Vardens by using the Flatfish and the Diamond Jim. I've taken many big brown trout on Garcia's Eelet.

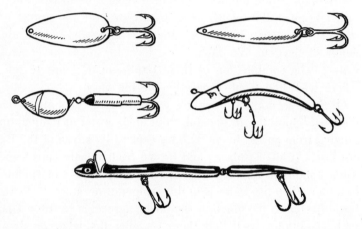

Spinning lures for big trout

Spinners work best when actively operating in a current, just under the surface. Wobblers are useful in all kinds of water, and can be fished near the surface or down deep. Sometimes they are very effective when employed as a jig.

Perhaps even more important than the kind of lure is the amount of flash it gives. Bright lures do well on dull days, or under swollen or cloudy water conditions. When the day is bright and the water is clear, a shiny lure may frighten more fish than it attracts. These are the times when a dull or tarnished lure should be used. If any metal lures become tarnished, I let them

43

stay that way. It takes but a few seconds to bring them to the desired degree of brightness with a bit of steel wool or a polishing cloth.

No matter what tackle we have, or how expert we are in using it, it won't catch fish for us unless we are fishing in areas and at depths where the fish are.

To determine where the trout are, let's start off by realizing that they are a lot more like people than people might think. When temperatures are too warm or too cold, people go where they can be more comfortable. So do trout. People like the protection of safe buildings. Trout like the haven of an undercut bank, a tree overturned into the water, or the safety from a stream's fast current offered by a large rock. People eat when they are hungry. Trout, too, like to be near where the food is, such as in a lake near the mouth of a stream, or over the gravel of a stream rather than its sandier areas. Trout also need an abundance of oxygen. We should not look for them in unaerated waters. The combination of these requirements helps to tell us where we'll find trout—especially the big ones!

Of these several requirements water temperatures are perhaps the most important. In general, trout enjoy water at temperatures ranging from 50° F. to 70° F. This especially is true of the Eastern brook trout. Rainbows and brown trout remain active under water conditions about 5° higher. We don't need a thermometer to tell us when the water is in this temperature range. If it's comfortably cold to the touch, it should be agreeable to trout. Under such conditions, we'll find them roaming the lakes or streams where we can reach them with surface or near-surface lures. But we'll find the really big ones where they also can enjoy protection and where food is nearby.

When temperatures are not in this ideal range, trout go where they can find it. If, for some reason, they can't find it, they become inactive. Thus, when surface waters are very cold or very warm, trout may go to depths where they are more comfortable. In lakes, we'll find them along shore lines or near ledges at this depth. When surface waters of lakes are too warm, trout also may seek spring holes or stream mouths where cooler waters enter the lake. When streams become too warm, such as in midsummer, trout will be deep in the pools or will be near spring holes. They

When it comes to catching big trout the spinning rig has it all over the fly rod.
*(Canadian Gov. Travel Bureau)*

may come to the surface to feed in the early morning or late evening when the sun is not bright and when surface waters are cooler than during the heat of the day.

The combination of these bits of knowledge helped to find the big Kamloops rainbow trout at Lake Pend Oreille. These big fish had been in the deep, cooler water all summer, but when we reached the lake in the early fall, the water seemed cool enough to tempt them to the surface. But it would be still cooler in the estuary of a mountain stream and such a place would bring food to them. The element of protection seemed a minor consideration for trout that big.

Thus, on studying the map, the logical place to go fishing at that time seemed to be in the bay made by the entrance of a small river into the lake. The logical lure to use seemed to be a long but thin wobbling spoon which would provide the flash and action of a baitfish of a size which might interest a trout that big. It proved to be a winning combination.

The combination of these bits of knowledge also helped to find the three big brook trout in Canada. At this time of year the surface water was warm, so only a few of the smaller trout could be taken on top—and these were taken by casting small wobblers to within inches of floating logs against deep and shaded shore lines.

To take big trout by casting spinning lures required finding cooler water in a spot where the fish could enjoy protection and preferably a supply of food. A stream mouth would have provided a solution, but this was a lake without an inlet.

On roaming the lake in a borrowed boat with my outboard motor, we had noticed a small cove containing a large spring hole. The wet rocks and verdant vegetation indicated its presence. Logs and stumps had blown into this little cove, thoroughly blocking its apex. It was a good-looking spot, with cooler water and plenty of protection for big trout. The vegetation and the logs also indicated a food supply.

We worked up to the cove slowly as the red sun neared the horizon and threw the water into shadow. Since the trout might be well out into the cove, we fan-casted to cover the entire surface, letting the brass wobbling spoon sink deep on alternate casts. Nothing happened until I made a long cast directly to the

Big trout are usually caught in our northern lakes and larger rivers and streams. Spinning tackle and lures are ideal for such waters. *Kiekhaefer Corp.*

logs. Then there was smashing strike and the big trout swirled before trying to reach the safety of the logs. Eventually, the 4-pound test monofilament, combined with the power of my rod and reel, led the fish into the cove, where he could be handled with less difficulty. He was a gorgeous hump-backed male, resplendent in early fall colors.

While admiring the trout, we rested the spring hole. Just before the sun set, the same tackle took another trout, identical with the first one. I removed the hook from his jaw and freed him without taking him from the water. Just before dark, I caught another which we also let go. I don't know how many big trout were in the spring hole because I went home the next day and never had a chance to return. Spring holes have fascinated me ever since. When the water is warm in a trout lake, these are excellent places to find trout.

Big trout in small streams require a very cautious approach. In New England, we often find very large browns under the undercut banks of brooks which can be stepped across without difficulty. Spinning gear is not at its best in these confined places but, if it is used, a very small metal wobbler should do the trick. Preferably we should explore the little stream a day or two before fishing it; marking on a sketch-map the deep holes, undercut banks, and other sanctuaries where big trout might be found. Then, when we are fishing, we approach such spots with the greatest caution, lest our shadow or our footsteps should disclose our presence.

In such confined places, usual casting techniques may be out of the question. A "flip cast" or the "bow-and-arrow" cast should put the lure accurately to the small distance necessary. Let it work to the bottom on a slack line, retrieve it slightly, let it fall back, allowing the stream's current to work it deep and into the side pockets where the big trout should be.

When a big trout is taken in any location, it's good strategy to make a note of it. Another one is almost certain to occupy the position before long.

In larger streams, big rocks provide excellent "holding water" for trophy fish—especially for steelhead in our western coastal rivers. The fast current must divide in passing a big rock, thus leaving a cone of quieter "holding water" both above and below. Using the "side cast" or the "overhead cast," drop the lure well above this position and let the lure sink and swing into it. A variety of casts from several positions both above and below the

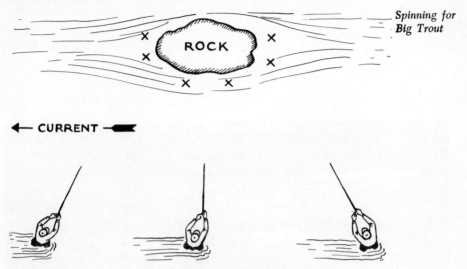

Angler changing positions to reach spots around rock

rock should be made to work the lure above. below, and beside the rock.

In fast streams, the error often is made of fishing too near the surface. Cast upstream or quartering upstream to let the lure sink deeply on a moderately slacked line. Then work it through the position as deeply as possible. In fishing runs, riffles, and channels this is called "bottom bumping." If the lure can be worked to where the trout are holding, sooner or later we'll be rewarded with a heavy strike.

Thus, the combination of a small amount of fishing skill and a large amount of knowledge of the habits of the various species of trout seems to be the secret of catching trophy fish with spinning tackle or any other sort of gear.

Smallmouthed bass thrive in pools below riffles and lie beside rock ledges. Drop baits in these hot spots.

*Chapter Four*

# LIVE BAIT FOR BLACK BASS

## *by* DON SHINER

THIS particular day I journeyed to a bass stream in north-eastern Pennsylvania to experiment with a new ultralight spin rod. The Huntington is a good stream, picturesque and productive of bass. Past experience indicated the new rod would be flexed considerably. Throughout much of its length the stream is drenched in deep shade from tall hemlocks that lean gracefully over the water. The day was warm and a dusty one. Rain had not moistened the foliage for the best part of two weeks; streams had shrunk into mere pools with only a thin film of water trickling over the rocks in the between sections. I knew the smallmouths would be skitterish, requiring one to maneuver along the banks with the soft, velvet foot of a lynx.

As I drove through several of the old, nostalgic, wooden covered bridges that lace this Keystone stream, I meditated on the best bait to use this day. All avenues of thought led to one conclusion. If I were to basket a few bass with this ultralight rod, the one positive way of accomplishing this end was to use bait —live bait, and it would be with hellgrammites that could be found under the stones in the thirsty riffles between the pools.

I parked the car in a small turnout point, one of the few along this narrow, twisting country road. From there I hurried down to the stream. As luck would have it, I picked up four hellgrammites under the first half-dozen rocks and bent the sharp hook under the collar of one of these "clippers."

The stream was indeed low and clear. A stream of bubbles poured into the pool, glided gently across the surface, coming to rest against a partly submerged hemlock that had fallen across the stream. My eyes rested on the log momentarily. There a squirrel tiptoed over the moss-covered log, stopping above the patch of foamy bubbles that had collected against the impoundment.

A gentle flip of the spin stick sent the hellgrammite sailing toward the log. It almost hit the squirrel but stopped short, dropping amidst the driftwood and foamy suds. The clipper barely sank below the surface when a fish struck. I played out line. The fish consumed several yards on its initial run as rapidly as the line could be uncoiled from the reel. When it stopped running I waited. Several tense moments passed. Taking up the slack in the line, I could feel a strong throbbing. The action that followed when the fish felt the steel was obscured by the log, but the fish leaped to the surface, sending a shower of water over the squirrel. The light rod bent double. The startled squirrel dropped whatever nut it was eating, turned and dashed madly across the log. The mossy covering was too slippery, for the squirrel lost its footing, turned a loop, and plunged into the drink. It splashed frantically about in the foamy deposit, clawing the water like a scared rabbit. It swam in my direction. When it brushed past my boot, the nutcracker recognized this fisherman and doubled its efforts to reach shore. The fish, apparently solidly hooked, continued to leap and race about on the opposite side of the log. I tried desperately to keep the line free of the driftwood and the fish from throwing the steel, yet I could not refrain from glancing over my shoulder at the little panic-stricken squirrel swimming frantically toward shore. It finally reached the pebbly bank, then dashed for the nearest hemlock, disappearing from view.

Turning back to the pool I realized that this was no smallish fish. Its tough tactics pictured an old moss-covered smallmouth that probably had hidden beneath the log for the best part of the summer. The constant line pressure, however, tired the fish until finally it submitted to being pulled from beneath the log and into the landing net. Four pounds of smallmouth flipped in the net as I waded ashore.

Bouncing a hellgrammite off a squirrel's back may not be the accepted method of taking smallmouthed bass. But bass men are firmly in agreement that clippers presented in most any orthodox manner will lure lunker-size black bass into the creel. Of course, like other baits, clippers have their off days, when bass simply refuse to display any interest in this larva. But those days are rare. In fact, when this strangely stubborn day is encountered, real shotgun-type action is gained by turning this bait inside out. It's a trick an old bass fisherman taught me many years ago. When bass won't take the natural clipper, turn the critter inside out so it assumes the appearance of a grub worm. This generally does the trick; old, smart bass literally swallow hook, line, and split shot in a frantic effort to taste this "something new" that has suddenly appeared in the stream.

Much of today's emphasis on black bass fishing is placed on artificial lures. Admittedly, flipping streamers, spinners, midget spoons, and plugs into quiet pools does creel plenty of bass. The gurgling, sputtering surface hardware and weedless spoons nail plenty of largemouths to the boat floor. But these celebrated methods should not be stressed continually lest the fine art of bait fishing becomes buried in the past pages of angling literature. Indeed, nothing is more relaxing, in today's dizzy world, than an unhurried afternoon spent astream dipping a baited hook into the pools for black bass. As one angler amply stated the case recently, "A fellow can toss in his line, relax, and catch up on his thinking, without having it interrupted every few seconds in order to recast a lure."

Much of the enjoyment of this style of fishing, aside from catching plenty of fish, is gathering the bait along the stream or lake shore line. There is no need for extensive preparation by gathering quantities of bait beforehand. An ample supply can be located in the field or along the stream bank, practically right under your thumb. Pick up the baits as you need them, always taking advantage of the variety that is present. One tuft of grass will hold a locust, a sun-lighted rock in the meadow will house several crickets, a moist rotted log on the bank will yield several worms; stones in riffles will provide hellgrammites; backwaters will hold schools of trapped minnows and frogs. These baits are effective for both short- and long-jawed bass. Differences among these two in no way affect their appetite. Both eat practically anything that doesn't eat them first. So let's run over the list of baits these two bass prefer and comment briefly on how to use each one. Let's start with the clipper, that popular bait for small-mouths that I happened to be using on this day when my prize bass nearly drowned that scared squirrel.

Top bait for the smallmouthed bass is the hellgrammite. Hook this bait under the hard collar.

*HELLGRAMMITE*. This larva is one of the natural foods found in most rivers and streams, living under the rocks in the riffle portions of the water. Bass grub for these like a miner pans for gold. Wild currents frequently roll and dislodge bottom stones, which in turn send the hellgrammite adrift. Unless the bass have just dined or are asleep, the dislodged larva rarely drifts far without some gasping jaws reaching out to intercept the bait to convert it to energy.

Use a light hook, preferably a No. 4 or 6 and a 4- to 6-pound test leader. Hook this bait under the hard collar just to the rear of the pincher-equipped head. Some fishermen prefer to remove the two tiny clawlike legs extending from the tail of the hellgrammite. This prevents the larva from catching hold and crawling under a stone on the bottom of the pool and thus fouling the hook permanently.

Permit this bait to drift with the current as though it were not attached to a line. A bass will normally grab the bait very lightly between its lips and run to some far-off corner to eat the prize. This maneuver reminds me of a barnyard chicken that has uncovered a fat worm and runs with it to some secluded spot so that it is unnecessary to share it with the busy neighbors. To set the hook immediately in the running bass invariably results in a missed fish. Give the bass plenty of line, yards of it if necessary. Then when it pauses, indicating that it now is in the act of swallowing the bait, set the hook hard. After that, hold on to your hat!

When bass refuse the hellgrammite in its natural form, turn this bait inside out. For all practical purposes the bait then resembles a whitish grub worm and this unique appearance frequently stirs action. This "reverse" technique is accomplished by cutting the head and collar from the larva. Then insert the hook in the tail, pushing or rolling the larva inside out as it slips easily over the hook.

Quantities of hellgrammites can be gathered by placing a large fine-mesh minnow net in riffles below rocks. Rake or overturn these stones. As the rocks are moved, the hellgrammites are dislodged and roll into the outstretched net.

They can be gathered just as easily, and with less damaging effects to the stream bottom, by placing a small hand net below a rock. Overturn this single stone. If there is a clipper present it will swim into the net. Most biologists, concerned chiefly with stream habitat, discourage wholesale raking of stones for hellgrammites. This kills countless nymphs and reduces the number of fish the stream can support. Most fish and game officials are prone to agree that removing large amounts of food from a stream is detrimental to good fishing. Exercise good judgment by taking only a few baits and then only as the need arises on a particular outing. Also check your local laws to make sure that the taking of such baits is legal in the waters you will be searching for bait.

The hellgrammite matures into a winged insect, known by the name dobson fly. This is indeed an ugly insect from man's point of view. However, bass are not inclined to reject this food on the basis of nonesthetic value. Let the dobson fly dip close to the

55

pool as it skims the water after sundown and the bass will nail it squarely. Look for this winged insect under the stones on shore in late July and August. Hook and leader it the same as the larva.

WORMS. The bait that is considered synonymous with sport fishing is the common earthworm. Izaak Walton, in his famous treatise, *The Compleat Angler,* gave rise to serious fly fishing, yet three hundred years later, the little soil-building worm remains the time-honored bait in the fishing world.

There are numerous varieties of these earthworms. The two most favored by bass fishermen are the common "red" worm found in the garden, and the dewworm, or night crawler, that comes to the surface at sundown to prowl through the moist lawns. In the absence of aquatic baits both of these worms will fill the angler's creel with black bass.

Immediately after a shower passes beyond the hills is a particularly excellent time to use worms for bass. Fish are conditioned over the years to expect worms to wash into the stream as currents rise to chew and erode earth from exposed banks. Whenever a worm appears, rolling and wiggling in the current, a bass just naturally cannot avoid reaching out and intercepting the tidbit. If the worm appears to be leadered to your line, pause a moment to allow the bass to run or at least enough time to amply swallow the bait. Then sock the hook home! The stinging steel always causes a bass to explode like a trapped bobcat.

The worm gang hook, popular in trout fishing, is also an excellent method of presenting the worm to bass. And, of course, a large dewworm fitted behind a small spinner is as deadly a lure as the angler will ever invent when trolled over weed beds and gravel bars. Throttle the motor down to a nice crawling speed or row sparingly while trailing the worm-spinner combination. Keep a firm grip on the rod for that electrifying blow from a striking bass.

MINNOWS. Both varieties of bass feed heavily on minnows. Smallmouths can be frequently seen chasing a luckless minnow right up to the edge of shore. Likewise, largemouths can be observed chasing schools of pond shiners, causing the panic-stricken minnows to jump and boil across the surface. When these signs are present, drop a minnow in the immediate vicinity.

The minnow is the main item in the diet of bass, with nymphs and terrestrial insects serving as trimmings or between-meal snacks. Two varieties of minnows hold the spotlight for small-mouths. These are the stone-catfish, or mad-tom, and the riffle chub, while the golden pond shiner is absolutely tops with the largemouth.

There are several ways of rigging this bait for bass. The man who prefers to still-fish usually slips the hook through the minnow's lips or lightly under the skin in the rear of the dorsal fin. The bait is permitted to swim about near beds of lily pads or rock-studded pools, in full view of nearby bass. Generally a small bobber is fitted to the line to suspend the bait at a desired height from the bottom. This accessory keeps the bait above the weed beds, where the minnow would most assuredly seek cover. Relax then and wait until the bobber does a sudden disappearing act. I must confess, the bobber action is very similar to that of a dry fly disappearing on the surface and every bit as exciting.

Used in the above manner, the bait will not withstand repeated castings without tearing from the hook. Those who choose to wade or boat to likely bass haunts and cast a minnow into these pockets to lure fish would do well to sew the bait to the hook in much the same manner as that illustrated in the section of this book dealing with trout on natural baits. Fixed in this manner, the bait can be spin-cast across riffles or pools and retrieved in such a manner as to suggest a live, but crippled, minnow that is trying desperately to swim away undetected. Sewn, so that the body is slightly curved, the bait will swim through the water with a peculiar rolling, darting motion so characteristic of a bait that is partly incapacitated. This creates the illusion of an easily caught meal which few largemouths or smallmouths can resist to chase.

There are several methods used to sew the minnow to the hook. Method No. 1 is accomplished by inserting the hook through the mouth and gill, wrapping line spirally around the body, and reinserting the hook in the tail. The reverse procedure is also a popular system. Method No. 2 is with a "safety pin" hook, or inserting a short piece of wire through the body to

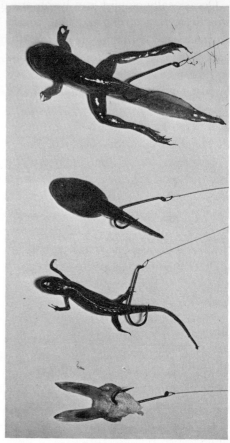

LEFT: The different ways to hook the ever-popular crayfish. RIGHT: Live baits used for largemouthed bass include tadpoles, salamander, and a fish fin.

pull the leader through, and attaching a double or treble hook near the tail. Minnows used in this manner can be cast much like artificial lures, thereby enabling the angler to cover far more water than the still-fisherman.

*CRAYFISH.* In the same category as the hellgrammite and minnow, the crayfish is another food that forms a large part of the diet of black bass. This small, fresh-water lobster is abundant in most streams and lakes throughout North America.

Occasionally crayfish can be observed crawling over the rocky aquatic terrain during daylight hours. Normally, however, they are nocturnal, emerging from their hiding places between and beneath stones late in the evening and at night, or heavily overcast days. Quantities of them can be gathered at this time simply by placing a piece of meat in the shallow water along shore. After a few hours have elapsed, return with a flashlight. Literally dozens of crayfish will be found feeding upon this flesh. Gather the smallish ones for bass bait.

Old-timers reveal that there are tricks in using this bait. For example, perhaps you have examined the stomach of a bass that was caught during the day and found remnants of an undigested crayfish. Using this as a clue, rocks are overturned in an effort to locate a "crab." But the bait gives discouraging poor success. The trouble lies in the fact that bass have fed on this bait the previous night—the active period for crayfish. Were you to use this bait when the sun sets in the west, the results would be entirely different.

There are numerous ways to fix the hook to this bait. A small crayfish can be wired to a long-shank hook. Or, the hook can be imbedded in the tail, as illustrated in one of the accompanying illustrations. In all cases, permit the bass an initial run or several moments after it has struck the bait to mouth it properly before attempting to set the hook.

The outer, hard covering on the crayfish is actually the bony, supporting structure. Periodically, during the growth period, this outer shell cracks and the crayfish molts this tough skin. It is after this molting process, when the crayfish is covered with a paper thin covering, that they are especially appealing to bass.

*SALAMANDERS.* Here is another bait that bass men rate highly for black bass. The black "lizards" or salamanders found under cool, moist stones in brooks and springs or among moist leaves in the confines of a marsh, are, in my book, a very fine smallmouth bait. Bass simply cannot let a wiggly salamander escape untouched. They also give surprisingly good results for trout.

The common newt, or red-spotted, olive-colored salamander of the pond is frequently found in the stomach of largemouthed bass. However, I have rarely experienced any outstanding success with this fellow. Perhaps this is due to its sluggish, lazy manner, in contrast to the energized fellow of the cool springs. I see no reason, however, why the pond newt cannot be used in the absence of other bait.

A No. 4 or 6 hook is about right for this bait. Insert the hook in the tail, just to the rear of the legs. Do not prick so deeply that the spinal cord is injured.

*FROGS.* Just as the hellgrammite is the capstone in the life of the small-jawed river bass, so is the frog to the long-lipped lake bass. Toss this bait in the midst of a lily bed, then hop it from one pad to another until it reaches the boat. No self-respecting mossback that happens to be loafing in the shade beneath the leafy vegetation will let the frog slide by without doing something about it.

In all cases, kill the frog before fixing the hook through its lips. I do not profess to have a faint heart, yet I dislike witnessing the frog using its humanlike legs and feet to grasp the object that is quite probably stinging its mouth. Instead, kill the bait beforehand, for having it alive on the hook serves no purpose in the pad-hopping technique. Permit the largemouth several moments to mouth the bait properly before setting the hook.

There are numerous frog harnesses made commercially for this pad-hopping technique. These hold the bait in such a position that the hook can be set immediately in a striking bass. These same rigs are also useful when using mice, if again, you have no personal objection to this bait.

The pollywog, forerunner of the mature frog, is another excellent bait for both species of bass. Largemouths cruise along the edges of coves and bays during the evening searching for these fat immature frogs. There is no trouble in catching this excellent bait during the month of July and early August.

*CRICKETS AND GRASSHOPPERS.* The chirping sound of the singing cricket, ringing from the sun-lighted stones in the meadow, is, I am quite certain, familiar to all fishermen. As an experiment for some afternoon, collect several of these chirping insects and drop them into a pool that harbors smallmouths. Stand on the bank in such a position to afford a view of the underwater world. After two or three strokes from the cricket's powerful legs it is lost in a swirl of water. A smallmouth lost no time in surfacing for this bait. Grasshopper or locust is in much the same category.

A popular method of fixing the frog to the hook. **Hook harnesses** are also popular.

A trick in using these insects, and one that obviously brings much excitement to bass fishing, is to fasten a cricket or locust to a small hook by means of a soft piece of wire. This method does not kill the insect. It therefore can jump or kick about on the surface causing a commotion exactly as though it were wind-blown into the stream. The entire procedure in presenting this bait is much like dry fly fishing for trout, with the result that the electrifying strike is in full view of the angler.

These baits are always available to the bass angler. A half hour spent in a farm meadow overturning stones that are warmed by the sun will uncover dozens of these chirping insects. The tall, unmowed grass also yields great quantities of locusts or grass-hoppers. Gather these in the morning when they are still stiff from the cool night air.

There are several other baits remaining that could be discussed in connection with bass fishing. There are many types of beetles, caterpillars, grub worms, and cicadas that will creel bass at one time or another. I would not hesitate using these whenever a search along the stream bank uncovers them. Bass eat practically everything that does not eat it first. Thus, the suitable baits are almost endless in number.

There is no question that these popular gamefish are most susceptible to hardware or artificial lures, perhaps more so than any other fish aside from possibly the pike and musky. Fickle though they are, preferring one particular colored plug over another at a given time, bass normally accept whatever bait is offered at the moment if they are the least bit hungry or playful. I am certain the bass, which almost drowned the scared squirrel, would have taken most any bait presented to it that day. I sensed that a well-presented hellgrammite would net results in that low, clear stream. Bait fishing is like that—it almost guarantees that a fisherman can slip a few bass and a handful of ferns into the creel before the day ends.

## Chapter Five

# BLACK BASS ON ARTIFICIAL LURES

## by HOMER CIRCLE

HOMER CIRCLE should know plenty about bass fishing lures, since he is
vice president of James Heddon's Sons, one of the leading manufacturers
of lures and fishing tackle. His work takes him all over the nation testing
products with leading anglers, learning secrets of these top bass fishermen. He finds plenty of time to fish for his favorite bass, largemouthed
and smallmouthed, and also serves as a director in the Outdoor Writers
of America. This know-how reflects itself in leading magazine articles
and is used to make better fishing lures. These bass were taken in Center
Hill Reservoir, Tennessee.

THE sport of fishing, species of fish, and the myriad ways to
catch them are as broad as the world, each with its own following.
Our choice after more than thirty-five years of probing is fishing
with artificial lures for one of the truly great gamefishes—black
bass.

We're talking about not one, but those three thoroughbreds;
the smallmouthed, largemouthed, and spotted bass. These anvil-
jawed roughnecks have every attribute required of great gamefish.

And they're canny fishes, too. Your first year fishing for them
can be as barren as a busted barrel. With some fish you can go
barging right up to the fishing spot, toss out the anchor, follow
it with a baited hook, and start pulling in fish. Not so with those
three husky peers; the largemouthed, smallmouthed, and spotted
bass.

Try barging up to a bass hole and you're in for some lonesome
fishing, for all you'll get is a good letting alone. Some skeptics
chuckle when we Midwestern fishermen give bass credit for being able to outsmart a green angler. They just don't know the
bass.

For instance, take any smallmouthed, largemouthed, or spotted

63

bass. Why, they can feel a vibration from the toe of your boot stumbling against a rock 25 or 50 yards away. If you doubt this just walk along the water's edge, stamp your foot, and watch ahead of you. You'll see those big wakes leaving the shore amazingly far ahead.

Which brings us to the first attribute of a topnotch bass fisherman—stealth. What good would the Indian's bow and arrow have done him if he couldn't have got within range of his game? Likewise with a bass fisherman. The deer has keen ears, the bass has a nervous system that is keenly sensitive to vibrations.

Let's don our fishing clothes and try our skill on a stream somewhere in Ohio, Missouri, Indiana, Illinois, Iowa, Kansas, Nebraska, Arkansas, or neighboring states. It doesn't matter which one, once you've learned to outsmart bass in one state, you can outsmart them in any state.

Let's wade the shallow side of the stream, and instead of stumbling along giving off telltale vibrations, we'll scoot our feet carefully, quietly over the bottom, always watching ahead for a feeding bass.

Instead of making long inaccurate casts we'll be shooting out short, accurate casts, probing every pocket, rock, drop-off, log, bush, tree root, weed patch, or other likely hiding places of the bass.

We'll use top-water or weedless lures in the shallow spots, deep-diving lures in the holes and along the drop-offs, and shallow running lures over the riffles. No telling where the bass will be on any particular day. Bass are where you find them, and just like rabbits you have to hunt them.

All old-timers know how important the quiet approach is, particularly on big bass that got that way because they were hep to a noisy approach. So, if you would catch the big ones, and plenty of the smaller ones, make your approach so doggone quiet that the only noise the bass will hear is that of your plug falling on the water.

These same rules apply to lake fishing. The unwise bass fisherman rows noisily up to within easy casting distance of a nice stretch of lily pads, throws over the anchor "kabloomp," scrapes the tackle box around, stands up in the boat, and heaves a plug hopefully.

Just slip into that bass's scales and weigh the situation for a moment. You've heard this same noisy approach dozens of times and know that man is out there. Where man is concerned you know fear and instinctively you back off into deep cover until he goes away.

Now, if man didn't make a single noise in approaching your lair but let his boat drift to within casting distance, and instead of tossing the anchor overboard he already had it only a short distance off the bottom, lowering it quietly until it stopped the boat, and instead of scraping the tackle box man already had his chosen lure ready to cast, sitting down, chances are you'd whack heck out of that little wiggling thing that suddenly plopped in front of your nose. Why? Because you wouldn't have a fear impulse but only the age-old impulse to eat that queer thing swimming away from you.

Such logic is called "thinking like a bass" and good bass fishermen do a lot of it. With commensurate results, too!

Accuracy comes next to stealth in bass-catching importance. In typical lakes and streams there is an abundance of cover in which bass will hide. You see, if the bass roamed around in open water, the little fish it hopes to feed on could see it coming too far away —and would scat.

So, to eat regularly, the bass hides under a pad, behind a rock, alongside a log, around a stump, and when an unwary fish swims by—Woosh—Mr. Bass has dined again!

Pin-point accuracy comes only to him who has tossed enough plugs to sharpen his eye and educate his thumb. It is wise to spend all possible spare time at home casting a practice plug around the back yard. See how close you can come to hedges, bushes, trees, etc., without getting tangled. Once your thumb masters feathering the spool of your reel and co-ordinates with your eye to stop the plug on your target—you're in!

Accuracy is so important! For instance, you're wading a stream fishing for smallmouthed bass which are lying along the deepest shore. You are wading the shallow side and shooting casts across stream. The nearest bridges are miles away and the stream is too deep to wade across. Therefore, if you haven't attained accuracy, you constantly overcast and lose plugs on the deep shore. To make it worse, you lose the bass, too.

Which lure should I use? Mr. Bass has the final say and you often have to try several until you find the right one. *(Florida State News Bureau)*

Also, in fishing lakes it is sometimes necessary to drop a surface plug into a lily-pad pocket the size of your hat. Hit it dead center and the pay-off is a dandy bass which has been waiting patiently below for an easy meal. Miss it and you miss the bass.

Or, you see a likely looking log. A cast laid at the back end of the log and brought along close to it means a big one might slam into your plug. Hit the log and you usually louse up your chance to fool the bass.

Again, you see a big swirl of water where a bass made a pass

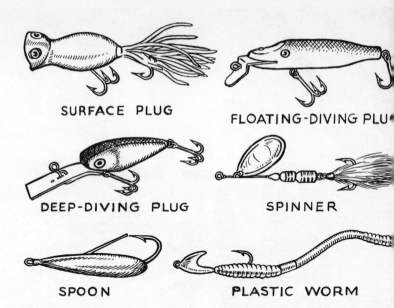

SURFACE PLUG

FLOATING-DIVING PLU

DEEP-DIVING PLUG

SPINNER

SPOON

PLASTIC WORM

Basic lures for black bass

at something. Drop your lure on that exact spot and nearly every time that bass will wham it, pronto! Miss it, or draw a backlash and you can guess the answer. Accuracy is a *MUST;* the less of it you have, the lower your score and the lighter your stringer.

The third requisite is lure selection and proper usage. Let's talk to the beginner at this plug-casting game, for we can take it for granted that the experienced plugger already has filled his box with accumulated lures, 8o per cent of which he hardly ever uses.

Don't let that showcase in the sporting-goods store awe you with the countless plugs on display—and don't let the clerk sell you everything in it, should he be inclined to do so. Here is a common sense approach.

Time and experiments have proven that the two most productive colors are yellow and red-white. Select these two colors in surface, floating-diving, and deep-diving plugs. Then add a bucktail spinner lure, a spoon, and a bottle of pork rind.

You have purchased only 8 lures and with these you can fish any kind of cover. But don't buy additional plugs unless you have

The black bass is the country's favorite fresh-water game fish. The bait-casting outfit shown here is used by many expert anglers when going after big bass. (*Minn. Div. of Publicity*)

a good reason, like seeing Joe Angler latch onto a nice mess of bass on a certain "Killer-Diller." At the end of the first year you won't have many plugs, but what you do have will be highly productive. And each will have a "reason for being."

This same foregoing logic applies to fly fishing, spinning, and live-bait fishing—approach, accuracy, and proper lures. The next logical bit of interest would be in proper tackle.

For all-round fishing throughout the nation's bass hotbeds, bait-casting and spin-casting outfits will take the majority of large-mouthed, smallmouthed, and spotted bass.

69

The rod should be 5½ to 6½ feet in length, light in action, and can be made of any material that suits your taste—tubular glass, solid glass, split bamboo, or metal. The tubular and solid-glass rods are wonderful if you buy a good name brand with a lively tip action.

The casting reel should have a lightweight aluminum spool so that it will start easily. The line needn't be more than 10- to 15-pound test—the lighter it is the easier it casts light lures. And very important is the use of a 3- to 4-foot nylon monofilament leader. This will stand up under many days' pounding, whereas a braided nylon line will fuzz up and weaken dangerously in a few hours of plug casting. A snap attachment at the end of your leader makes it handy to change lures. The swivel is superfluous because good lures don't twist your line and it's just that much more for a bass to be suspicious of.

And, if you want to catch the greatest possible number of bass with the greatest possible amount of pleasure, try a 6-foot, light-action rod, with a small, fast reel equipped with 6-pound test line, and cast some of these fine miniature plugs designed for spinning.

These miniature plugs are deadly and many of them are designed after larger, famous bait-casting lures that have been taking the bass for several decades. These small lures will take a greater total of bass and the lightness of the outfit will transmit to your hand the thrill of every fighting surge.

Spin casting requires about the same rods and lures as bait casting, but the push-button type reel is the big difference. It's great for a beginner and fairly trouble free. The line is 8- to 12-pound test monofilament.

Spinning gives the same thrills as casting or spin-casting except the lightness of the rod and line will test your skill in playing a fish. This form of light lure casting experienced a tremendous growth in popularity, particularly when American-made plugs became so widely available, replacing those early concoctions that twisted heck out of your line.

The reel is open face, free casting, equipped with 6- to 10-pound line. The rod from 6 to 7 feet long, and we prefer the fixed reel seat to sliding bands.

Fly fishing with a powerful 8½- to 9-foot rod, using a GAF torpedo taper line and popping bugs or feathered minnows, is great if you're husky enough to handle one of these outfits. It takes a stout back and a powerful arm to whip a bass-bugging outfit throughout a day's fishing.

It also takes a stout heart to stand the excitement that takes place when a 4- or 5-pound largemouthed, smallmouthed, or spotted bass blasts a hole in the water and erupts in a tail-dancing frenzy with your bug in its gaping mouth!

Also not to be overlooked as a steady producer of nice bass is the cane-pole outfit, particularly when backed by an old-timer at the art—and it is an art! You'll watch fascinated as the cane-pole expert kneels in the bow of the boat and noiselessly slips his lure down all sides of a stump, weed bed, or other promising cover.

He doesn't miss a single angle where a bass might see his offering. His fishing partner rows the boat ever so quietly, and every half hour they change places. Their lures take in about everything including plugs, spinner-fly combinations, pork chunk, spoons, and all kinds of live bait. Here is a mighty deadly way to fish for bass.

Adding to the enjoyment of bass fishing is the beauty of the country in which the bass are found. Deep, clear, fast flowing streams coursing through valleys, flatlands, gorges, woods, and swamps that have been materially unchanged for centuries. Also, some beautiful new waters created by dams, especially in Tennessee and Arkansas.

Nothing cleans the fast-pace fatigue of the city from your veins like greeting dawn afloat on a spring-fed lake or wading a stream of water so pure you can safely drink it.

When you go fishing here, you go for the day, and you go prepared to enjoy it—a parka for that unexpected storm, a change of clothing should you get dunked, and lunch should it turn out to be "one of those days."

Nearly all veteran fishermen have a family boat, motor, some a trailer, and many prefer to rough it in tents or sleeping bags. They just start out on a weekend fishing trip and stop where their fancy and the road takes them. Lakes and streams are plentiful in most sections and it's a challenge to fish new waters.

And now, let's take a quick look at those objects of all these angling machinations—the largemouthed, smallmouthed, and spotted bass.

By far the most popular and abundant is the largemouthed bass, found in most of the United States. It is recognizable by the jaw joint which ends behind the eye, and the distinct dark marking along the lateral line. Here is a powerhouse on fins, a roughhouser with your tackle, and the heavyweight of the sunfish family. It is hardy and apt to be found in any livable piece of water. One of the truly great gamefish of the world.

The smallmouth is conceded by many to hit harder, run faster, and fight longer than its two brethren. Be that as it may, here is an admirable fighting fish. It will stay only in cleaner, cooler waters and has a better eating flavor than the other two, ordinarily. Recognized by the jaw joint ending below the middle of the eye, and the vertical bars which usually mark the sides. Found mostly from Tennessee and Arkansas north into Canada, especially in the Mississippi tributary system and Great Lakes area.

The spotted bass is difficult to identify, except for those who have caught enough of all three species of bass. Jaw joint ends at back edge of eye and body markings are a series of diamond-shaped splotches along the back and lateral line. Easier to raise than either of the other two but harder to find. Found mostly in southern Ohio, Indiana, Illinois, Kansas, Tennessee, Kentucky, Arkansas, and the deep South. A grand antagonist, it will sometimes scare your pants off the way it smashes into a surface lure or murders an underwater lure.

Interestingly, just to muddy the waters a bit, the largemouthed bass, smallmouthed bass, and spotted bass aren't true bass at all but members of the sunfish family, which includes the crappies, bluegill, warmouth, rock bass, etc. The only true fresh-water basses are the white bass, yellow bass, and, hold your hat, the white perch!

All of which means nothing to the bass fisherman, for no matter what family they belong to—the largemouthed, smallmouthed, and spotted bass are top bananas for his stock of artificial lures.

Deep water alongside rocky cliffs often attracts and holds big bass. Deep-running and sinking lures worked way down usually work best here. *(Johnson Motors photo by Dick Matt)*

Now, let's talk about when and how the largest bass are consistently taken. Most fishermen think early spring is when the lunkers are taken. True, plenty of big bass are caught early, but the old mossbacks are racked up in the warmer months—at night!

That's right, in dead dark, and here's why. At this time of year the water is warmer in general. Oxygen content is higher where the cooler water is. The surface waters cool at night and that's where small fish cavort in search of food. Where small fish mess around, there you'll find the big fish ready to take them in for supper—all the way in!

The best fishermen we know don't start fishing until most other fishermen are quitting. About "first dark" until after midnight is best. And here are a few tricks to remember.

First, make sure your line is at full strength. Break off any fuzzed portion, because if Old Calijah latches on, you're going to need every pound that line tests. Then check over your equipment and make certain it is working smoothly. Night is no time to have your fishing outfit acting up.

It's sensible to fish a lake where you are familiar with the shore line, for here is where the majority of your fishing will be done. However, if the lake is fairly shallow and has cover near the surface, you can fish most anywhere.

You can take these big tackle-busters two ways—fishing down and fishing on top. For fishing down you'll want a fairly weedless lure like a jig and worm, bucktail-spinner combination, or a weedless spoon with pork rind. The pork rind is good because even fish like to chew the fat once in a while.

For surface fishing use a noisy lure with plenty of commotion. One of those that go "bloomp" when you jerk on it, because it has a cupped head, or one that goes "swish" because it has spinners fore and aft. Color is immaterial because they strike the point of commotion, not the pattern. If you don't believe this, try painting your favorite night plug a repulsive color and you'll find it takes just as many fish.

Start fishing when commotion on the lake has died down. You'll be just barely able to see the shore line. Keep an easy casting distance from shore and be extremely quiet. Let the fish know you are around and you'll never catch a lunker.

Have the anchor over the side of your boat so it can be eased down and keep the oars inside the boat when not in use. Here is where a sculling oar is ideal. It's quiet and effortless, never making a splash to give you away.

When you get a strike, set the hook good, then ease down the anchor. Otherwise you might drift too close to shore and spoil your chances of taking more fish from the same spot. Many times, at night, it's possible to take from two to a half-dozen fish in the same spot, if you work it right.

And here is a most important point to remember when you're working a surface lure after dark. Cast twice into each spot. That's right—two times, and there's a logical reason. Many times your lure lands 10 to 20 feet from the fish. The fish hears it land and starts moving in that direction. By the time the fish arrives there you have retrieved your lure and tossed it into another spot. This way you run that fish skinny trying to catch up with your lure.

However, if you cast twice into each spot, notice how many times you catch fish on that second cast—it'll surprise you! It's just because the fish moved in there when it heard your first cast light, then, when your second cast dropped near, the fish was there to bust it.

And, when working a surface lure, don't get into the rut of working it just the same all the time. Vary your retrieve from time to time.

Try leaving it lie motionless for 5 to 10 seconds, then move it very slightly, teasingly, as if the fish were right beside it. It might well be and a loud noise at this point would probably scare the fish rather than attract it. However, a very quiet jiggling would bring you an immediate strike.

If the quiet, slow retrieve doesn't do business, then step up the pace. Make it a bit noisier and faster. Here is a good rule that is fairly consistent. The calmer the water, the slower and quieter the retrieve. The choppier the water, the louder and faster the retrieve. In other words, you've got to make your lure heard above the noise of the wave action.

When fishing down with those weedless lures, just drop them along the shore, around weeds, rocks, logs, lily pads, or other cover and retrieve them very slowly. So slowly that they almost stop working. And, at times, let the lure settle to the bottom for 5 to 10 seconds before starting it in. Again, this gives the fish time to get there.

Night fishing is an art, and those who have become proficient at it usually are artists with their fishing outfits. It will amaze you how much even your ears play a part in nighttime accuracy, for just the sound of your reel tells you approximately when to thumb it down to keep from overshooting your mark!

But, night or day, bass fishing with artificial lures is one of the most challenging and rewarding ways to enjoy fishing. All men should know its joys.

If you haven't done it, hurry, you're missing much. If you have, you know what a great fraternity it is, wherever the bass are found!

*Chapter Six*

# BUGGING FOR BLACK BASS

## *by* TOM MCNALLY

TOM MCNALLY is a newspaperman and writer who spends all his time fishing or writing about it. Pick up any outdoor magazine and chances are there will be a feature story by Tom in it. He travels all over the country and to many parts of the world to gather material for his stories. At present he is outdoor editor of the Chicago *Tribune,* where his column is popular with many anglers and hunters. Currently he is on an ultralight spinning tackle binge in fresh and salt water, taking fish on hairlines and rods weighing a couple of ounces. But his favorite method is fly-rod fishing for black bass, about which he writes so clearly and knowingly.

A largemouthed black bass is a large mouth that swims. A smallmouthed black bass is a smaller mouth that also swims. Each of these fin-propelled mouths patrols a watery world filled with a squirming abundance of minnows, crayfish, worms, newts, frogs, nymphs, eels, and hellgrammites. These subsurface foods—because of their availability and abundance—make up the bulk of a bass's diet.

But both the largemouthed and smallmouthed black bass like nothing better than to tip back on their caudal fins and rise to the surface, sweeping it clean of insects, large bugs, wounded minnows, mice, and so on. Even though the greater part of a bass's menu consists of underwater life, he's happiest when feeding at the surface. More bass are taken on surface plugs and popping bugs than on any other lure!

Surface lures seem peculiarly designed for the bass—particularly the largemouth. When a southern cracker boy is minted into manhood, he inherits a squirrel gun and a surface plug. The plug may be a battered, tooth-pocked chunk of wood blunted on the nose and pointed at the tail, or it may be a wood sliver 6 inches long, covered with chipped paint, and sporting tarnished metal propellers fore and aft. He may fish the plug from a short length of stout string tied to a long cane pole, dabbling the lure here and there in lily-bed pockets; or he may use a stiff, 3-foot rod and rusty reel to heave it, side-arm style to the edge of weeds and stumps. Regardless of his poor tackle and method of presentation, the southern angler's addiction to surface lures attests to his understanding of bass fishing.

Nothing raises the ire of shallow water bass more than fussing, sputtering, gurgling surface lures. And of the various surface lures, nothing breaks up a bass faster than a fly-rod bug.

I believe there is no deadlier system of taking bass than fly fishing with popping or similar bugs *when the fish are in the shallows.* I've fished with many men who were devout spin-casters and pluggers, but I've never known one who didn't take up bass bug fishing after seeing poppers in action on days when the fish were shallow. Naturally no surface lure is very effective when bass are deep—which is much of the time—but when they're close enough to the top to spot a floating bug they'll go for it fast and hard.

Probably it is the small size of bugs that makes them especially appealing to bass. Bugs hit the water with a slight, lifelike "*splat*," instead of a loud, fish-scaring splash as do some oversized heavy plugs. A fly-rod bug acts natural on the water, much like a real locust or grasshopper. Because they are light, fly-rod bugs are extremely realistic on the water. Each time you twitch or "pop" a bug a stream of bubbles filters down into the water, then curves to the surface again. This *bubble trail* draws fish, causes them to investigate, and helps arouse the peculiar emotions bass seem to have.

Many fishermen try bass-bugging briefly, then give it up as a bad job because of casting difficulties. Bass bug fishing is the most difficult form of fly fishing. Because of the big, wind-resistant bugs used, what amounts to a minor fault in ordinary fly casting becomes a major problem when bugging. Each error in casting form is magnified when casting popping bugs.

The would-be bass fisherman must first take the time to de-

Tom McNally

velop his casting skill. The angler who spends most of his time on the pond fighting his tackle, instead of concentrating on working his lure, will not enjoy much success. Many more bass are taken at ranges of 40 to 60 feet than on casts dropping within

20 feet of the boat. It is not necessary to be a tournament-type caster to take bass on bugs, but you must be able to handle your tackle reasonably well. And, if you master the "double haul" of fly casting so that you can chuck a popper 100 feet, you'll be in the bass-busting game with a fistful of Aces. An adept fly caster, letting his tackle do the work, is able to fish heavy, wind-resistant bass bugs from dawn to dark without fatigue. This is opposed to the inept caster who, after only an hour or two of sawing his fly line through the air, is completely bushed; fighting the fly rod has beat his arm and shoulder muscles so badly he's forced to pick up a spinning or bait-casting rig.

This is not a discourse on how to fly cast, since it's impossible to teach fly casting via the printed word, but I wish to impress that casting *IS* important in bass bug fishing. If you are not a reasonably proficient fly caster, go out and become one before going further into the business of bass-bugging.

Most starting bass-bug fishermen "under arm" themselves, choosing equipment so poor that not even a tournament champion could cast bugs with it. A "balanced" outfit is needed, meaning the line should be of the proper weight to bring out the action of the rod. And a fly outfit that is just right for small stream trout fishing won't do for bass-bugging. It is not necessary to arm yourself with the biggest fly rod you can find, but you need a rod and matching line sufficiently powerful to handle bugs well. Rods 8 to 9½ feet in length, weighing 4½ to 6½ ounces and taking size GBF or GAF lines are preferred. For years I used an 8½-foot, 5-ounce bamboo rod with great satisfaction. Then I went to a bamboo stick 9½ feet, 6 ounces, but eventually decided it had too much authority for bass fishing. I finally settled on a 9-foot, 5-ounce glass rod—and have used it exclusively for the past six years. It takes a short-bellied GAF line, has a fast tip action that helps put line out quickly, and a slow power reserve in its butt section that makes casts of 100 feet possible with a minimum of two false casts.

Accuracy and distance come with practice, but remember that a balanced outfit is the first step to casting ease. Learn the "double haul" and how to "shoot" line—you'll do better at bugging.

Assuming you have the right tackle and know how to use it, allow me to move on to leaders and bugs. Leaders can be dispensed with quickly. Use tapered leaders. Mine range 8 to 14 feet, depending on the clarity of the water. Tapers are altered according to the size bug and wind conditions, but as a rule leader butts usually are 25-pound test, then 20, then shorter lengths of 15, 12, 10, 8 and 6. Tippet sizes vary according to popper weight or its resistance in the air, wind, average size of the bass, or whether fishing reasonably open water or water infested with weeds, stumps, and snags.

Bugs are more complicated. Doubtless the ones in your box are all little bass killers, but not 5 per cent of the commercial bugs available today are worth the space they take up in your local tackle emporium. You're better off if you make your own.

The best bugs are made of cork, not balsa wood. Balsa is soft, will break from around the hook before you land many bass, and hooks turn more easily in balsa bodies than they do in cork. Some plastic materials such as "styrofoam" make good bug bodies.

One of the prime requisites of a good bug is that it be mounted on a long-shank hook. Hook sizes 1/0 and 2/0, 3X long, humpshank are best and I mount them in cork bodies at a downward angle. The length of the hook and angle of mounting make for surer hooking. The majority of commercially made bugs have hooks too short and with too little "bite" to make for certain hooking. It's smart to be sure any bug you use has a hook long enough to take a bite back at a rising bass.

A good bug must "pop" well and pick up off the water easily on long casts, and not have too much hair or feathers. A lot of frilling may make a bug attractive to you, but normally it means little to a bass. Too much hackling creates excessive wind resistance, and makes a bug difficult to cast.

Bass fishermen are suckers for accumulating lures and I was that way too when I first took to bass-bugging. But over the years, I've whittled the number of my favorite bugs down to six. Of course, I occasionally use others, but day in and day out these six account for the most bass.

I tend to use large bugs because I dislike baby bass or bluegills interrupting my thinking when I'm concentrating on big stuff. A

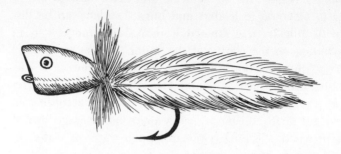

A good bass bug has long-shank hook and a wide gap between the hook point and cork body

large popping frog, with cork body and bucktail hair legs, has accounted for more big bass for me than any other fly-rod lure I own. The bug is built on a 1/0 or 2/0, 3X shank hook, with its cork face angling back so it pops well, yet picks up easily. Its bucktail legs are about 2½ inches long and when mounted in the cork correctly they open and close as you work the bug. This kicking action is important. I've seen bass rise under this bug and follow it along, staring. But they wouldn't hit until the legs were wiggling like a frog's.

Getting this frog bug's legs to "work" right is a matter of feel. Since none of the bugs you make will be identical, the legs of one will kick at one speed, those of another at a different speed. It's best to allow these frog bugs to rest for a moment after hitting the water, then pop them gently by raising the rod tip to make the legs jump. Let the bug sit motionless while its legs flutter, and if a bass doesn't wallop it, work it a few feet more, then pause again. Finally pop it along steadily just fast enough to make the legs open and close.

Another excellent bug is a simple yellow popper. It has yellow saddle hackle feathers extending about 1½ inches beyond the hook, usually tied so they splay outward in "breather" style. This way, the hackles wiggle actively when the bug is worked. The bug has no unnecessary frills to build up air resistance. It casts accurately. It can be made to gurgle, splutter, pop, or skitter along until it raises the temper of a bass.

Five of Tom McNally's pet bass bugs: top left, green frog with bucktail
hair legs; top right, Gerbubble Bug; center left, Bullet Bug; center right,
standard yellow popper; and bottom, Powder Puff.

Tom Loving of Pasadena, Maryland, invented the Gerbubble
Bug, a zany-looking creation unknown to most fly rodders. This
bug is flat on the bottom and top, with hackles buried in slits in
its sides. These side hackles add to the bug's air resistance, making it more difficult to cast than ordinary bugs, but they give it
a fluttering appearance on the water. The thing looks almost alive
even when sitting still. This is a bug that just can't be fished too
slowly.

83

Another bug that should be in every fly fisherman's kit is the Bullet Bug. I originated it years ago for striped bass and bluefish in Chesapeake Bay, then discovered almost accidentally that it was death on bass. One day on a Maryland pond, Chuck Besche and I found a school of largemouths riding herd on minnows, but they ignored every popper we threw at them. When I finally tried a Bullet Bug—which doesn't pop but skitters along like a wounded minnow—the bass climbed all over it. Four inches long, the bug has a bullet-shaped head and flowing saddle hackles. Two feathers are wound palmer-style behind the cork body. They should be made on flat or ball-eye hooks, which don't make a bug dive as some hooks with turned-down eyes do.

The Marm Minnow is another excellent bug for use on schooling bass. It's a mere sliver of a lure, yet is one of the deadliest I've seen in recent years. This bug, about 2 inches long, is shaped like a minnow and acts like one on the water. It has a blunt head, and when stripped across the water darts and splashes like a frantic minnow. The bug originated in Florida for use on the famed St. Johns River when the bass are running rampant after shad minnows.

I have a strong dislike for so-called "weedless" bugs and most deer-hair bugs, since nearly all of them have poor hooking qualities, do not perform well on the water, and usually cast badly. A bushy, deer-hair (untrimmed) creation called the Powder Puff works well in extremely weedy water. Strictly speaking, this one should be classified as a fly, not a bug. It is made by tying gobs of deer hair on a short-shank 2/0 hook. The billowing hair causes the bug to ride high, right over lily pads, stumps, grass, and weeds. Though the hook point is covered, a striking bass forces the soft hairs down and the hook goes home.

Color is comparatively unimportant in bass bugs, yet fishermen everywhere seem to prefer yellow, black, white, and brown, or combinations of those colors with red. Cork bugs with only a coat of clear lacquer often take as many fish as colored bugs.

How to work bugs is something learned by experience. You can pop them too hard or too easily; some must be fished slowly, others fast. It's necessary to experiment until you find the best method for fishing each bug and this can vary one day to the

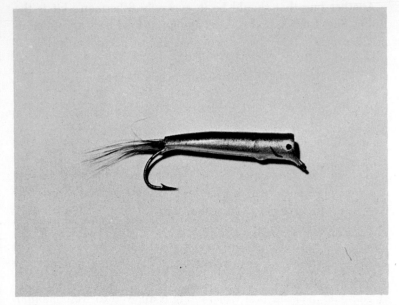

Marm minnow is one of the deadliest fly rod surface lures. Bug looks like a minnow—and acts like one on the water.

next, or what is right during the morning's fishing may be wrong that evening. Most important to realize is that you have put a dabble of cork and feathers out onto the water and you must handle it in such a way as to make it look alive to a bass. In "playing" a bug, imagine that always there is a bass lurking below it. Concentrate on animating that inanimate piece of cork and if there are any bass around they'll do the rest. In working a bug I attempt to project my mind to the bug, thinking of nothing else except making that cork and feathers come alive. It is this mental projection that gives the expert his heralded "touch." This concentration and "feel" that a successful bug fisherman develops is difficult to explain, but it is real. Many casters dislike unnecessary conversation with an oarsman because it takes their mind away from what they're trying to do with a bug.

At the start of a day's fishing it is well to experiment with different actions, many of which can be tried on a single cast. The bug can be rested for a long time, then popped slowly, then quickly, then rested again. You can make a cast and swoop the bug across the surface in a single, fast retrieve. Most important is to break up your retrieve, making the bug wobble and waggle until it looks alive. When a bass hits during a particular kind of lure play, stay with that method as long as it continues to pay off.

In general try to put your bugs down lightly by stopping your cast before the bug hits the water. This is done by halting the rod at the ten o'clock position at completion of the forward cast, then raising the tip up and back slightly as the line drops. The line will fall lightly to the water, and the bug will hit with a gentle *splat*. Remember that real bugs such as locusts, big beetles, moths, and grasshoppers are light and settle to the water without heavy splashes. Your bugs should settle lightly too, without any fish-scaring *"thunk."*

Normally bass hit best when a bug is allowed to "rest" motionless for some time after first striking the water. Think of a bug falling to the water and being momentarily stunned. After a few minutes he collects himself, realizes his predicament, and starts kicking furiously.

A bass usually swims off a few feet when an object falls to the surface nearby. If the object doesn't move, the bass's curiosity is aroused and he swims back, staring. He lurks below the item, watching and waiting for signs of life. When the object—in this case your bug—is twitched gently, the bass takes it for a struggling insect and comes roaring up behind with that big mouth of his.

Most fishermen allow a bug to sit perfectly still until all the rings caused by its falling to the water have subsided. When the surface again is glass-calm they twitch the lure—but not before. When retrieving, bass most often are taken by working the bug lightly and slowly, with frequent pauses between twitches. Sometimes it's good to just tighten the fly line enough to make your bug nod its head a little—repeating this maneuver over and over.

Much of the time it's best for a bug to remain absolutely motionless just after striking the water. I wish to emphasize this because many fishermen *think* their bugs are motionless after

Ideal bass-bugging water with lunker largemouths lurking under the lily pads.

hitting the water. They do not deliberately twitch or "pop" the bug after it falls, hence they think it is still. I've observed that the average bug fisherman, however, makes his cast and then unconsciously moves the rod tip up—causing the bug to slide a foot or so across the surface. Most times the bug should be *dead still* after striking the water, and this can be accomplished only by continuing to lower the rod on completion of the cast. Most fishermen also take slack out of the line carelessly, which also causes the bug to slide.

After delivering a cast, take slack out of the line as quickly as possible without moving the bug. Keep the rod tip low so that if a fish hits you can raise the rod sharply to set the hook. If a bass doesn't rise, raise the rod tip slightly but sharply enough to make the bug jump ahead and "pop." Allow it to remain motionless again, then pop it again. Always be sure to strip in all slack line without moving the lure, so that you'll be prepared to strike a rising fish at any time.

Sometimes rocking a bug just a little is very effective. The popping, resting technique should be repeated constantly until the bug is near the boat. Some fishermen then strip line in steadily until the bug is close enough to roll it up for another cast. But often bass follow top water baits, so it is better to just pop them all the way in. This way a bug is "working" all the time, not just when it is against the bank in the shallows. Most bass taken on bugs are caught around shore-line cover, but many are hooked almost at the boat when bugs are fished on a full retrieve.

Sometimes, particularly in the fall, a very fast retrieve works well with popping bugs. On this kind of retrieve the bug is popped along steadily and fast. You make the water fly—but not so much that a bass thinks a water buffalo is swimming over him. The fast retrieve can be varied, too, by popping the bug along steadily and fast for 3 or 4 feet, then resting it, then moving it again fast for several feet, then resting it again—this time waiting a long while before popping it again. Normally when my bug is about halfway back to the boat—past the area where I believe the fish are—I work it straight in to the boat with steady twitches of the rod tip.

It's not possible to overemphasize the necessity of keeping slack out of the fly line once your bug is on the water. If you have slack and a bass hits, chances are you won't hook him. Keep slack out of the line, and when a fish hits raise the rod tip fast as you can and with considerable authority, to drive the hooks

A bass rises from beneath lily pads to take a yellow popping bug.

home. A swift strong movement of the rod is absolutely necessary if you are to hook most of the bass that come to your bugs. I strike so hard and fast when a bass engulfs my popper that, if it's a small bass, I will likely skitter him right across the surface. Some anglers, even ones of experience, believe that a fisherman should delay setting the hook when using surface lures. I've tried this method, but most of the bass merely spat out my bugs when I delayed setting the hook.

Bugs have a way of upsetting a bass's equilibrium. For example, you can often cast repeatedly to one spot and make a bass so mad he'll come rushing up to knock your bug silly. Whenever you find a submerged stump, log, or other cover that you think must surely harbor a bass, keep casting to it, and chances are if there's a bass there he'll eventually come up fighting mad. Sometimes it takes 20, 30, or more casts to a spot before a bass is unnerved enough to strike. The important thing in making repeated casts to one place is to be certain only your popper and leader fall on the spot where you believe the bass to be. Never cast so far beyond a stump, for instance, that your fly line settles by the stump. There's nothing stupid about a bass, and if he's a big fellow he's got fourteen or fifteen summers behind him. A bass can learn a lot about fishermen in fifteen years.

Too many bug fishermen work their poppers only by twitching the rod tip. But it's possible to make a bug really perform by working the fly line with the left hand. It's also possible to combine rod tip work with left-hand action to make a bug struggle across the top in a very lifelike manner. Try casting a bug and allowing it to rest, then pop it by jerking the rod or line. Next make the bug swim rapidly over the surface for about a yard by pointing the rod at the bug and hauling quickly on the line. The bug will bounce and skitter over the top, much like a wounded minnow that's lost his marbles.

Making a bug "splat" when it hits the water is sometimes a killing technique. The Gerbubble Bug is great for this because it's flat on the bottom and makes a resounding "splat" when put down on the water properly. To make a bug "splat," throw a wide-bow cast, and as the forward cast straightens pull back hard on the line with your left hand, simultaneously raising the rod tip. This causes the leader to straighten quickly, pulling the bug backward and down so that it hits the water and goes "splaaaaat!" On such casts, bass often strike the moment the bug hits the water.

The Gerbubble Bug is great around lily pads. Cast it directly onto a pad, putting an extra push into the rod so that the bug plunks down hard. Bass lurking beneath the pads will know something has landed nearby, and frequently swim over to the pad waiting to see what happens. After a few moments, pull the Gerbubble Bug off the pad—and it may drop right into the gaping mouth of a bass.

Fish bugs slowly around lily pads, trying to make them act like some injured creature struggling to reach a pad and climb off the water to safety.

There are days when bass won't take regular bugs. Standard poppers are best when the water is glass-calm, but you must frequently fish under conditions of riffled water. Perhaps bass can't see a floater well when the surface is rippled by wind or perhaps they don't like to rise under such conditions. On such days the Bullet Bug or Marm Minnow work wonders. Cast them out and sweep the line in quickly so the bugs scoot across the surface. They'll dive under occasionally, where they act like feather minnows or big streamers. You can make them dart along under the surface for 3 or 4 feet, then let them rise slowly to the top. Bass hit them most often when they're floating "dead" toward the surface.

Retrieving Bullet Bug just under the surface of water. It should be allowed to rise to the top every foot or so

If you get the right cadence into your retrieve, you can make a Bullet Bug or Marm Minnow swim in sawtooth-fashion just under the surface. They're fished like a minnow that's been injured and can't stay down. Cast, let the bug sit a moment, then yank it under. It will go down about 4 inches and move forward a foot, then float to the surface. Keep this up and the bug will move sawtooth-fashion, diving, darting, surfacing.

The Marm Minnow can give you a riot of fishing under conditions of calm water too. Every fisherman has seen tiny minnows on the surface. Their noses break out of the surface film, and as the minnow darts along he leaves a "V" wake. When the water is table-top smooth, these tiny "Vs" can be seen great distances.

The Marm Minnow, when worked properly, makes a "V" wake exactly like a minnow struggling over the surface. The bug should be fished with a high-floating line, and stripped over the top by pulling line in with foot-long hauls.

Bugs should be fished around logs, stumps, underwater obstructions, fallen trees, weed beds, lily pads, and so on. Pick out a likely spot, and try to make your first cast good. Generally its the first cast that produces. A good second cast, following an initial presentation that is sloppy, rarely produces adult bass.

Boat handling is important, too. Approach bassy spots carefully, and with a minimum of boat disturbance. Do most of your casting sitting down, particularly if you are unable to toss a long line. Bass rising to a surface lure in clear water can spot a fisherman standing in a nearby boat.

Bass bug fishing has its limitations, since it's most productive when the water is calm and when bass are in the shallows. Thus bugging is no cure for all of your bass fishing ills, but there are times when no other system will produce as well.

After all, there's a kind of affinity between bass and bugs.

Chapter Seven

# HOW TO CATCH STEELHEAD

## *by* DON HARGER

DON HARGER of Salem, Oregon, is right in the heart of the steelhead country. He has fished for the mighty steelhead in most of the well-known rivers of the Pacific Northwest. A skilled fly tyer, he has tied many trout and steelhead flies commercially. Until recently he wrote an outdoor column in the *Oregon Statesman*, published in his home town of Salem. Don has also contributed articles to outdoor magazines and fishing encyclopedias.

FLASHING brilliantly in the late autumn sun, against a gaudy background of frost-tinted leaves, a steelhead cartwheeled in a breathtaking leap and slammed back into the current, free from the frightening, unknown force which had been holding him against his will. He turned quickly, heading into the current of the stream, working his jaws deliberately, and realizing that he was rid of the unseen torment. With a flip of his powerful tail the steelhead quartered the stream current and took a position below a slanting ledge of rock which knifed itself through the stream bed. Sheltered from the main force of the current, the silver and blue fish finned lazily, totally unaware of the angler on the far bank of the stream who was hurriedly reeling in a slack line and who was apparently far more annoyed than was the steelhead from the pulse-quickening experience just ended.

Pacific Coast steelhead (*Salmo gairdnerii*) have probably excited, thrilled, and humiliated more anglers year in and year out than have any other fresh-water game fish of North America. He (the steelhead) is every angler's fish, and every angler wants him. For twelve months of the year steelhead may be found in many of the rivers of the Pacific slope. For twelve months of the

93

year steelheaders will be along the banks of those rivers trying their own pet methods and baits and lures. It matters not to the steelhead angler whether it be raining, snowing, sleeting, freezing, or stifling from a hot summer sun. Give him fishable water and he will be on his favorite stream clothed for the occasion and ready to do battle should the gods be so favoring as to put him in contact with one of the most magnificent fish in the world.

I have known many steelhead fishermen over a period of years who have fished patiently if not wisely season after season and who have counted the years until they ran out of fingers and they still have a first steelhead to hook and land. To this heroic never-quit band of steelheaders there grows ever stronger with the passing of the seasons a gnawing certainty in their minds that there lives a deep, closely guarded secret governing the taking of steelhead. A secret shared by a minority of the steelheaders who catch fish on nearly every trip and who rarely if ever go through a day of steelheading without at least hooking a fish.

As strong as this belief may become over the years in the minds of these steelheaders, there is really no basis for it regardless of how many fishless seasons may have gone by. The only secret, if it may be called such at all, is held by the steelhead themselves and may be openly shared with any angler who will devote a little time and thought to the fish himself and to the "whys" of his never-changing stream habits, which are as reliable year after year as the day itself.

The stream habits of the great Pacific Coast steelhead may be learned at the same time one is learning to "read" a stream, which is of greatest importance in being consistently successful when fishing for any member of the salmo group. Being able to read the character of a stream bottom by carefully studying the surface currents is not as difficult as it may seem. A few odd hours devoted to observing just what it is on the stream bed that causes the many rifts, bulges, slicks, and other surface disturbances will be time well spent and will graduate the seemingly luckless angler to that group of fishermen, who, if there is a fish in the stream, will seldom fail to find him.

The bulk of an erroneous cloak of mystery which has clothed the Pacific Coast steelhead ever since the late Zane Grey intro-

Don Harger

95

duced the fish to the angling world may be eliminated if the angler will accept the fish as he really is, nothing more than a rainbow trout that has chosen to spend a portion of his life at sea where he grows to tackle-straining proportions on the rich and abundant food life of the Pacific Ocean.

As a matter of fact, the large resident trout found in many of the rivers and lakes of North America are often far more difficult to take than is the steelhead. The resident trout have become overly suspicious and may be put down or frightened by a bad cast or by the steady parade of wader-clad anglers shuffling through a riffle or quiet run. A steelhead, on the other hand, will quite often be hooked by an angler who may have been preceded by a dozen or more fishermen who failed to touch a fish while working the same stretch of water. Therein lies one clue to successful steelheading.

To simplify the problem, which seems to confront so many frustrated anglers bent on taking steelhead, it can be broken down into three smaller or subproblems, each of which can be digested more easily than can the problem in the whole. (A) The steelhead and his stream habits. (B) Learning to read water. (C) Presentation of fly, bait, or lure. The answer to any one of the three subproblems by itself will not aid materially in the taking of steelhead unless it be the latter, presentation of fly, bait, or lure. Even then it would be more on the side of luck if the offering were fished within striking distance of a steelhead no matter how perfect the presentation.

In taking subproblem (A), the steelhead and his stream habits, we must first be made aware of his precarious position in this predatory world. From the moment the steelhead is little more than an eyed egg starting life on his parental spawning bed, he is constantly besieged by scores of natural enemies and is constantly harassed by man and by the many man-made monuments of progress along with the many fishery-destroying blemishes left on the land by man in his greedy efforts to exploit the continent's natural resources.

On his downstream migration the steelhead, in schools of fingerlings, is under constant attack by large families of mergansers and other birds of prey, who, in this world of diminishing wild-

Steelhead fishing is often done in picturesque country such as this Oregon stream. Steelhead move up most of the coastal rivers in successive waves from spring to winter. *(Oregon State Highway Dept.)*

life habitat, are also struggling for survival. Anglers, in those waters where the minimum size limit for trout is 6 inches, also take a heavy toll of the young downstream migrants. As soon as the steelhead reach the sea, those lucky enough to have overcome the hazards of nonscreened irrigation ditches, high dams, flagrant stream pollution, and scores of other hurdles, they immediately become prey for fish of the Pacific Ocean.

With this constant fight for survival it is little wonder that the steelhead use every precaution, by instinct, to avoid the many dangers awaiting them on their travels to the sea and on the return to their parent stream on the inevitable spawning migration. It is little wonder too that they choose the deep, fast currents in their journey upriver and choose every bit of protective cover offered by the various discrepancies of the stream bed itself. As is the case with all of God's wild creatures, the steelhead has been endowed with a powerful instinct for survival and he uses it to the full extent of his ability.

To give an example of instinctive fear, I recall the only time I ever witnessed the sudden and hasty departure of a trio of steelhead alarmed by no more than a fleeting shadow of a large steelhead fly hanging momentarily in the air before its descent to the water.

I was fishing Oregon's Little North Fork one day several years ago with John Clayton of Salem, Oregon. It was early March and the trip was one of investigation to learn if there might possibly be any steelhead in the river at that time. The day was bright and sunny and the stream low and clear, making it a memorable day to be in the open whether the fish were there or not.

We left the automobile and made our way to a large point of rock where the river gathered speed after a short rest in a deep, green pool before it burst its way into a white water chute some distance below. Directly below us, lying in a narrow pocket between the upward thrusts of bedrock, were three beautiful steelhead. As they finned lazily in their protective pocket away from the main force of the current, I hurried to get my fly rod.

After assembling the rod and tying a large red and white weighted steelhead fly to the end of a 9-foot leader, I walked a short distance upriver and picked my way down the steep bank

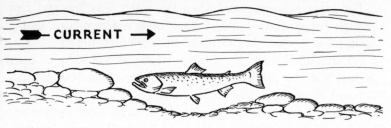

In fast water look for steelhead in the deeper pockets and small holes

to the water. In my fevered excitement I had given no thought to
the brilliant sun in relation to my casting position. It was a bad
oversight. I could see the three beautiful fish through the clear
water, where they held position near the center of the stream
and some 50 feet below me.

Stripping line from the single-action, steelhead fly reel I made
a few false casts up across the deep pool to get out line and then
I slowly turned while continuing the false casting. The dark,
streamlined shapes of the three steelhead were still there when
I shot the line out across the river some distance above them. At
the end of the cast the rod was pulled back slightly to give a bit
of slack line and the big fly hung for a split second in the air.
The sun was in exactly the right position, or rather wrong position. At that instant the large steelhead fly caused a shadow,
magnified some by the water, to flit across the vision of the steelhead. As one, the three fish shot out of the pocket with incredible
speed and disappeared into the green, protective depths of the
pool.

Those steelhead had chosen that resting or holding spot because it offered them everything desired. The depth of the water
at that point was about 6 feet, and it was gathering speed enough
to mix and contain sufficient oxygen. The pocket between the
two upward thrusts of bedrock afforded a sizable area where the
main force of the current was deflected, slightly upward, allowing the steelhead to loaf with a minimum of effort. Most important of all, the position offered an open escape route to the nearby
pool and the safety of its dark depths.

99

For many seasons since, when the water was low and clear enough for good visibility, I have observed steelhead in that same pocket, which has changed little through the years. Each successive small wave of upstream steelhead will leave as many as half a dozen fish in that pocket as preceding tenants move out and make their way farther upriver.

In stream after stream, from Alaska to as far south as Southern California, the habits of the steelhead remain the same year after year, unchanged except when a stream or river itself is changed by the untiring and often careless efforts of man in his conquest of nature.

Steelhead will instinctively seek out the places of rest which afford them protection from the main current forces and which offer them a quick retreat to safety. Rocky outcroppings in the stream bed, underwater rock ledges, submerged logs, large scattered boulders, all offer respite from the main current and will invariably shelter one or more steelhead provided the water is of sufficient depth to add to the safety factor. This depth may range between 5 and 15 feet, give or take a little, depending upon the speed of the water.

When streams become swollen and discolored from heavy winter rains and the normal currents change to rushing torrents, steelhead will change their positions and seek the quieter, less turbulent waters of the back eddies, or they may seek the shelter of some deep pool, which, rather than an unattractive stretch of stagnant water, has suddenly become alive with the wild deluge. The deeper pools will often afford shelter from the smashing freshet as the main force of flooding river will normally embrace the upper currents, leaving the bottom level more or less undisturbed.

Too, a sudden rising of the rivers will often bring new runs of steelhead from the sea and will send most of the fish already in the river many miles farther upstream. The great majority of steelheaders feel that it is a waste of time to fish a rising river. I go along with that line of thinking, as the chances of hooking a fish in water which is rising and rapidly becoming discolored are very slim indeed.

Once the storm has passed and the rivers start to recede and

Steelhead often rest beside or below a submerged boulder

clear, it is time to don steelhead clothing and lose little time in getting to a favorite stream. The steelhead will begin to move back into normal resting areas once again and will usually hold in those locations until a new storm brings further rising of the waters and then the process will be repeated. And so it shall continue as long as our rivers contain steelhead and as long as our streams remain physically unchanged.

Subproblem (B), learning to read water, is probably the least difficult of the three and yet I know few anglers personally who can travel from stream to stream and with little more than a casual glance at a stretch of water tell whether or not it should hold steelhead. However, few though they may be, these anglers who are adept at reading water could be dropped on the gravel bars of a stream never visited before and they would catch steelhead, assuming of course that steelhead were in the river.

The easiest way in which an angler can learn to read water, one by which a few fishing acquaintances have learned, is to select a stream not too far from home for a lengthy study period. For best results the stream should be of a size and depth that can be waded easily during the low-water months but could not possibly be waded during the high-water months of winter.

The angler should choose a stretch of the stream where the bottom offers a study of every possible obstruction, depression, or discrepancy that may be encountered when angling strange waters many miles from home. The study area or areas should be covered as completely as possible during the low-water period.

A small sketch pad and pencil and an observing eye is all that is needed.

The study area may be broken into several sections on the sketch pad for easier consumption at home. Draw in every single boulder, rocky outcropping, submerged log, and deep pocket. If there is a small hump in the stream bed, sketch that in on the section where it belongs. Leave out absolutely nothing that may deflect or alter the current in any way. An uneven stream bank on the deep-water side of the stream will often provide a pocket or two, each large enough to harbor a fish from the main force of the current.

As soon as the stream bed obstructions are sketched you may begin your reading lesson. Begin in the low-water period and study carefully the surface currents and their reactions to the immediate underwater obstructions. Make notes of those reactions on your first observation. With the first slight rise of the stream go over the area again. Once more note the surface reactions of the stream current in relation to the underwater obstructions. Keep going over your study area again and again at various water heights until you know at a glance what causes each glassy slick, each gurgling whirlpool, each riffle collar, as the main currents struggle to go over or around some solid obstruction. Learned in this manner your knowledge will never stray, and you should read at a glance any stream you may choose to fish.

In coming to the subproblem (C), presentation of fly, bait, or lure, we get into the most important part of the main problem. Once you have knowledge of the steelhead and his stream habits and are skilled enough at reading water so that you will know where the fish are most likely to be holding, there is no further problem than that of presenting your offering so that it carries the best possible chance of inviting a strike. It matters little what your skill may be in casting record distances with fly rod, spin rod, drift rod, or casting rod. More important is what you do with the offering once it reaches the target area.

I seriously doubt if many anglers have ever been subjected to such a painful, thorough, and dramatic lesson on the importance of presentation as was your writer some years ago on the

Klamath River in California. I was most fortunate in having been able, along with my wife, to spend a wonderful five weeks of fly fishing on the Klamath with the late John Atherton, well-known artist and author of *The Fly and The Fish,* and his charming wife, Maxine.

We fly fished daily from early morning until late evening for the beautiful summer steelhead of the Klamath which ranged in size from 2 pounds to 8 pounds. Though smaller on the average than the winter steelhead, the summer fish more than makes up for his size with his spectacular acrobatics and his willingness to take a fly.

There was a most attractive piece of water some distance upriver from our camp which rarely failed to produce a steelhead or two. It was our practice to fish this water nearly every morning, the four of us spacing ourselves at wide intervals and fishing slowly, but thoroughly, downstream through the fishable area.

At the very head of this stretch, beyond casting range from our usual fishing position, an outcropping of jagged rock thrust itself through the surface, forming a small island running lengthwise with the river. It was approximately 30 feet in length and perhaps 8 feet in width. The main current slammed into the upstream face of this obstruction curling mostly to the near side and bouncing along hurriedly to rejoin a lesser current skirting the far side to form a quiet eddy where the stronger current gathered it in again to race off to the sea many miles away.

The eddy was a natural station in which steelhead could rest until the cover of darkness offered safe passage upstream through a fast but extremely shallow stretch of water. It was a difficult spot to reach from where a fly might be presented properly, and only after a frustrating period of trial and error did we discover a route across the shallow riffle which would allow us to cover the spot from directly above.

Numerous stretches of the Klamath River present difficult wading problems because of a thick coating of algae on the rocky stream bed. With a bottom nearly solid with rocks ranging from the size of a baseball to that of a basketball our particular route to the casting position was quite tricky and many times during our wading we came within an eyelash of losing our footing and sprawling headlong into the river.

Atherton was the first to pick his way across the shallows and take a fish from this challenging piece of water. I was not the least bit surprised at his success since he was, without question, the most accomplished fly fisherman it has ever been my pleasure to watch and fish with.

On the following morning I drew the honor of fishing the island first while the remainder of the party fished on down the stretch of good water below. For more than an hour I cast steelhead flies into that choice area, changing patterns several times, and was finally convinced that, although my efforts had very carefully covered every inch, I had spent a slippery, straining interlude casting to barren water.

Noticing Atherton and our wives plodding back upstream along the gravel bar bordering the lower run, I slipped and stumbled my way back across the slick shallows to greet them and exchange notes on the results of the morning's angling. Atherton seemed quite surprised that I had not hooked a fish, and he turned to gaze out across the water toward the little rocky island. The ensuing few moments will live with me for the remainder of my angling years, a vivid picture of the always present importance of presentation.

Atherton shook his head as if unable to accept my "barren water" theory, continuing his fixed stare across the river. "There just has to be a fish there," he said to no one in particular, and with a sudden decision, based on an unparalleled knowledge of fishing and all of its counterparts, he fought his way across the treacherous footing to the far side of the river while I relaxed on the gravel bar with the ladies and waited for him to fare as I had.

As we watched, Atherton made a long, beautiful downstream cast, halting his fly rod with a sudden reverse motion just as the fly reached the maximum limit. Line, leader, and fly snapped backward several feet to drop gently on the water in a series of slack line loops. I noticed then several large coils of line held in Atherton's left hand as the fly rod again flipped forward to toss additional slack line on the water. Suddenly he was fast to a good fish which raced off downriver bringing him stumbling through the slick, difficult stretch of water in splashing pursuit.

A few moments later, whipped by a master angler, a beautiful 6-pound steelhead was brought to beach a short distance from where I sat, red-faced and unable to understand my recent failure. After releasing the fish to the safety of the river, Atherton headed once again through the swift water to the preferred casting position on the far side. Mingled with the soft, musical gurgling of the Klamath I was certain I heard, "There ought to be another fish there."

It was a repeat performance as we again watched a skilled angler shoot a long line unerringly downstream. Once more the vigorous backward snap of the fly rod to force the heavy forward tapered fly line into a series of loops that dropped gently to the choppy current. A gentle downward flip of the rod again sent additional loops of slack line into the stream. There could now be no possible hint of drag to interfere with the drift of the fly as it sped past the little island, free to follow every natural whim and fancy of the currents.

The fly rod bent once again into a throbbing downstream arc as another steelhead accepted the fly and shot into the air with an explosion of spray, then fell back again into the heavy current to the exciting hum of a fly reel. This steelhead, too, as did the preceding one, forced the angler to follow it down through the swift, shallow riffle to the deeper water below, where it soon submitted to the skill of the rod and allowed itself to be beached on the gravel bar. Smaller by nearly 2 pounds than the first fish, it was no less a beautiful steelhead as Atherton held it aloft for us to admire a moment before it too was returned to the river, where it would regain its strength for the journey far on up the Klamath.

I was greatly subdued on our trip back to camp for lunch, and I ran and reran a mental movie of my recent whitewashing on our favorite morning steelhead water. My long period of casting to no avail was picked apart and placed alongside the only two casts which Atherton had made to take two fish. Every phase of our casting procedures were exactly the same with one slight exception. That exception proved to be the deciding edge between my casting to barren water and Atherton's "There's really nothing to it" taking of the two steelhead.

Fishing both wet and dry flies for many seasons over Atlantic salmon, a far distant cousin to the Pacific steelhead, had given Atherton a sort of "sixth sense" governing the action of his fly every second it was in the water. Where he was experienced enough to observe immediately what must be done with rod and line to allow the fly a natural, drag-free drift, I was either not observant enough or too dense at the time to realize that my method of adding slack line to the drifting fly was too amateurish to have fooled even a blind squawfish.

Atherton had stripped enough line from his reel in preparing for the one important cast to allow him to hold three or four large, free loops of line in his left or noncasting hand, while he still had enough line available to cast a few feet beyond his target and to pull back for the initial loops of slack so important on the first few feet of the drift.

My own casting had been comparable until it reached the point where additional slack was called for to avoid the inevitable drag and accompanying unnatural drift of the fly which simply would not interest the fish. Rather than strip off and hold reserve loops of loose line to toss after the rapidly diminishing slack allowed for on the cast, I chose to strip additional line from the reel itself. Although the latter method may work under some conditions, I simply failed (unknowingly) to strip line off the reel rapidly enough to keep pace with the river current.

On every single cast I made, even with the few feet of slack line to start with, the fly would be almost to the strike area when it would suddenly run out of free-running line. At that point, and I must have thought it was soon enough to have kept at it all morning, I began stripping line from my reel. It was already too late, and I was doing no more than locking the barn door after the horse had been stolen. The heavy current had already snatched the fly away from its natural drift and it was immediately a lifeless, unnatural nothing which nullified any interest the fish may have shown.

Continued and duplicated casts merely caused a succession of uninteresting and harmless blobs of color suddenly to go dancing away in direct defiance of the natural flow of the currents. They (the flies) neither frightened nor alarmed the fish, and they cer-

Some of the best steelhead water is accessible only by boat. Such boats and guides can be hired on many of the more popular steelhead rivers in the northwest. *(Oregon State Highway Dept.)*

tainly did not interest the fish. Rather they became a strange and small foreign object which the fish simply ignored since it bothered them not at all.

It must follow that it matters little what type of tackle may be chosen for steelhead fishing or what method may be employed, the presentation of fly, bait, or lure holds the number one position in importance. There will always be that day or that river which will produce a steelhead who for some unexplained reason chooses to take an angler's offering though it has been presented in a manner normally guaranteed to drive every fish in sight under cover for the remainder of the season. But no angler in his right mind would think of continuing his fishing in an upside-down manner simply because one single fish with a suicide complex may have chased and caught a lure halfway up a perpendicular waterfall.

When fly fishing for summer and early fall steelhead where deep-water wading is necessary to place you within casting distance of your fish it is usually wise to employ a fly rod with at least a 9-foot length and with backbone enough to shoot a heavy forward taper steelhead line at distances up to 100 feet. When casting a fly with heavy water swirling around your waist, the longer rod is necessary to keep your line up and out of the near currents so that your fly will have the needed freedom of a natural, deep running drift.

Standard steelhead fly patterns of the Pacific Coast have taken fish for years and will continue to take fish so long as there are fish to take. New patterns may come and go, but the old patterns continue to keep their prominent places in the steelheaders' fly boxes.

Some anglers prefer their steelhead flies weighted under the body dressing with lead fuse wire, claiming that the weighted flies sink more rapidly in heavy water. We have always carried some weighted flies with us and have found them to be most useful at times.

In the matter of fly leaders I prefer a tapered leader at least 9 feet in length and at times a 12-foot leader will be even more effective in allowing the fly to drift with the conflicting currents

in a more natural manner.

In drift fishing with salmon egg clusters, which has long been the accepted method of winter steelheaders, the principle of presentation is the same. The bait is usually cast in a quartering direction upstream and across where, with the necessary weight, it drops quickly to the bottom, where the heavy current will carry it bouncing along the bottom as line is fed from either a smooth running casting reel or spinning reel.

In fishing any of the numerous artificial steelhead lures the practice more or less remains the same as in the other methods of steelhead fishing. Lures, weighted or unweighted, are normally cast upstream and allowed to bounce and roll along the bottom. In all cases it falls back to the importance of presentation.

Winter steelheaders may expect to, and usually do, lose a lot of terminal tackle. The big winter steelhead hold to the bottom and are seldom inclined to move very far from their position to take a bait or lure. The offering must be fished along the bottom, where the fish are or there will be little to show for a day's angling.

You may cast aside the phony cloak of mystery which seems to have enveloped the mighty steelhead over the years. There really is no cloak of mystery at all. It remains a simple matter of mixing knowledge of the fish, stream habits of the fish, and presentation of the offering into a big, black kettle. Bring to a thorough boil and then cool, drink to the very last drop. From then on you'll find that steelhead are relatively easy to locate and much easier to catch. Just avoid being stubborn to the point where you will drink the tonic before reading the directions.

Bob Pinkowski (right) and guide George Bazso

*Chapter Eight*

# FISHING FOR MUSKELLUNGE

### *by* BOB PINKOWSKI

BOB PINKOWSKI, a sports writer for The Milwaukee *Journal,* has sought muskellunge for 16 of his 30 years. During this period he has fished in most of the lakes and rivers in the United States and Canada where muskies are found. But most of his muskie expeditions have taken place in his home state of Wisconsin, where he has fished with some of the best guides in the state. After having caught hundreds of 'lunges and having studied their habits and habitat he is well qualified to write on the subject. He has written a book called *Muskie Fever,* which was published recently.

So you are dead set on catching a muskie, are you? Brother, have your head examined. It's not the muskie that's a maniac, it's the people who fish for them that are nutty. Or if you aren't nutty when you start this game, you'll have a head start over everyone else in a relatively short time.

The muskie is a ferocious thing with more glamour than a Hollywood movie star. It is a tricky, temperamental, unpredictable devil that can lure you into a false sense of security by continually following your bait but not striking. And when you have run out of cuss words and are dead tired and ready to throw in the towel, he will hit. And 99 out of 100 times he will catch you napping. You will lose the fish but you will return home with a fish story and vow revenge. You will have contacted the muskie bug. There will be no stopping. You will have to whip this insolent dog to save face and erase frustrations.

How does a beginner go about catching a legal-sized muskie ( 30 inches in my home state of Wisconsin)? First of all it's a good idea to tote a prayer book and use it often. Next comes expe-

111

rience. The more you learn about old *Esox masquinongy*, his habits and habitat, his behavior, the easier it will be to hunt him down.

For instance, you will learn that if you have raised a decent-sized fish from a certain deep weed bed, but the fish merely followed instead of striking, it probably will not venture far from that spot. You may not find him in exactly the same place on your next venture, but he'll be in the neighborhood. If you have the time keep after him until you get him.

You will learn that a muskie has a jaw that is as bony as a skeleton's and that a gentle little set, like you might use on a walleye or northern, will not get you a fish. Once you have hooked one you will learn how high and long it can perform an aerial circus before the hook holes in its mouth are torn enough to allow him to spit the bait back in your face. You will learn that the easiest way to catch one of these creatures is to get it into the boat as soon as possible once you have hooked it. Muskies don't tire fast. You will find that the sight of man will not rattle this fish, and since it doesn't it must be a pretty damn brave and cagey critter.

You will learn to keep a sharp eye out for guides and the spot their parties pound hard. This is where the fish are. For the newcomer, it is best to acquire, if possible, the services of a good guide who can show you around to the various weed beds, rock bars, and other spots muskies frequent.

Above all, you will get a rapid education regarding what a downright, malicious, crafty sneak a muskie is and why you must hunt him down rather than fish for him. And again, you will learn to ram the hooks home hard into anything that might nudge your lure—weeds, snags, rocks, logs. You will find quickly that what you considered a mild snag is Old Snagglepuss.

Probably the number one reason that a muskie is lost when it hits is because the fisherman is not alert. Despite the fact that he knows there is an excellent possibility of catching a fish, he is sun gazing or watching the birds flit about, so that when the strike comes, the angler is caught unaware and sets the hook halfheartedly, like trying to drive it into a hunk of balsa wood. If he has fished muskies long enough and knows them thoroughly,

Muskies are continually being tagged, measured, and studied by the state conservation departments in an effort to provide better fishing. This one is being handled by Ohio biologists. *(Ohio Dept. of Natural Resources)*

he realizes that he has had a strike, but he is semiparalyzed for the moment—perhaps even mildly scared—and the hooks don't hold. The fish boils to the surface, shakes its head once, and the bait zooms past the angler's ear. He can't figure out what happened.

This has happened to me many times and undoubtedly will occur again, mainly because I am not prepared for the strike. A muskie will do one of two things: It will shoot up from the bottom and hit the lure broadside with its viselike jaws (in which

113

case you will feel a severe jolt) or it will follow the bait and make an instinctive dash to nab it and nip the trailer hooks hard enough to cause the bait to stop dead for a split second.

In conclusion to this, I can say only one thing. Keep that rod down and pointed in the direction of the lure and when you feel a bump, set the hook like your life depended on it. Anybody, large or small, can catch a muskie providing he is in the right mental state. If he is not, he might as well lumber over to the nearest carp pond and try his luck there. Muskie fishing is not a lazy man's game.

With this in mind, keep your hooks razor sharp. Pulling a bait through weeds and setting it into deadheads can dull the hooks in no time flat. A good idea is to check them before starting out each day. Also replace rusty, weak hooks with new ones. Dull and rusty hooks lose many fish.

During one of my earlier years I once lost a muskie, that I knew was more than 40 inches, because I did not have anybody else in the boat with me. Rather than have the wind-blown craft bang against an overhanging rock ledge, I tried to use one hand to row free and the other to keep a tight line. This was impossible. I saved the motor but lost the fish. Should you get a good fish on, you can use both hands on the rod to fight him if somebody else is available to scoop him up in a net or gaff him. You yourself will find it darn near impossible.

Aside from a few isolated patches here and there, most of the weed beds on this continent's muskie waters are large enough for you to take advantage of a favorable wind drift and still enable you to cover the bed adequately. If you are by yourself, drop the anchor 3 or 4 feet down the gunwale nearest to the side you are casting on. This will slow the speed of your drift. A favorable wind also will enable you to make two or more passes over the same bed using different type baits, giving the fish a chance to look over a variety of lures.

Many muskie anglers, successful or otherwise, have expressed their opinions in print on the best way to get a muskie into the boat once it is hooked and you are fairly assured that you have whipped it. Learn how to handle a net. Use a gaff if the fish is too big for the net. Never use a pistol because this is not sporting.

To sum up all of this qualified opinion, I will say this: If the muskie is small enough and not particularly robust or savage, try to get it into your net, always head first. You would be surprised what a muskie can do in a net when netted tail first. If the fish is fairly heavy and is not too capable of making long runs or jumping, but tends to bore deep, be ready with a gaff. Get him alongside the boat and run it through his jaw rather than his side, for if you do jab him in the jaw you will have more leverage should he decide to swim away. If the muskie is an unusually large one that could fall through the net or wouldn't fit in it, or that you can't work close enough to gaff, use a .22 pistol. This takes practice. A head shot rarely will stop a big fish. A shot which fractures its spine will rob it of its vigor and it won't be able to execute power dives—the kind that tax your heart.

And for the purist, I suggest a billy on the order of a cop's night stick, with which you can bop a fish atop the cranium and stun him long enough to get him into the boat. Choose a hardwood such as hickory or oak, carve the hunk of wood out to desirable size, smooth it down, lacquer it with a resin to harden it, and you have a weapon.

Regardless of what you have heard, muskies strike at the time they are supposed to—and follow the solunar tables—moonrise, sunrise, tides, etc., pretty closely to schedule. Contest records, to me, are fallacious. Most vacationists fish hard between about 10 A.M. and 1 P.M. and between 3:30 or so and dusk. This obviously is when most muskies are caught. This always is not when the fish are moving, so consult the solunar tables when possible. I have found them reliable.

The best times of the year are the last two weeks in June and the first two in July and after that any time after Labor Day, when the water starts to cool off again. In May and early June, when the first fish wander off the spawning beds, they still haven't shaken off the cobwebs of winter and usually will follow the lure only until the water starts to warm up a bit.

The three different types of muskies all belong to the pike family (*Esox*). The true muskie, found in most waters, usually is rather dark in color, with a bronze-olive tinge. The fish's environment actually determines its coloration, so even a true muskie

115

often has faint stripes. The most abundant of the muskies is a hybrid, the "tiger." It is a gorgeous-looking specimen, especially in its early years. The tiger is a cross breed between a true muskie and a northern pike. Olive-mottled stripes streak down its silvery-bronze sides to make this mean-looking brute a handsome gent.

Third, but not lacking the fighting qualities of its brothers, is the spotted Ohio River muskie, found chiefly in Michigan and Ohio. It has dark spots in place of the stripes and is not a hybrid. A fourth variety found in several lakes in Canada, including Vermilion, has been termed the silver muskie. It is a variety of tiger, but water conditions have wiped most of the stripes off its shiny sides, giving it the appearance of a barracuda.

The easiest place for me to catch muskies is the Manitowish Waters chain in Wisconsin's Vilas County. This can be attributed to the fact that I was weaned on muskie fishing there by a gentleman named George Bazso. He was once trussed up and tossed in a coal cellar by one of John Dillinger's mob when that gang sought refuge in those parts while trying to escape Eliot Ness's good guys. Since that scare, Bazso has become one of the state's top guides.

Other excellent places I have found to be great producers, not in the order of importance, are the Chippewa Flowage, St. Germain and Arbor Vitae area, the Wisconsin River near Rhinelander, the Eagle River and Boulder Junction chains, the Gile Flowage, Pelican Lake, Lac Vieux Desert and the Presque Isle and Crab Lake areas all in Wisconsin; the Chautauqua and Finger Lakes chain and the St. Lawrence River in New York state; Lake St. Clair, which borders on part of the Motor City in Michigan; the Little Kanawha and Elk rivers in West Virginia; the gorgeous Lake of the Woods in Ontario; Leech Lake in Minnesota, and Vermilion Lake in Ontario between the Sioux-Lookout-Dryden areas.

For the record, Art Lawton of Unionville, New York, holds the present world's record, 69 pounds 15 ounces. Two other anglers have held it three times each on previous occasions. They are Percy Haver of Detroit and Louis Spray of Rice Lake, Wisconsin.

Haver nailed three big boys in near succession while motor trolling on St. Clair. In August of 1938 he got a 56-pounder. In

Even when dead, a musky is a formidable looking creature with huge gaping mouth and long powerful body. The 44½-pounder on the left and the 32½-pounder on the right were caught in Wisconsin on suckers for bait.

June, 1939, he got a 58-pounder and in June a year later he got a 62½-pounder. Spray also had three muskies recognized by *Field & Stream*, but not that close together.

Women muskie anglers are on the increase. My wife, for instance, can wield a heavy rod almost as well as I can. Kitty Dombrock, a charming little mother from Winter, Wisconsin,

117

catches about 50 fish annually. Dotty Lapp, whose husband is one of the sharper guides around Vieux Desert, has caught several fine fish, including a 50-pounder in 1951.

You will hear so much about muskie baits that it would seem almost fantastic to the beginner regarding what a muskie will hit. This bait is terrific and that one is a killer. When they point to the pink polka-dotted job adorned in powder blue on the sports shop shelf and proclaim it a killer, it is because the bait itself has tantalizing action. The pink and blue has to be pushed.

Actually, you should try to duplicate the color of a muskie's natural food. You can count on one hand the number of muskies caught on a red and white plug as compared to the darker variety. First of all, going back to what the fish faces in its natural environment, there is nothing red and white (natural food) that a muskie sees, so why should it give your gaudy-looking plug a second look, unless perhaps it is a surface lure worked slowly.

The old stand-bys will never fade out. You need not fill your tackle box to the brim either. For fishing deep there is the Go-deep Pikie Minnow and the large Helin Flatfish. For medium running baits I would recommend the medium running Pikie (in which the spoon can be set according to the depth desired), the Vamp Spook, and the LeMaster Shiner Minnow. For working over shallow weeds, a dark colored bucktail, either natural or black, is tops. Here, a good, full bucktail which covers the trailer hooks is a necessity to keep the muskie from spotting a forgery.

The Suick bait (a wooden replica of a sucker) and a harnessed sucker itself are excellent baits. The casting sucker will be dealt with later. The Suick bait, dreamed up by a fine muskie man from Wisconsin's potato empire, Antigo, is a killer for the angler who wants to work up a sweat.

Retrieved in short, sharp jerks this bait would make any muskie in the right frame of mind hungry. It resembles a wounded fish in its death throes. It has large gang hooks, however, and these are especially tough to set unless you have a stiff, deep-sea type rod. As I said, it is grueling work to obtain the proper zig-zag action, and only an old hand can obtain the proper results.

Of all the baits mentioned, bucktails seem to be the best enticers. So much of a muskie's food duplicates what a bucktail has to offer. Reeled fast at the right time it results in many thrills.

Vouching for a bucktails effectiveness is this report from Resort of the Woods at Boulder Junction, Wisconsin. The owner keeps an accurate record and statistics on all muskies caught by his guests. In the last ten years, 1369 muskies have been brought in. Of this number 708 were caught on bucktails, 124 on a Pikie Minnow, 60 on a Suick, 102 on other artificials, and 375 on minnows and suckers.

The Mickey Finn, Marathon Musky Hawk, and Slim Jim are my favorites, largely because they have the lead weight hidden near the swivel snap rather than the treble hooks. You will seldom "foul up" these bucktails when casting.

Many have argued on how fast to reel a bucktail or for that matter any muskie bait. Slow? Fast? Medium? Vary the retrieve? The last idea is probably the best. Normally a muskie will stalk its quarry like a cat watching a canary. Why the fish will follow the bait with that killer look in its eyes, then swim calmly under the boat without smashing it, is a mystery. I have watched this happen more than a dozen times in one day, and if you have ever hunted muskies, you know how frustrating such futility can be.

My study of the fish reveals that it is extremely curious. I had one follow my drifting boat for fifteen minutes one day. It showed no interest when I emptied my tackle box at it, but the boat seemed to entrance it. Many times swimmers have reported muskies sunning themselves within rock-throwing range. If the fish merely shadows the bait on the retrieve, speed it up. Let that bait fairly zip through the water and often this is enough to excite the fish into making a headlong charge. Don't stop reeling at the boat, either, if you see a fish coming. Slow the bait down to a walk, but keep it in the water and *moving!*

The fish's eyes are focused on its intended meal, not on you. If the bait stops short at boatside, he may be distracted from the lure, see you, and sink out of sight. A good idea to follow when a muskie is in pursuit is to either swish the lure in front of him or transcribe a figure eight with your rod. I have caught many fish, some of which had already disappeared from sight, by using this desperate method.

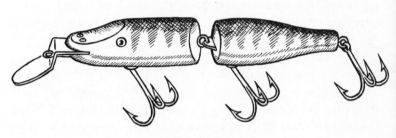

## SURFACE

## UNDER-WATER

Two proven muskie plugs

Regarding surface baits, I would vouch for the effectiveness of these four. They are the Heddon Flap-tail, the Pflueger Globe, the large Jitterbug, and large Heddon Crazy Crawler. The Globe, yellow with silver spots, and the black Jitterbug are my favorites. Reel the Globe in fast spurts and the Jitterbug very slowly so that it creates a paddling noise.

Spin-fishing manufacturers contend that spinning is the only way to fish. This is nuts, and the first man I heard admit it was a gent from one of the country's leading tackle manufacturers. Unless you have spin-fished for years and know the capabilities of the tackle and the fish you are after, you will be lost with a muskie at the other end.

You will hear reports of good muskies taken on 8- or 10-pound monofilament. These probably were caught unconsciously, because I have seen several taken by novices who didn't know what they had hooked and horsed the fish beyond the test limit of the line. Luckily it didn't break. I would say that about 8 of 10 muskies hooked on spinning equipment are lost and the really big ones are safe because the manufacturers still haven't devised leaders long enough or thick enough to keep a muskies teeth from shearing them.

A good, stiff, bait-casting rod about 6 feet long is the best way to throw artificials. The rod will have enough backbone to enable you to set the hook hard. A rod with more of a pool cue action is needed for heaving suckers and larger artificials.

A solid reel like the Pflueger Supreme is essential for muskie fishing. Keep it well oiled from day to day and grease it thoroughly before each trip. Tossing heavy baits with a bulky line is a severe test for any reel. There are many models out, but an inexpensive Swedish model, which has a fine star drag, is a good bet for a guy who likes sucker fishing.

A dacron line of between 20- and 30-pound test is about right. I prefer dacron to nylon because the latter has a tendency to twist (from the revolving action of spoons and bucktails) and gets frizzy. A nylon line also will stretch a lot and this won't help you when you get a strike. And don't forget to check the last 2 or 3 feet of your line, where it is knotted to the leader, before starting out every morning. Flinging heavy lures all day places extreme strain on the line. More than once I have had a lure fly into space because the line wore thin.

One evening, guide George Bazso and I were leaving Rudy List's supper club at Manitowish Waters when some guy sitting at the end of the bar hailed George. He turned out to be one of George's steady customers. Following a quick introduction to me, George informed his friend, Bert, that it was impossible to tarry any longer because the muskies were waiting. Bert downed his shot, fingered his bottle of beer, then turned to Bazso.

"You mean you're goin' pike fishing, not for muskies, for walleyes," he said, looking at his watch, then at us quizzically.

"It's damn near nine o'clock. C'mon, have a drink. Muskies quit bitin' an hour ago. The pike'll wait. You got all night!"

Convinced that we weren't spoofing in relation to our destination, the sober little man reached into his pocket, hauled out a fin, and tossed it on the bar. "You catch a muskie out in this dark and this bill is yours, and a round of drinks with it," he said cockily, a wry smile on his face.

Poor Bert really didn't know what he was up against. I did though. I had gone through the mill long before this stuffy August night in 1960. Three years before, I was accustomed to hauling my muskie tackle into the cottage as soon as it became totally dark. It was later, on a night excursion with Bazso into Clear Lake, that I became aware that night fishing for this giant was almost as productive as daylight fishing—in fact sometimes better.

For some unaccountable reason, the popular opinion seems to be that members of the pike family tend to call it a day after sunset. Bazso, especially, has poked holes in that theory and proven it to be fallacious.

Bazso has averaged more than 50 keeper muskies a season during the last ten years. Of this number, one third were nailed at night, when other muskie men had hung up their rods. I have caught a 20-pounder off the rock bar in Clear Lake at the stroke of midnight, when the plop of the Pikie Minnow turned the glassy surface into a seeming wall of waves. Only a year ago my wife caught a 35-inch fish from water so shallow you couldn't have gotten your knees wet if you had waded it. The muskie must have taken advantage of the quiet night to hunt crawfish and other small morsels which sneak into shallow water to escape their bigger brothers when the moon comes up.

Here are several things to remember when hunting muskies under moonlight:

1. Try the spots in which you have raised fish in the daytime. Chances are that other fishing parties besides yours excited the fish into following. If he expressed passing interest during the day, he could be fooled in the dark, providing you sneak up on him.

2. Don't ignore deep weed beds, rock bars, and the like— choice spots which guides work daily. Guides know their business. They wouldn't work a certain spot unless they were rea-

sonably sure there was a fish there. Use a surface or shallow running lure and work it slow. The quieter the night the better, especially for surface baits. A fish can hear the noise a long way off.

3. If you hook a muskie at night, the fish probably will not be as aggressive as he would be during the day. Why? It's anybody's guess. Perhaps it's because he has a difficult time locating you and the boat. Keep the rod tip down and the line taut and chances are you can horse him within netting range. If you observe other fish surface feeding, work hard. The muskies may be moving too. If not, hit the choice spots and head for home.

On the particular night we met Bert, I got a 37-inch fish after missing two that would have gone over 40 inches. Poor Bert is now a believer too.

The mere mention of fishing with suckers will cause many of the muskie purists to throw a temper tantrum. They want their fish caught only on artificials. This is the way I too would like to have it, but often there comes a time when you have to scrape the bottom of the barrel to have any fun. I once fished with a wealthy chap who was so proud he'd spit at a sucker. It was that time of year—the dog days of August—when the big lunkers would just not chase an artificial. They wanted to be teased with something juicy like a sucker. At 10 bucks a fish, I milked $90. from him in two weeks, and I had fun doing it. Fourteen days later he was frustrated, in a state of mild poverty, and has since switched to tossing suckers when muskies beg for them.

It is nigh impossible to toss a pound or pound and a half sucker all day. You can only do it in spurts, so you should keep one stiff rod baited with a sucker and another with an artificial in the boat so that you can change when the biceps start to ache. Another maneuver which I have found to be quite fruitful is to trail a sucker, hooked through the lips, buoyed by a small float some 5 yards or so behind the boat while you're casting. Many times a muskie will follow the bait, get scared by the boat or your shadow, and sink beneath the craft. This doesn't mean he wasn't hungry. He probably was spooked. About 50 per cent of the time he will nail the trailing sucker in a rage of madness.

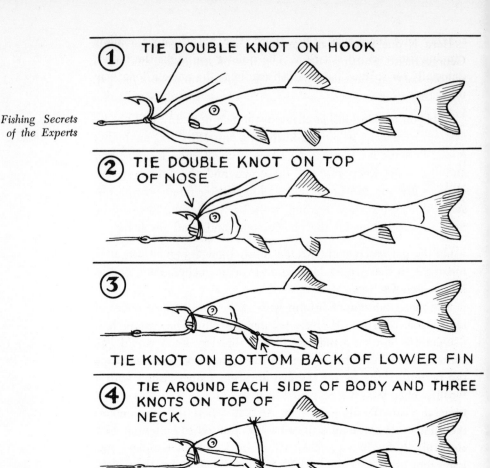

1. TIE DOUBLE KNOT ON HOOK

2. TIE DOUBLE KNOT ON TOP OF NOSE

3. TIE KNOT ON BOTTOM BACK OF LOWER FIN

4. TIE AROUND EACH SIDE OF BODY AND THREE KNOTS ON TOP OF NECK.

How to harness a sucker

Harnessing a sucker is simple once you have learned what to do. The main thing is to tie down the fish's head and gills securely so that the head can't be ripped from the body by repeated casts. This is done with fish string. Once it has been accomplished, and it takes about five minutes, you have to tie the sucker's snout tight and insert a long-leadered sucker hook through the snout with the barb aimed upward so that, when you set the hook, the tip of it is aimed directly at the muskie's throat.

Here is one method of harnessing a sucker used by guide George Bazso. Starting with 2 or 3 feet of strong fish line, tie a double knot on the sucker hook. See illustration (No. 1). Next, wrap the string twice around the sucker's snout and tie a double knot (No. 2) on top of the sucker's nose. Then run the remaining free line on the bottom and back of the lower fin and tie knot (No. 3). Finally, bring the string up twice around each side of the body and tie three knots atop the sucker's neck (No. 4). Cut off loose fish string. Harnessed this way the sucker should last half a day providing it isn't mangled by a muskie.

Obviously a good-sized sucker wielded on a strong line and a stiff rod can be heaved a long way. The number one thing to watch for on the retrieve, which must be a pumping motion to make the sucker slice through the water, surface, dart, and dive, is a boil behind the baitfish. Secondly, if the sucker stops suddenly on an underwater retrieve, let the line go slack immediately or the fish may feel the tension and drop the sucker.

Once the muskie has hit the sucker and taken it down and started chomping on it, never let the line slack. Keep it fairly tight so that you can feel the fish munch on the sucker. You actually can do this. It won't drop the baitfish if you don't put too much pressure on the line. This way, if the muskie has swallowed the sucker sooner than anticipated, you won't be caught with slack line lying all over when he surfaces in an attempt to disgorge the baitfish.

When you feel the muskie starting to move fast after five minutes or so, be sure to row up behind it and set the hook hard, not once, but at least twice. It will drive the barb deep into its throat. By all means don't let the muskie swim toward you before you set the hook for fear you might pull the hook out of its throat when you finally set it. Keep to the rear or side of the fish.

In the first week of June, 1961, my wife and I pounded the Manitowish chain to a froth without catching a fish for seven days. On the eighth, when we were about to depart, I took a tour of the chain with Bazso. On my third cast on Stone Lake I nailed a 29¾-inch fish, a quarter-inch shy. George and I didn't see a muskie for the next four hours. We whipped underwater lures and suckers against the wind on a slightly overcast day

without success. We couldn't raise a fish. In a last desperate
try, we tied on suckers and finally sped over to Manitowish Lake
to exploit a rock bar adjacent to an island near the bridge on
Highway 51. Here is where I was taught another lesson.

A monster about 50 inches or so had been haunting the bar for
several years, but nobody could quite drive the hooks deep
enough. George told me to peg the sucker out as far as possible,
let it sink completely to the bottom, then retrieve it to the surface in short, sharp jerks. This, he said, would usually infuriate
any muskie in the vicinity. It did. On my third cast a fish hit in
15 feet of water and fifteen minutes later I had myself a 15-
pound, 37-inch tiger, not the one we were looking for but still a
dandy fish. Remember this hint, especially when fishing rock
or sand bars in deep water.

A dead sucker on a casting line looks as limp as an overripe
banana when you impart no Oomph behind the retrieve. On rock
bars, when a normal retrieve doesn't work, let that sucker sink
like a dying walleye, then bring it up fast—and wait for the
strike. When the sucker stops you stop—and wait.

The world record fish, caught by Mr. Lawton, came out of the
St. Lawrence River. Art and his wife probably nail more muskies
each year than any other twosome, but they troll for them with a
motor. I do not consider this half as sporting as casting, because
the fish is all but hooked when he strikes. We'll let the motor-
trolling issue die here. Wisconsin has fought off the outboard
motor lobbyists for years and its muskies have prospered. Chautauqua in the Empire State once had so many muskies swimming around it you could have got one with a landing net. The
motor trollers have cut deep into its annual production.

Lawton's record is far from safe and he probably would be the
first to admit it, for he has seen bigger fish. Whopper muskies
have long been legendary in Wisconsin and Canada.

You can take with a grain of salt most of the fish stories you
hear. In most of them the fish reported was 60 inches long when
he was actually only 40. There is no question, however, that there
are muskies swimming this continent that would dwarf Lawton's
catch. Back in 1902, two Wisconsin fisheries men, in the process
of stripping spawn, caught a 102-pounder in their nets on

Many muskellunge are caught each year with the Lake of the Woods the most outstanding region. *(Ontario Dept. of Travel & Publicity)*

Tomahawk Lake and an 80-pounder on Minocqua Lake. These two probably are dead and decomposed by now, but surely there must be others to take their places in nature's cycle.

Getting back briefly to what a muskie will eat, and how fast, when he is hungry, try these three stories from the Boulder Junction area for size. They are true:

On slicing open a 23-pound muskie just a few hours earlier, a young man and his wife were astonished to find a 24-inch muskie in the larger fish's tummy, which just goes to show you what a large cannibal will tackle when his appetite calls for it.

Here's a case of vice versa, going back on what I said earlier on fishing for muskies with pike minnows early in the season. The opening day at Boulder Lake recently found two anglers working hard—one fishing for walleyes with a 4-inch minnow, the other for muskies with a pound sucker. So what happened? The walleye angler got a 42-inch muskie and the muskie man got a 10-pound walleye.

Two other men fishing the Boulder area on the same lake, within spitting distance of each other, each had a strike at about the same time. Both set the hook and started to reel in. A few yards short of their respective boats, their lines crossed. No wonder! Both had hooked the same 19-pound muskie on opposite sides of the mouth and both on walleye bait of about the same size.

Odd things like outboard-motor hub caps, forks, various denominations of small change, key chains, parts which slipped loose from outboard motors, Langley De-Liars, a man's wedding ring, a woman's bracelet, along with other goofy items, have been discovered in muskies' stomachs.

I personally am waiting for the day I'll catch one of these gluttons with a bottle of Canadian Club in its belly so that I can work off the frustrations encountered thus far.

*Chapter Nine*

# ATLANTIC SALMON FISHING

## *by* LEE WULFF

LEE WULFF needs no introduction to many of the nation's anglers, who are already familiar with his angling achievements. A talented artist, photographer, fly tier, lecturer, and expert angler, he has made many contributions to the sport of fishing. Although a skillful all-round angler in both fresh and salt water, he has acquired a world-wide reputation with one fish—the Atlantic salmon. Each season without fail he journeys to Canada to enjoy salmon fishing and acquire more knowledge about this challenging game fish. His latest book, *The Atlantic Salmon*, contains the most up-to-date and complete information written about this fish.

FISHING for Atlantic salmon is not quite like fishing for any other species. To begin with, Atlantic salmon are anadromous; like the sea-running trout, the Pacific salmon, the smelt, etc., they move from fresh water to salt, from bay to river, from ocean to stream. The sea is the salmon's great source of food. Entering it with several years of stream feeding behind him the salmon "smolt" is about 6 inches long. At the end of a year of sea feeding he'll be about 2 feet long; at the end of two years at sea he'll be 30-odd inches in length and at the end of three years of steady sea feeding he may be 40 inches long and weigh over 30 pounds. When returning to his river on his spawning journey he loses interest in food. He's fat and amazingly strong. Rarely will he take anything to eat. As a result he loses weight and after many months in fresh water his weight may drop to half of what it was when he re-entered his river. (Atlantic salmon may survive to spawn several times although the spawning ordeal is arduous and only a small percentage of each year's run live to spawn a second or third time.) Whether he has been steadily at sea for only one year or for four, there is still the possibility that either a recollection of his earlier years of stream feeding—or some other whim—will cause him to rise to take an angler's fly.

Most anadromous fish will take a lure imitating the food of their youth, at least to some degree, when they return to the fresh-water streams. The Atlantic salmon's delicacy of taste and the relatively small lures he will take make him a most difficult fish to hook and to land. By law Atlantic salmon must be fished for with unweighted flies and fly fishing tackle practically everywhere they exist on this continent. This increases the difficulty of catching them. There are no such restrictions on the steelhead, a very similar fish, and the sport is not judged to be as high, for fish taken on bait and hardware do not require as much angling skill. No one would pay the high rates involved to get good Atlantic salmon fishing if it were not a top sport. The basis of which lies in that innate resistance to a fly fisherman's wiles that all salmon have to a high degree, even though they may never have seen a fly before.

Salmon are found in big rivers, moderate streams, and sometimes in very small brooks. They choose certain pools to rest in, year after year, usually lying in the same spots as did their predecessors when water conditions were similar. As the water level in a river rises or lowers, the salmon shift their lies and they may move swiftly, or slowly, on their upstream travel. To have even a fair understanding of the Atlantic salmon an angler must fish on many rivers, high waters, and in summer drought. Even then, he will find much to puzzle him. However, when he becomes experienced he will recognize that there is less luck in Atlantic salmon fishing, except for sudden freshets or unusually high water, than in almost any other type of angling.

This fairly complete understanding of the fish and his habits takes years to accumulate. Meantime, here are some suggestions from an old hand who is still puzzled by this paradoxical fish, yet who would give up almost everything else rather than miss his annual salmon fishing trips.

If you are a fly fisherman the chances are you can use the same fly rod and fly line you use for other fish. The chances are, though, that you'll need a larger reel and a lot more backing for

Lee Wulff    131

a salmon. An angler fishing in open water may require more than 250 yards of line to keep contact with the fish he hooks. These fish, with thousands of miles of sea migration behind them, take off swiftly on long runs. They're too powerful to be stopped by any reasonable tackle in mid-run. The normal size of the fly they'll take is about a No. 4, though it may run as large as a 3/0 or as small as a 16 or 18. The problem is that of playing a big, fast fish on much the same tackle that would be used for trout in a brook.

The average length of the rods used to catch salmon is about 9 feet. Its weight will be about seven ounces and quite often it will be equipped with a detachable butt that will lengthen the rod and make it easier to play the fish. The butt can be rested against the body while holding the rod with one hand and reeling with the other. Other satisfactory rods may be as light as an ounce and three-quarters at 6 feet and as heavy as a pound or more at 16 or 17 feet. Take your choice and the best advice is to fish with the type of rod you are used to. If you are not used to fly fishing, pick a 9-footer. A detachable butt can be helpful but is not at all necessary.

The line must match the rod's power and make casting easy. The backing should be a little stronger than the strongest leader you plan to use. A 15-pound test braided line makes a good backing when leaders up to 12-pound test are contemplated. Those who fish light may reduce their backing strength to 8 or 10 pounds. Leaders for salmon are rarely less than 9 feet long and may be much longer. My preference is from 12 to 15 feet.

It is the reel that is the key to the salmon fishing tackle. It must run smoothly and have just the right drag. Many old-timers set their reels at a very light drag, just enough to keep the spool from overrunning and they apply additional pressure to suit the moment, using their fingers either against the fly line as it passes through them, or against the turning spool.

A net big enough to land a salmon is pretty bulky. If you fish from a canoe or boat it is easy enough to carry such a net. If you walk and wade you'll prefer to carry a tailer: a snarelike device which will lasso a tired fish by the tail in a way that will let you drag him ashore or slide him into a boat. A gaff, a big hook

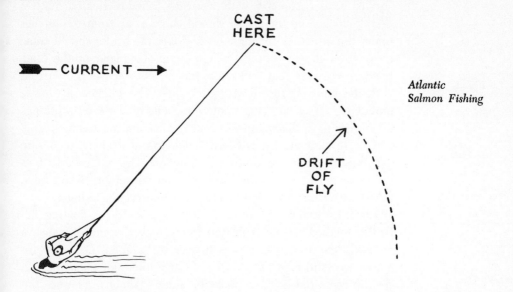

CAST
HERE

◀━ CURRENT ━▶

DRIFT
OF
FLY

Using wet fly for salmon

fastened to a wood or metal handle, is still used frequently to hook the tired fish and bring him ashore, but gaffs are outlawed on many waters as barbaric. Beaching a fish is safe enough, when a beach is available, but the beginner will want a net or a tailer handy.

There are several methods of fishing for salmon. The oldest and still the most common method is fishing with a wet fly. In the standard wet fly method the fly is cast across and downstream at an angle of about 45°, then allowed to swing with the current in an arc until the line hangs downstream in the current. Then another cast is made. The wading angler will usually fish a cast or two and then move downstream a few feet and fish again, thus working over the likely water. Where there is a particularly interesting spot the angler should concentrate his casting there for a longer period.

The Portland Creek hitch is the name given the practice of taking two half hitches behind the head of the fly with the leader to make it skim across the surface instead of sinking below the

133

surface as is customary with wet flies fished normally. With a double-hooked fly the leader should come away from the hitches under the throat. With single-hooked flies the leader should come away from the fly at a 45° angle from the plane of the hook bend on the side that will make the fly skim across the current with its point on the downstream side. The hitched fly has a tantalizing effect on many salmon and one of the exciting things about fishing in this manner is that the salmon must come to the surface to take the fly. Often it is moving at a fairly good rate and the salmon makes quite a commotion. The hitch works better on some rivers than on others, but on no salmon river I have fished in recent years has it failed to interest the salmon.

The third major method is to fish with a dry or floating fly. In this method the fly is drifted freely with the current, always on slack line, in order to pass it over the salmon. Dry flies are most successful when the water is fairly low and when the fish are concentrated in the pools or other salmon lies and the fisherman need not spend a lot of time floating a slow-moving fly over empty water.

There are thousands of casts made for every Atlantic salmon captured. Often a week of fishing will not produce a single fish for an angler and this can happen on normally excellent water at

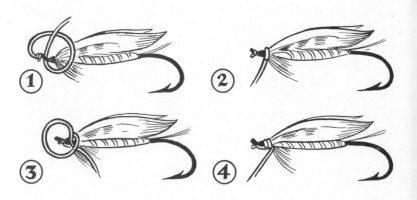

Tying the Portland Creek hitch

a normally excellent time. Usually, salmon are easiest to catch when they first come in from the sea. As their time in the river lengthens they become more wary and less likely to take a fly. In the early part of the season larger, brighter wet flies are usually most effective. In late season or in low water the smaller more somber wet flies take more fish.

Among the more popular wet fly patterns are the Jock Scott, Silver Doctor, Silver Rat, Cosseboom, Silver Grey, Black Dose, Dusty Miller, Thunder and Lightning, and Blue Charm. The first mentioned and the last mentioned could well be taken as the key flies to be carried in a variety of sizes. Wet flies for salmon are available in both single- and double-hooked types. Single-hooked flies are generally preferred, being easier to carry in a book or box, less expensive and just as effective if not more so than the doubles.

There are not too many dry fly patterns available on salmon hooks. The Rat-Faced McDougall, The Irresistible, Surface Stone Fly, Pink Lady, White Wulff, Grey Wulff, and Royal Wulff are among those most readily available and most popular. The range of dry fly patterns is still expanding and should continue to grow for many years. Although large wet flies rarely work well in low or warm water conditions, large dry flies often work well then. It is possible to have a salmon roll up to take a No. 16 fly on one cast and then have another come up to a No. 2 on the next. A No. 2 dry fly is a pretty big butterfly to cast.

Salmon often make false rises. This is especially true with the dry fly. A fish may come up and seem to take the fly time after time although in actuality he is merely playing with it. Salmon have poked my flies out of the water on their noses without opening their mouths—and after I learned to restrain that almost irrepressible impulse to yank—I had some of them lift the fly up out of the water and then, as they sank low again, let it float on down the stream. It takes a cool cucumber to watch a rise like that and strike only when he has determined that the salmon has actually closed his mouth on the fly. Usually, if an angler does not offend a salmon by striking when the fish is only playing with the fly, the fish can be tormented into actually taking it into his mouth on a future cast.

Lee Wulff is playing a big 30-pound salmon which will probably be grabbed by hand around the narrow part of the tail. Experts can do this, but beginners had better stick to a net or tailer when landing a fish.

Salmon fishing is often done on long, wide pools where the water looks alike for yard after yard. A marked line is of great advantage in this type of fishing. If there's a line mark at 30, 40, 50, and 60 feet, then when a fish rises and is missed, the exact direction of the rise may be noted as well as the length of line out. The angler can then rest that fish by shortening or extending his line to fish other water until he is ready to make another cast identical to the one that drew the rise. Many anglers like to rest a salmon that has risen and failed to take the fly. Others, and I am among them, cast back to the same spot several times before giving the fish a resting period. I've caught a lot of fish on that return cast or I wouldn't feel that way.

There is also considerable difference of opinion on the value of fine leaders in taking salmon. Many successful anglers continually use leaders of 10-pound test or heavier. I like to use leaders that vary with the conditions. When the rivers are clear and small flies are in order a 3- to 4-pound test leader seems to draw more rises and such a leader is adequate for landing the largest of salmon if the fisherman is skillful—and fortunate. No heavier than 6- or 8-pound test leaders should be used when flies of size No. 6 or 8 or smaller are used, I believe.

When a salmon is hooked he is still a long way from landed. More anglers lose their first salmon than land them. The biggest cause of losing salmon is the failure to get one's hand off the reel handle swiftly enough to let the fish run freely when he starts to travel. A beginner should be gentle with his fish, keeping abreast or below him wherever possible. As the fish tires he can be held a little more tightly, but even though almost exhausted he's likely to have enough speed left to break away before the unwary angler can release the pressure. The greatest loss of fish comes at the strike, when the fish starts his first real run. The next greatest loss takes place when he starts his last run—the one the fisherman didn't believe he had strength enough to make.

Salmon should be played directly from the reel because any loops of line between the reel and first guide, left over from casting, can cause a tangle that will let your fish go free. It is good policy to strike a salmon only hard enough to set the hook. With small, sharp hooks and dry flies this need be only a sharp twitch

Catching an Atlantic salmon is one of the greatest thrills and achievements in fresh-water fishing. This one was taken in Canada's River St. Jean on the Gaspé Peninsula. *(Canadian Gov. Travel Bureau)*

beyond the taking up of slack. With the wet fly many anglers feel that no strike is necessary, that the current and the salmon's own movement will set the hook. If the pressure is relaxed immediately after the hook is set, and the setting is not harsh, the fish will often settle back toward the bottom before moving off slowly. This gives the fisherman time to reel in the slack and ready himself for the swift runs that are sure to come when the salmon realizes he's in real trouble.

Be sure your leader is spliced to the end of your fly line or is joined by locking loops or by some method that will allow you to bring the leader part way into the guides if you plan to land your own fish. That's the most sporting and exciting way to land a fish. You'll find it a bigger thrill than having to share the capture with another person. Salmon fishing is considered by many to be the highest form of individual angling. It is not always easy for a man to land a salmon unaided, but the best fishermen are likely to do it as a matter of course.

To read an article like this can help a beginner to understand some of the problems involved in fishing for Atlantic salmon. To read a book can give him a greater knowledge of the techniques and the tackle involved. The best way to understand salmon is to find and hire a good guide, one who knows salmon fishing and is particularly well acquainted with the river on which you'll fish. Every river is different and on any given river conditions will vary by day and by week. When you have fished one river in low water it may not prepare you for another under the same conditions or for the same river when the water is high. Once you have a basic understanding of the wide variety of problems involved in getting a salmon to take a fly and realize, too, there is no salmon that may not be coaxed into taking one, you can go on to experiment wisely. Then you can fit your special experiences into the general fishing pattern or vice versa. Salmon fishing is a complex game and a strange one. You may have a lot of luck at the start—or very little—but over the years you can pretty well count on having the number of salmon that take your fly become a pretty accurate measure of your skill.

Emmett Gowen. *(Photo by Pete Barrett)*

*Chapter Ten*

# CATFISHING KNOW-HOW

## *by* EMMETT GOWEN

EMMETT GOWEN, of Lavergne, Tennessee, has been a Marine, news reporter, publicity man, and novelist. His pursuit of fishes for sport has led
him to Quintana Roo, Mexico, where he operates his own guiding and
outfitting business, organizing and leading expeditions (for sport, archae-
ological, and undersea explorations) into the virgin areas still to be found
in Mexico and Central America. He has recently published a book called
*The Joys of Fishing*, and has in the works a book on the hunting and fishing of Mexico and a novel. His articles and stories have appeared in the
leading outdoor and general magazines.

I COLLECT methods of catching catfish as some people collect antique guns, old bottles, or carved-ivory miniature ele-
phants. I wheedle fishing secrets out of mellow *afficionados* and
try them out. It is like doing research for one's own practice of
an art or other endeavor. Catfishing, to be frank, should be considered "other endeavor"; it is scarcely dignified enough to be
called an art. With catfish, to the true catfisherman, the idea is
to catch them, and any way it can be done is acceptable to him,
although often not to the game wardens. Even angling is permis-
sible, and we will come to that, but the old-fashioned ways never
lose their charm in catfishing. It is an old-time sport. Take trotlining, for example, the method by which the biggest catfish I ever
saw was caught. It weighed 104 pounds, and was blind.

J. K. Walker and his son, Paul, devotees of catfishing any way
it can be done, but especially of trotlining, had been finding their
trotlines broken, the trots snapped off, and slimy places left on
the line. The meaning of this was as obvious as a hunting writer's
opening gambit describing the disappearance of goats and cattle

in tiger country. A big catfish had taken up residence where the Walkers fished, and was living off their labor. Apparently catfish, as they grow tremendous, also grow somewhat cumbersome and slow, unwilling to catch their own food, and they take to robbing trotlines. This fish night after night had swum along the line, swallowing whatever had been caught on it—carp, buffalo, or his own cannibalistic kind—breaking off the leader lines as he went. There doubtless were some fish hooks in this diet, but intestinal punctures are not fatal to fish. Stomach acids and corrosion dissolve the hooks, and anyway a catfish can turn its stomach wrong side out and empty it of incidental rubbish at will.

The Walkers would have gloried in the catching of this fish in any case, but they had the added incentive of a $500. reward for any fish that weighed over a hundred pounds. This prize money was promised by the businessmen of Savannah, Tennessee, in an ingenious publicity stunt. On the theory that anything bigger than its counterpart in Texas would be news, the reward aimed to procure a newsworthy catfish for Texas, to present to the aquarium of the Fort Worth Botanic Gardens.

The Walkers finally caught the fish and brought it to Mr. Cecil Parris, chairman of the town's Catfish Derby. They transported it wrapped in wet sacks in a pick-up truck. Mr. Parris put it in a goldfish pool he had in his back yard. A crowd gathered. The highway patrol had to get on the job to keep the main street clear, as the street was also a through highway.

Toward evening the fish began to list, obviously in a sinking condition. Somebody suggested there might not be enough oxygen in so small a pool for so big a fish. Toward midnight the crowd was still there and men dashed off to get an air compressor to aerate the pool, while electricians put in wiring for the compressor and for floodlights. Mr. Parris and other leading citizens were in the pool with the fish, trying to revive it. At this point the sick fish disgorged a 2-pound carp. This reduced his weight from 104 pounds to 102 pounds—still over a hundred and (Mr. Walker thought) still in the money. Mr. Walker stood around wondering how long it was going to take them to find a spare moment, in all this business, to hand him the $500. reward.

Toward dawn the fish died.

Now the Savannah folks thought of another publicity angle. Mr. Parris was a manufacturer of toy rifles, and he had originated a boy's drill team. Now he called the drill team to its popguns, and rallied the contestants for the queen's title in the Catfish Derby. They would have a funeral for the catfish.

All that Sunday people swarmed to the shindig, the catfish funeral. The catfish queen aspirants served prettily, in bathing suits, as pallbearers. The drill team, wearing coonskin caps, fired a popgun salute. The catfish was purgatoried into the town's locker plant, to be resurrected for photographic and publicity purposes again during the month of the Catfish Derby. All this goes to show what a to-do is made over big catfish, what adventures fall to a knowledgeable catfisherman.

The Walkers did not get the $500. reward. The verbal equivalent of the fine print read that the reward would be payable upon delivery alive to the Fort Worth Botanic Garden. The fish having died, they were paid 50 cents a pound—about double—for their catch.

The Walkers were good sports about it, as becomes heroes. They divulged their secret of how to catch the biggest catfish in Kentucky Lake to me, there with my press card in my hat, along with reporters from Memphis and Nashville, Tennessee, and Corinth, Mississippi.

But to lead into this secret, we must absorb some poop about catfish and their varieties, for the secret in this instance was the bait, and it pertains to catfish themselves. Catfish are known as *Ictalurus, Pilodictis,* and *Ameirus.* According to the encyclopedias there are 1200 kinds of catfish in the world, 35 kinds in the United States. We are concerned here with just a few kinds, especially the blue catfish, the Mississippi white catfish, the yellow, or flathead catfish—all of which get big; and the channel cats, willow cats, and bullheads, which reach nice game fish size. The bullheads are smaller and are named yellow bullheads, black bullheads, brown bullheads, and hornpouts (New England).

There is also a very tiny and very black bullhead, which makes the best bait for catfish that anybody ever put on a hook. These are hard to come by. In the Tennessee River, however, catfishermen occasionally have the luck to find a colony of these little

143

fish, usually inhabiting a rocky point. Either they are scarce or they are seclusive, for few people have ever seen them. But any time a man can bait a hook with one of these, he can sure catch a bigger fish. The Walkers knew of a place along the river where they could catch these black pigmy catfish on a small hook and cane pole. They had put the small children of the family to fishing for them, saving them alive in a minnow bucket to reinvest in larger fish.

Big catfish of a hundred pounds and up are rather scarce in the nation's principal catfish habitat, which is to say in the waters known as the Mississippi drainage system. One of 105 pounds was caught early in the history of the TVA below Wheeler Dam. In 1946 a commercial fisherman caught a yellow catfish of 130 pounds out of the upper part of Kentucky Lake. Mark Twain in his *Life on the Mississippi* writes that a 150-pound catfish was caught in his day near St. Louis. Some big ones, yellow catfish of over 100 pounds, have been pulled out of the bayous of Louisiana. Texas insolently challenged Mr. Parris' aspiration of proving that the Tennessee River had the biggest catfish by publishing the claim of Arley W. Cumings, of Texarkana, that he had caught a 138-pound blue catfish out of the Red River. All of these big catfish were caught on trotlines.

The reason for the rarity of hundred-pound catfish in the United States is undoubtedly the fishing pressure. Wherever there are catfish it would be hard to go a hundred yards without encountering a fish net, a trotline, a snagline, or at least a couple of fellows floating fifty jugs. Over twenty million people buy fishing licenses every year. Of course there is no way of telling how many individuals will fish primarily for catfish, except that any fool knows it will be the most of them, if you count the Yankees who fish for hornpout, and the old colored women who line the drainage ditches and the borrow pits to cane-pole for small ones.

It is therefore rare for a catfish to survive in the wilderness of hooks and other contraptions designed to catch him, and get to be over a hundred pounds. I collected a method whereby a 110-pound catfish was caught in the Cumberland River above Nashville. The man saw it on its spawning bed in an indentation in

Monster catfish like this one lurk in the depths of some of our larger southern rivers. Although the big ones are not as numerous as in the past, there are still plenty of small- and medium-sized fish to go around. *(Photo by Claire Gowen)*

the river bank and gigged it with a pitchfork. The "how-to" of catfishing has much variety! The lips and face of this fish were covered with hooks and bits of leader and line, like a beard. He was the big one that had many times got away.

Blue catfish seem to live with considerable violence in a rather delicate balance, and will die quickly out of water, almost immediately if in the sun. On the other hand I have brought home yellow catfish from a couple of hundred miles and had them still alive when I got home. Blue catfish prefer clear and swift waters, and in this compare to yellow catfish as smallmouthed bass compare to largemouths. Thus the TVA, which changed the Tennessee River into a chain of lakes connected by relatively short stretches of swiftly flowing streams, vastly improved blue catfish habitat and made catfish angling a popular sport below every dam along the Tennessee River—Kentucky Dam, Pickwick, Wilson, Wheeler, Guntersville, Chickamauga, all the way to Watts Bar Dam high up in East Tennessee. Here catfish are concentrated in vast numbers and are catchable in large sizes now and then, and in great quantities nearly all the time. We call the small ones fiddlers.

When I first began to fish below Tennessee River dams, back in the 1940s, I established a method there. My most recent fishing phase had been surf casting for oceanic striped bass and I took that tackle catfishing. The secret of the success was the tackle; it was heavy enough to handle a sinker of from 4 ounces to a pound. With that size sinker one could feel the bottom in the swift water below the turbine exits, and feel into holes in the river bottom where the catfish lay, presumably not to be washed away by the swift water. We would let our boat drift, hunting for these holes and dropping a variety of baits into them.

I have never been above any method of catching catfish, and the only one I have never tried is that of shocking them with the generator of an old-fashioned wall telephone. This method had a vogue and proved itself so effective that the fish and game division passed a regulation by which it would confiscate boat, motor, and all fishing gear of anyone found using it. That was a little too sporty for me, too much to lose for the game if you failed to win, and so my most sinful way of catching catfish has been grabbling.

Catfishing requires strong and fairly heavy fishing tackle. Many anglers are now using salt-water rods, reels, lines, and hooks for the larger catfish. *(Photo by Claire Gowen)*

147

I have had great grabbling days with Forrest Bell, a lifelong fishing companion. One day while we were resting in wet clothes on the river bank, I asked Forrest if he had ever been caught and arrested for grabbling. Clearly, avoiding arrest is part of the secret of this method, so I include his reply.

"Have I ever been caught? Listen, they got us one day with a hundred and ten pounds of blue catfish, me and three friends of mine.

"We were grabbling down along the Harpeth River. I had just put my hand in a hole, a nice clean one so I knew a catfish had taken up there. Catfish won't take a muddy hole, they'll find one with sand at the entrance, and then sweep it clean. Well, we'd been doing fine all day and I was feeling mighty good till I looked over to shore and seen this old boy raise his head up in the hoss weeds, and squat back down. I got to looking then and they was men in the weeds all around us, and on both sides of the river. 'Boys,' I said, 'they got us!' It was half a dozen of 'em. Held they guns on us, too. Said, 'Don't run, damn ye, or we'll shoot!' Took us to a magistrate there. They fined us right smart. They was going to take the fish, too, but I called the judge here at home and he chewed that magistrate out. Told that magistrate that when a thief is arrested for stealing, it ain't proper for the judge to take for himself what was stole. Them game wardens will run it over on a man, if they get some little old bass-fishin' magistrate to workin' with 'em, some fellow that when he does his fishing he has a servant to paddle him and pass him his bottle. Aye gosh, I work for my fish, and I figure the man that does the work to git 'em is the one entitled to 'em."

The grabbler's secret is the knowledge of the nesting places along the streams. Often these sites become a father-to-son legacy. Sometimes a man will set out and choose a rock or old stump and prepare a catfish hole himself, so he'll know where to go. Knowing where there are a few such holes, a man can go each spring and get himself some catfish every day, like a farmer's wife steps out into the corn patch to get a mess of roasting ears. Naturally a grabbler just won't listen to the law trying to tell him he must not.

A recent encounter between Forrest and the game warden is

illustrative. In the good way of courtesy prior to animosities, they passed the time of day. Then the warden noticed Forrest's hands. They were scratched and skinned, one arm chewed up where he'd had hold of more catfish than he could handle. With his hand in a big catfish's mouth and out past the gills for a hand grasp, Forrest had that day had to pull loose by main force when he hadn't been able to dislodge the fish. His whole lower arm was sore from where he had pulled against the rasp of the fish's teeth.

"Ah, ha!" the warden said. "You done taken to grabbling again," he said.

"Ah, ha! you peckerwood," Forrest replied. "They been dynamiting just up the creek early today and I even heard the blast. Looks like that there blasting would be bigger to attract your attention than these here little old scratches on my arms. Looks like that muck the chemical plant runs into the Duck River and ruined the fishing there would keep you busy so's you wouldn't need to go around looking for a few little old sores on my arms."

Nowadays the grabbling situation is somewhat confused, in that it is legal in many states. In Tennessee and a few other states, however, it is prohibited. In either status, grabbling is a solid sport and in the waters of practically the whole of the Mississippi drainage system it is solidly entrenched. In the lowlands, however, the fish are somewhat harder to locate than on up the tributary streams to which the fish migrate to spawn. When the fish have moved up out of the navigable rivers into the shallows, into the rocky and cluttered-up tributaries that are no more than wading depth, the fishing is fine.

Catfish begin to spawn late in April and through May, but they do not have to lay their eggs at an immediate time; they can lay them when they want to. They can pick a time of low, clear water, which is of course very nice for grabblers who want that kind of water, too. When it rains and the river rises and is muddy, the catfish come out of their holes, for they realize that mud could wash in and stop them up in there. This may account for the fact that a rise of muddy water is the best time to fish for catfish with bait, the time when they bite the best, and irrefutable proof that they don't have to see the bait to find it.

Catfish family life is idyllic and monogamous, there in a hole under a rock at the bottom of the river. A pair of catfish will get together and work to clean out a nest. They don't mate for size, and an 8-pound hen blue catfish is apt to have a suitor that wouldn't weigh a pound. A team of scientists discovered that in captivity the female will lay about 2000 eggs and that within five days some 1900 of these will hatch.

Along with the fun of catching them, with catfish the sportsman has a gustatory connection. I know a man who for a curious purpose likes to get hold of rainbow trout, generally considered the most delicious eating fish of all, and keep them frozen along with small catfish, 6, 8, and 10 inches long. He likes to have both kinds fried up to perfection, and then demand of a guest if the catfish is not better.

Inland people get cravings for fish. One of my methods comes from a boyhood incident of a time when we were plowing corn, back in the mule and double-shovel days, and we were stopped by a thunder shower. We unhitched the mules and led them to the river to drink. It had already been raining upriver, and the water was becoming muddy, although not rising much.

"This here water is just right," remarked John Nipper, a sharecropper. "I'm plumb catfish hongry. How about you all?" The three other sharecroppers were fish hongry, too, and I was of an age to be hongry for excitement. I volunteered to go get the seine, and rode off on my mule, the trace chains jingling. When I got back with the net, somebody had gone to his house and got a skillet, salt, and grease. We got into the river with the net and would work from the middle to the water weeds growing along the sandbars. Catches become the more ideal the longer remembered, but it does seem that every time we upped the net we had four or five catfish a couple of feet long.

After that, whenever I would see John Nipper, even thirty-five years later, we would reminisce about those wonderful catfish, for we ate as many as we could there on the river bank before dividing up the rest. John would always say, "We et catfish thar til we pooched out."

I learned a lot about catfishing, angling division, from a fabulous hole which no longer exists. Pickwick Dam now has six turbines, but at that time had only four, with the foundation laid for the remaining two. The draft tubes, through which the water would rush from the turbines, at that time constituted something like quiet submarine caverns, which were full of big yellow catfish. I used to go there at dawn, while waiting for the coffee water to boil at the fish camp, and almost without fail would catch a catfish of 30 or 40 pounds.

Fishing there one time with Forrest Bell, he hooked his first big one, which turned out to weigh over 50 pounds. The bait, a theory of baiting for catfish, is the secret here. Rigged for big catfish, using a big-game rod and reel with 100-pound test line, in his excitement Forrest raised that fish to the surface in almost nothing flat. It got around the anchor rope and he raised the anchor along with the fish. Thus, in the catching, it weighed as much as the fish plus the anchor. In the recounting over the years it never lost a pound.

Ever since then I have had much quiet amusement listening to Forrest's accounts of the finesse with which he played that fish. In these accounts I have known him to fight the fish for forty-five minutes, while it towed the boat all over the river. The whole matter has become, by subtle revisions of history, entirely as elegant as a trophy sailfish catch. But Forrest would not have caught that fish, except for my knowledge of the proper bait to use.

One reason for the plentitude of catfish is that a catfish will eat just about anything, and thus has an easy time of making a living. Catfishermen are traditionally ingenious about killer-diller baits —trying everything from doughballs made of corn meal and molasses (with a banana and fifteen drops of oil of valerin added) to chopped-up worms mixed with asafetida and packed into chicken guts—and they have yet to come up with a bait that a catfish will not bite.

Such fellows are inclined to secrecy about their potent baits. A man might give out that he used slaughterhouse blood, salted and set to congeal, but this apparent candor is to mislead the competition, for actually he uses a mixture of skunk fur, Limburger cheese, and chicken feathers, bonded with casein glue.

Below the hydro dams, where hickory shad swarm and are catchable with special dip nets made of a kind of wire netting known as hardware cloth, these baitfish are used in various ways. Sometimes the fish will seem to bite best on shad guts. Other times the man who has caught the most will say he was using pieces of shad, cut-up and bloodied. To the various ways of preparing shad for bait, some add stink oils, asafetida, or commercial preparations, such as one which is brand named Doodle-oil. Others think bait should be red, and use cake coloring, red ink, mercurochrome, or poke-berry juice. Blue catfish, Mississippi white catfish, channel catfish, and willow catfish bite readily for them all.

Yellow catfish, however, are entirely different in their bait-taking habits. The safe rule for yellow catfish is to use nothing unless it is alive. Yellow catfish will take live minnows, stunted pond perch (this is really great bait for them), cicadas in a cicada year when all fish gorge on this bug often known as the seven-year locust (but the cicadas must still be kicking when they are offered). They also take catalpa worms, frogs, crayfish, hellgrammites, and baby catfish. The young of hickory shad known as shad minnows are superb, but are so difficult to keep alive that they are impractical except when they are available right at the hydro dam where they can be caught as needed. Steelback minnows or sucker minnows caught out of a creek and carefully kept lively are hard to beat for yellow catfish, and the other varieties will take live bait, too.

I mention this in the hope of bringing catfish baits back from the foul-smelling concoctions human ingenuity has devised, to some semblance of decency. The bait that turned out to be the most effective for those big yellow catfish in the submarine caverns, however, was so natural and obvious that nobody else thought of it: worms.

*Chapter Eleven*

# HOW TO CATCH CARP

## *by* RUSSELL TINSLEY

RUSSELL TINSLEY lives in Austin, Texas, where he writes an outdoor column for the *American-Statesman.* Having such a big state to cover he naturally gets around, fishing in the fresh-water rivers, lakes, reservoirs, and in the salt waters of the Gulf of Mexico. In addition he also does a lot of hunting in Texas and neighboring states. This provides plenty of material for his newspaper column and for many outdoor magazines in which his writing and photos appear regularly.

THE carp is a paradox. Although man originally introduced this oriental alien into the United States, today he looks upon it as an undesirable pest. The carp is a prolific scavenger that soon populates waters with its own kind, forcing out the game fish.

The carp is justly maligned, yet there is one obvious overlooked fact about this widespread piscatorial inhabitant. It is fun to catch on fishing tackle.

Catching carp is specialized fishing. Because of its peculiar habit of rooting along bottom with its suctionlike mouth in search of food, the carp requires a different angling technique than those associated with game fish such as bass and bluegills. A carp doesn't actually strike a bait. Rather, it sort of mouths it, telegraphing a bite up the line in a series of light, short taps. The angler who catches carp consistently must have a sensitive touch.

But once the carp feels the bite of a hook it loses this timidness, becoming a bulldogging submarine that fights tenaciously in grudging spurts near bottom. On appropriate tackle the carp is a sporty battler, indeed.

There's nothing flashy about the carp. It doesn't jump once hooked, nor does it zig-zag in speedy runs. The carp is a slugger and its front-line defense is brute strength.

153

I recall an exceptionally large carp I once caught on spinning tackle equipped with 6-pound test line. My wife, Marjorie, and I were fishing a deep, placid pool in the Llano River of central Texas. This carp didn't gingerly mouth the bait, but instead grabbed hold greedily, almost yanking the rod from my grasp. I heaved back on the Fiberglas stick and it whipped almost in a full circle. For a brief moment it was a stalemate. Nothing moved.

My wife said, "You've hung a log."

"It's the first time I ever saw a snag swim upstream," I answered, grinning.

At first the carp didn't realize it had been hooked. It swam leisurely upstream. Then, abruptly, it felt the sharp steel. Shifting into high gear the fish bored deep, making the spinning reel-drag sing in protest.

For perhaps ten minutes it was a give-and-take duel. It was difficult to determine who was fighting whom. The fish would take a couple of dozen yards of monofilament and I would slowly regain it. Then the rod began to sap the fish's strength. Shortly I had it coming my way, but when the carp glimpsed land it turned and headed back toward the middle of the river, its broad tail churning the water.

After three such runs the fish's stamina was spent. But it had enough reserve strength to more than hold its own. I worked the fish to within 20 yards of shore, but it refused to be coaxed any closer. I couldn't gain line, nor could the carp. I dared not put any more pressure on the tackle without risking a broken line. The fish remained stationary, its long bronze body hovering just under the surface, fanning with its powerful tail and fins, refusing to quit. We must have remained in this stand-off position for a full five minutes before I started gaining line again, only a few inches at a time. When I had the fish pulled into the shallows it still tried to get away, jerking feebly.

This one weighed 20 pounds, an exceptionally large carp. Anything exceeding 10 pounds in size is a whopper.

"That fish didn't know when to quit." Marjorie remarked respectfully.

Russell Tinsley

In rivers, carp like the quieter sections and pools, where the current isn't too strong. This one was taken below a dam, another good spot.

This gameness makes me wonder why the carp is overlooked as a sport-fishing prospect. In most of our waters, the population ratio is balanced in the carp's favor, yet almost without exception anglers are after the minority—the game fish. The person who catches carp is serving a dual purpose: he is having royal fun and is aiding in fish conservation.

Certainly most fishermen would rather catch an aerial-minded trout or bass than a lowly carp. But there are times when the

Bill Corley holds an average-sized carp, although many smaller ones and bigger ones are also caught.

game species simply refuse to co-operate. This is the time when Mr. Carp comes to the rescue. If you locate a concentration of carp you can usually catch them. They know no seasons or feeding periods in the South. It seems the carp is always on the prowl. Of course, in northern waters they are not very active during the winter and there your best fishing is from May to October.

The real secret, then, of carp fishing is finding the fish. In a large body of water, which carp prefer, it is easy for the fish to get lost. A carp doesn't necessarily seek out a bait, like a trout or bass does. Instead, it is more likely to suck it up during its aimless wandering in search of food. A person who catches carp consistently must have his bait pin-pointed in an area where carp are feeding.

The most popular method of congregating carp is to "bait an area." A likely location is a spot that is calm and secluded, not necessarily very deep. Cottonseed meal or cake, used for livestock feed, and stale corn are the two most popular baits. But probably the best is a combination of the two. This is placed in a wire-mesh basket (or a loose mesh cloth sack) and weighted so that it remains on bottom. The mesh wire keeps turtles and small fish from stealing the bait. The ingredients are mixed at a ratio of two parts cottonseed cake or meal to one part corn. A cup of sugar and a small box of anise seed are added. In about two or three days this bait should attract a big gathering of carp. This is a more permanent bait, one which will keep carp in one area for several days.

But for a more temporary bait, improvised only to attract carp into a limited area for a short duration, simply toss out pieces of cottonseed cake or kernels of stale corn, scattering them over an area roughly 30 yards in diameter. Drop your baited hook right in the middle. The carp will move back and forth, sucking up the bait, and eventually one is apt to pick up your baited hook.

Almost any type tackle is suitable for carp fishing. However, something on the medium to stiff side is recommended. A medium-action rod with lots of backbone down near the butt, 5 to 7 feet long, equipped with a reel loaded with 15-pound test line is about right. Either spinning or casting tackle is okay.

Some of my sportiest carp fishing is done with a 9-foot fly rod. A fly reel is filled with 10-pound test monofil and a tiny treble hook is tied on the business end. A split-shot sinker is added about a foot above the hook. This rig can be cast adequately with the fly rod and there isn't much dragging weight for the carp to feel when it picks up the bait. Also, on the delicate tackle it is easier to "feel" the light touch of a biting carp.

Dough bait is the favorite of most carp fishermen. The treble hook is recommended when fishing dough bait, either the home-

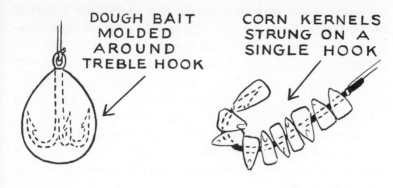

DOUGH BAIT MOLDED AROUND TREBLE HOOK

CORN KERNELS STRUNG ON A SINGLE HOOK

Hooking baits for carp

made or commercial variety. The bait is molded into a ball, completely hiding the hook, and it remains in one piece longer on this type hook. When fishing with kernels of stale corn I like to string them on a single No. 4 or No. 5 hook (the carp has a small mouth) like beads on a necklace. The corn should be soaked beforehand so that it is pliable and goes on a hook easier. The carp also prefer soft moist corn to the hard kernels.

Above the hook, either type, is added a "slip" or "sliding" sinker. This is a lengthy potbellied sinker with a hole running through it horizontally. There are a couple of ways for rigging

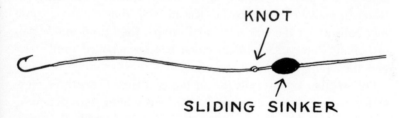

KNOT

SLIDING SINKER

Rig for carp fishing

this type sinker. One is to tie a knot about a foot above the hook, the other is to add a bead before tying on the hook. Both methods are designed to keep the sinker from slipping down over the hook on the cast.

This sinker provides sufficient weight for casting, yet when a carp mouths the bait the line will slip through the sinker un-

159

hindered. Often a carp will drop the bait immediately if it feels any hindrance. I've had a carp pick up and drop a bait as many as five or six times before it takes it for good.

The bait should be fished directly on bottom, as this is the vicinity where carp feed. They're always rooting for food and a bait dangling even an inch off the bottom will be ignored.

There are many commercial concoctions on the market designed to attract carp. Most of them are good. Some already have moisture added; others are of the dry variety and water must be mixed in before using. The former is more convenient, but the latter lasts longer.

But the enterprising angler can concoct his own dough bait in the kitchen at home. Here's one homemade recipe: Mix one cup of yellow cornmeal, one cup of flour, and one teaspoon sugar with just enough water to make a heavy dough. Roll into small balls. Add one quart water and one cup Karo syrup in a saucepan and bring to a boil. Drop in the dough balls and allow to boil for two or three minutes, being careful not to add too many since they have a tendency to stick together. After cooling, the balls can be stored in the leftover water.

Another formula calls for one cup flour, one cup yellow cornmeal, one-fourth cup grated cheese (the canned variety is best), and one teaspoon sugar, mixed while dry. Add just enough cold water to make a thick mixture. Knead well. Roll the dough into tiny balls about the size of a small grape, then drop into a pan of boiling water in which an onion has been boiled until done and then removed.

Still another recipe calls for mixing two cups flour, three cups white cornmeal, one cup sugar, two egg whites, one cup cold water, and one small box anise seed. Thoroughly sift the flour, cornmeal, and sugar together. Beat the egg whites and cold water together, add the anise seed, then combine the dry and damp mixtures. Add enough flour and cornmeal, or a little water, to make a stiff dough.

Flatten the mass into an even spread about an inch and a half thick. Place in a cloth sack and tie the mouth shut with a string. Drop this into a pan of boiling water. Cook about three minutes on one side, turn and repeat on the other. Lower the fire and

A nice string of carp, especially when taken on a spinning outfit. They put up a sustained and thrilling battle on light tackle.

allow to simmer for about fifteen minutes. Remove the bait from the sack and let cool on a piece of wax paper. Portions of the bait can be pinched off and rolled into balls as you fish. This mixture keeps indefinitely under refrigeration.

Stale corn is effective at times, as are mulberries. The latter are particularly good in season, and if the angler can find where a mulberry tree hangs over the water of a stream or lake, he probably has located a carp hot spot. The fish congregate to feed on the ripe berries as they fall into the water.

The carp (*Cyprinus carpio*) was originally from China. It was brought into this country by way of Europe in 1877 when it was propagated in ponds at Washington, D.C. From this original stock of 345 carp, enough fry were obtained to distribute them widely throughout the United States in 1879 during the farm-pond program of that era. The carp has been thriving and multiplying ever since.

A female carp will lay as many as two million eggs, and the young fish grow to 8 or 9 inches the first year under optimum conditions. Carp migrate into the shallows in either May or June to spawn. The carp is a cousin to the common goldfish. There are three varieties in this country: the common carp, mirror carp, and leather carp. They can be distinguished from native American minnows by the strong spinous rays at the front of both the anal and dorsal fins, and by the long dorsal fin. The common carp has thirty-two or more scales and two barbels on the sides of its mouth. The mirror carp has relatively large scales while the leather carp has none.

The skin of a carp's mouth is leathery and tough. The angler should strike a biting carp forcefully to drive a hook into his hard skin.

If prepared correctly a carp is fairly good to eat. One way is to skin the fish and remove the dark meat along either side. Cut into large chunks and cook in a pressure cooker until done. The large bones are easily removed while the smaller ones become soft. Roll the meat into patties and fry.

Another method is to dress the carp as mentioned above, cut the meat into pieces of 1½ inches thick and 2 inches square, soak for three hours in milk (salt water is a good substitute) to which salt and pepper has been added, roll in yellow cornmeal, and fry to a rich brown.

Canned carp is prepared by cutting off a carp's head, fins, and tail and cutting the skinned meat into chunks. One teaspoon of salt is added to a pint jar of water holding the fish chunks. This is cooked under ten pounds of pressure for two hours. The bones soften like tuna or salmon.

Catching carp is fascinating in an intriguingly odd sort of way. Patience is the main requisite. An angler can't hurry a carp. He's got to wait one out. It's peaceful, relaxing fishing. That is, until a belligerent fish picks up the bait.

The carp likes to slug, and it always loses on a decision, never by a quick knockout.

*How to*
*Catch Carp*

Vlad Evanoff

164

## Chapter Twelve

# SURF FISHING TIPS

## *by* VLAD EVANOFF

VLAD EVANOFF, the editor of this volume, enjoys all kinds of fresh- and salt-water fishing. But he especially favors surf fishing and has spent twenty-five years seeking such gamesters as striped bass, channel bass, weakfish, and other species from the beaches. He was recently featured in *Life* magazine as one of the country's leading surf anglers. He has written several books and many magazine articles on fishing. His book *Surf Fishing* has been in print for twelve years and is considered the surf angler's bible. He has written two chapters for this book, one on surf fishing and the other on bottom fishing.

ALMOST everyone who has tried surf fishing will admit that of all the different kinds of salt-water fishing, casting from the beaches, jetties, or rocky shores is one of the toughest ways to catch fish. You really have to know what you are doing and you have to work hard for your fish in the surf. In fact, many anglers have tried surf fishing a few times and then have given it up as too unrewarding in the terms of the number of fish caught for the effort expended. Still other anglers, determined to master surf fishing, have been trying for years to acquire the skill and knowledge necessary to become a good surf angler.

Many beginners in surf fishing get off to a bad start by buying the wrong fishing tackle and accessories. Or they try to skimp and save money by not getting *all* the equipment that they need. Some of them, for example, will buy a good surf rod, reel, and line—then they'll buy one or two lures and think that they are all set to catch fish in the surf. Most of the expert surf anglers that I know rarely carry less than a dozen lures with them every time they go out. Others carry two or three dozen. And in their cars they'll have several dozen lures to choose from. Still

165

other surf anglers try to fish the surf without boots when they really need them. Or they use boots when the spot being fished calls for waders. I could go on with more examples—but you should know what I'm driving at by now. If you plan to take up surf fishing get *everything* that you need for this game. If you have been fishing with makeshift tackle or doing without certain important items go out and buy them before you try surf fishing again.

We won't go into too much detail on exactly the type of surf rod, reel, and line you need for surf fishing. You can obtain this information from books on the subject. Or ask a tackle dealer to recommend an outfit for you. For best results buy your surf outfit from a coastal store where the owner does surf fishing himself or caters to experienced surf anglers.

Most surf anglers today use a surf spinning rod anywhere from 9 to 12 feet in over-all length. For jetty fishing or sandy beaches where casts are short you can use a medium-weight outfit. But in some areas you may need a heavy surf rod. The spinning reel should be made for surf fishing and should hold at least 250 or 300 yards of line. The monofilament line can test about 15 pounds for the medium weight rod and about 20 pounds for the heavy rod.

Surf anglers also need boots, waders, waterproof parka jacket, small pouches or bags for holding lures, a head light, ice creepers or wading sandals for fishing from jetties or rocky shores, a gaff, and a knife.

If you fish along the Atlantic Coast for striped bass, bluefish, weakfish, and channel bass you'll need an assortment of metal squids, jigs, plugs, and a rigged eel. If you fish with natural baits you'll need an assortment of hooks, wire leader material, monofilament leader material, swivels, and pyramid sinkers.

If this sounds like a lot of stuff remember that surf fishing is one of the least expensive forms of salt-water fishing in the long run. In the beginning you might have to invest up to $150. or so to be fully equipped. But from then on the cost of transportation, bait, replacement of lines or lures, care of tackle, etc., is negligible. Of course, possession of the right surf rod, reel, line, and lures doesn't automatically make you a good surf angler. You have to know how to use this equipment. Practice casting until you can hit a small area with accuracy and reach the maximum distance with a particular rod, reel, line, and lure. You should become so familiar with your outfit that you can use it on the darkest night without any difficulty.

To be prepared for changing surf conditions and the different species of fish, you must carry a good assortment of lures. You should not only carry them, but know when, where, and how to use them. The metal squid for example comes in various sizes and weights. When sand eels or silversides (spearing) are present the smaller, narrow types should be used. When mullet, herring, or shiners are present the broader, heavier types resemble these fish more closely. Metal squids work best in the daytime, at dusk and in the morning, especially when the water is fairly rough and white. They should be reeled slowly for such fish as weakfish, channel bass, and big striped bass. For small striped bass they can be reeled a bit faster. While for such fish as bluefish, bonito, albacore, and mackerel they can be reeled very fast. When the water is clean and clear, reel the metal squids faster than when it's dirty and discolored. They should also be reeled faster along rocky shores than along sandy beaches.

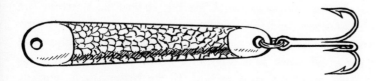

HOPKINS NO-EQL lure

Another lure, similar to the metal squid which has proven a killer in the surf for many species, is the heavy spoon-type lure such as the Hopkins No-Eql. This is made of stainless steel and casts like a bullet. For best results it should be reeled at a moderate or fast speed to bring out the action.

In recent years the jigs have proven to be versatile lures for surf fishing. They are especially deadly for small striped bass, bluefish, weakfish, and channel bass. Jigs are highly adaptable lures and can be reeled in straight near the surface to simulate terrified baitfish. This will often take fish when they are chasing baitfish near the surface. But when the fish go down deep the jigs can be allowed to sink and are then reeled at varying depths in a stop-and-go fashion with plenty of rod action. When the fish are down on the bottom, the jigs can be bounced along the bottom very slowly to get strikes.

When fish are chasing baitfish on the surface in the surf you can't beat the surface-type plugs such as the swimmers, poppers, and propeller plugs which cause a commotion when reeled and jerked. They come in various sizes and weights. The big 2- and 3-ounce surface plugs are used for big striped bass. The smaller plugs are used for small striped bass, sea trout, bluefish, and many other fish in southern waters. For best results keep these surface plugs moving fairly fast and jerk them often so that they splash and make plenty of fuss. Surface plugs will often raise fish when the water is flat and calm even in broad daylight. However, they can also be used at night when the water is fairly flat. Also at dusk and at daybreak. They'll take fish when the water is rough, too, but are less likely to be seen at such times.

When surf fish do not respond to surface plugs try underwater plugs. These also come in various sizes and weights. Here, again, the big plugs are used for big striped bass, while the smaller ones are used for various small species found in the surf. When using underwater plugs it is important to feel the plug working at all times. If a wave or the tide pushes the plug toward you, speed up your reeling. If the backwash or current pulls on the plug, slow down your reeling.

My favorite lure for big striped bass along the Atlantic Coast from Massachusetts to New Jersey is the rigged eel. And I like the big ones measuring anywhere from 12 to 18 inches in length for use with a conventional surf rod. But with a spinning rod you can use the smaller ones from 8 to 12 inches with good results.

Rigged eels can be prepared at home if you can catch or buy the smaller salt-water bay eels. If you want a tough rigged eel get it alive, kill it, and rig it and use it the same night. A freshly killed eel will last all night and you can often catch two or three fish on the same bait. If you must keep the eels for several days freeze them immediately after killing them and rigging them. When a frozen eel thaws out it is still a tough bait. Eels can also be pickled in heavy salt brine and kept in airtight jars for several months or longer. However, such eels usually soften and fall apart after a few hours fishing. So bring along plenty of spare rigged eels if you are using pickled ones.

I've caught plenty of small stripers on rigged eels, but usually they are best for the big bass from 15 pounds and up. And the rigged eel is mostly a nighttime lure. Actually, they are also very good at daybreak and at dusk too, but what I mean is that rigged eels aren't the best lures to use in the middle of the day.

The rigged eel is a difficult lure to use and it usually takes a while before you get the knack of working it effectively. Reel it as slowly as possible—remember that it's a natural bait and you can give a striper plenty of time to look it over. But don't reel it slowly all the time. Speed up your reeling at regular intervals for a second or two. Then slow down again and let the eel settle and sink once more. Some anglers like to jerk the eel at regular intervals, but I feel that it's less tiring on the arms to speed up the reeling to get the same results.

Rigged eel

A rigged eel without any added weight is a versatile lure that can be manipulated and worked at any desired depth from the near surface to the very bottom. I've had stripers also strike it on top when it was rippling across the surface of the water. Some of these fish were solidly hooked and landed—but a lot of others have been hooked and then immediately lost because they weren't securely hooked or the fish thrashed around on top and tore off. For best results try to keep your eel down below the surface a foot or two or at least a few inches. In fact, such a retrieve is a must over rocky bottoms where the boulders are of

169

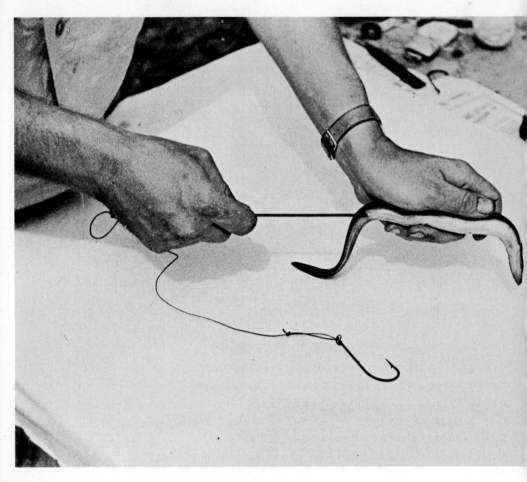

To rig an eel you need a long needle to run the line holding the hook through the body cavity of the bait.

varying sizes and are numerous. Here you can't let the eel sink too deep or you'll get hung up.

Along sandy beaches, however, you can often try sinking the eel almost to the bottom and then retrieving slowly just off the bottom. You may not get a strike all the way out and down deep, but you may catch the eye of a striper that will follow the eel into shallow water or the surf near shore and then grab it.

With the great emphasis on artificial lures these days for surf fishing, bait fishing for striped bass, bluefish, weakfish, and other species has been neglected. But these fish can often be caught with natural baits when they won't strike the artificial. During the summer months of June, July, and August, for example, you can't beat bottom fishing along sandy bottoms on Long Island and New Jersey with soft-shelled or shedder crabs. The best crab for this is the lady or calico crab. These crabs are found buried in the sand in shallow water along the beaches. They can be raked out with a combination rake and scoop net. Then they must be tied to a hook with fine thread so that the soft meat of the crab doesn't fly off on the first cast. Sure, it's a lot of trouble to get the crabs and it requires patience to wait for a strike with the bait. But this shedder or soft-shell crab often works when other lures and baits fail. Other baits which can be used for striped bass include whole squid, sea clams, bloodworms, pieces of menhaden, herring, butterfish, and mullet. These fish baits will also catch bluefish and channel bass. We won't go into detail on using them for channel bass because this is covered thoroughly by Claude Rogers in Chapter 15 of this book.

You can't catch fish in the surf unless you fish the spots where fish are present. So the most successful anglers spend hours trying to locate the fish and follow up every lead. They scan the outdoor columns of newspapers, talk with other surf anglers, query tackle dealers. If these fail to provide the necessary information they cruise along the beaches looking for signs of birds working, breaking fish, and keep an eye on other surf anglers and boats trolling offshore.

Once you know that fish are being caught in a certain area then it's a matter of waiting and sweating it out. Fish hard at daybreak, dusk, and during the night. If the water is flat and calm, wait until a wind comes along and creates some white water. Or if the calm period persists, fish mostly at night with rigged eels or natural bait. Stripers usually bite best immediately before, during, and right after a storm. If the water is very dirty you may have to wait a day or two before it clears up. But don't wait too long! Try to catch the period when the water is a milky green. Then it's easier to fool the stripers than when the water clears up completely.

When fishing for stripers always concentrate on the white water spots, where the surf is roughest and the water turbulent. Along rocky shores even when the water is fairly calm, there are usually some pockets, holes, or reefs or rocky points where a wave breaks and creates a little white water. Cast into these or work your lure so that it passes through this white water.

The best tide to fish will depend on the area being fished, type of bottom, and shore formation. As a general rule fish the change of the tide at both high and low water. In other words, fish the first hour or two of the incoming and the first hour or two of the outgoing. Around rivers or inlets emptying into the surf the last two or three hours of the outgoing tide are usually best.

Study the winds and how they affect your fishing area. Usually you'll find that along the Atlantic Coast winds blowing from the east, northeast, and southeast will result in big waves and a heavy surf, if they are strong and continue to blow for any length of time. This may create good surf fishing along rocky shores during the storm or right after it. But along sandy beaches these onshore winds will tend to ruin the surf fishing by creating brown or dirty water. Winds from the north, northwest, and west calm or flatten the surf. The fishing may be good the first two or three days that these winds blow. But later on they may flatten the surf too much and clear the water, making surf fishing less productive.

Many veteran surf anglers who have studied and observed through the years claim that the moon has an effect on surf fishing. Most of them agree that the period from the first quarter through the full moon is best for surf fishing. I, personally, have found that some of the best fishing and the biggest stripers are taken around the full moon period in the fall of the year.

Your chances are also better in the surf if you choose the peak fishing months for a given location. Thus if you are interested in catching channel bass you should go to North Carolina during April and May and again in October and November. For stripers you can fish the New Jersey and Long Island beaches in May and June. During the summer months fishing slows down in most places, but may be hot in Cape Cod in Massachusetts on certain days. During the fall months stripers are active from Cape Cod

This surf angler on a jetty is trying to reach the sand bar where the breaking waves create white water. Such spots are especially productive of striped bass.

to New Jersey. Fish New England during September and October, especially Massachusetts and Rhode Island. Then later shift to Montauk Point on Long Island, New York, and the beaches of New Jersey. Here the fishing often lasts well into November.

And try to spend more than a day or two at these surf fishing spots. Too many anglers come down for a day or a weekend and expect to find good fishing. This happens at times, of course, if you're lucky, but your chances are much better if you spend

173

The wise surf angler fishes on the bottom with bait when the fish are not hitting artificials on top.

several days at a surf fishing spot. This is especially true if you are fishing a new or strange spot. It usually takes a day or two to become acquainted with the area. The anglers who catch the most fish in the surf spend many days and hours living or camping on the beach. Or they cruise up and down in cars and beach buggies, checking on the various spots, trying to locate the fish.

Once they catch fish or see fish caught, they go to work and fish hard.

And I mean fish hard! Surf fishing isn't for the lazy or comfort-loving angler. When the fish are running the regulars fish day and night, during rain, storms, cold, or heat until the action stops. These men know that you rarely get continuous action for more than a day or two. Then there's a long wait before the next hot fishing period.

Surf fishing is never easy. True, there may be bonanza days, when the fish are thick and you get one on almost every cast. But such days are pretty rare. Most of the time you have to make hundreds, if not thousands, of casts for a few fish. And when it comes to the big fish, many are hooked, but not all of them are landed. Fighting and landing a big striped bass, channel bass, bluefish, or weakfish in the surf is difficult and the odds are in favor of the fish. But when you do finally beach a trophy-size fish you can take a bow and feel you've really accomplished something in the fishing world. One big fish caught from the surf is equal to a dozen of the same size caught from a boat.

*Chapter Thirteen*

# THE ART OF BOTTOM FISHING

*by* VLAD EVANOFF

SOME who read the heading of this chapter may question my calling bottom fishing an "art." In fact, it's a common belief that bottom fishing is easy and all you have to do is lower the sinker and bait, wait a short while, and the fish will come swarming to get hooked. On certain days, this, of course, happens with certain species—they are so thick and hungry that it doesn't take too much skill or trickery to hook them. On such days almost anyone, novice or expert, can catch a bagful of fish.

But there are also many days when the fish are scarce or playing hard to get. At such times it may require a specific technique or method, or bait, or stage of tide to get results. On such days you'll often hear some of the bottom bouncers who have caught few or no fish wailing, "Look at that lucky guy—he's catching all of the fish. What's the matter with me? I'm using the same bait and fishing right next to him."

Well, when this happens it is usually not luck. Nine times out of ten, the so-called "lucky" angler knows all the tricks for the type of bottom fishing he is doing. And he puts them to use every chance he gets. You'll see these anglers fishing from party boats, private boats, piers, and shore. They often win the pool or prize on the party boats or catch more and bigger fish than the rest of the anglers. These men are the "regulars" or "old-timers" who go out often and through the years have acquired the skill and knowledge which makes them better than average bottom fishermen.

The tackle used for bottom fishing will vary according to the location being fished, whether you fish from a boat or shore or pier, the weight of the fish being sought, the depth of the water, the strength of the tides, and the weight of the sinker needed. For small fish in shallow water from shore, pier, or boat a light salt-water spinning outfit is usually best. You can cast with such an outfit and use thin lines testing anywhere from 10 to 20 pounds. You'll feel the lightest nibbles and wary fish won't see your line. You can also use light sinkers weighing a couple of ounces in many areas with such an outfit.

For medium-sized fish from piers, shore, or boats a so-called "boat" rod is a good all-round outfit. They run from 5 to 7 feet in over-all length. I, personally, find a somewhat longer rod say about 8 or 8½ feet in length better for casting, handling rigs, and for keeping the line away from piles, rocks, or the boat itself. The boat rods are used with conventional reels holding anywhere from 150 to 300 yards of line. Monofilament lines testing from 30 to 50 pounds can be used depending on the type of bottom and size of the fish being caught. On rough, broken bottoms where lines get fouled often and where you expect big fish, the heavier lines are best.

A spinning outfit can be used for bottom fishing from piers, shore, or private boats. They are especially good where you have to cast your rig some distance. Spinning outfits aren't too good if you get hung up on the bottom often or when fishing from crowded party boats.

The rig or terminal tackle being used for bottom fishing is very important in this type of angling. There are so many different kinds of rigs it would take too much space to cover them all here. Each rig is designed for certain kinds of fish or fishing. Rigs should present the baits naturally, keep them away from the main fishing line, and offer the baits at the proper level. There are ready-made rigs for sale in many coastal fishing-tackle stores and on party boats. Some of these are excellent, while others may be too clumsy, with all kinds of hardware such as snaps, swivels, and spreaders.

Most veteran bottom fishermen learn how to make their own rigs. It's easy and all you need is nylon leader material of the proper strength, swivels and snaps, and the right size and pattern of hooks. Sinkers are needed, too, to complete the rig. When you tie such rigs yourself pay close attention to the length and strength of the nylon leader material being used. Notice how high up the hooks are tied from the sinker. If you are on a party boat don't hesitate to ask the captain or one of the crew members to show you how to make the right kind of rig for the fishing you will do.

After you learn how to tie the correct rig for the fishing you will do make up plenty of such rigs. And make them up in advance. Don't go bottom fishing with only one or two rigs in your bag. Make up at least a dozen ahead of time. Then if you lose a rig you won't waste valuable fishing time working on rigs when the fish are biting. The same goes for sinkers. Bring along plenty of sinkers to replace those which are lost. And make sure that they are the correct weights for the location being fished. Usually you'll need sinkers from 2 to 6 ounces for light tackle and inshore fishing in shallow water. While for offshore fishing in deep water, strong currents, and with heavy tackle, you'll need sinkers ranging from 6 to 12 ounces.

To catch bottom fish you have to know where to fish and when to fish. If you hear of a run of fish at a local pier or beach you already know when to go and where to go. Likewise if you go on a party boat the captain will take you to the best spot. And if you rent a rowboat or skiff the owner of the place will usually direct you to the most productive spots.

Bottom fish of all kinds tend to gather where food is plentiful. They usually feed on clams, oysters, mussels, crabs, worms, shrimp, and small fish. So most bottom fishermen look for rocky bottoms, oyster, clam, or mussel beds, and so-called offshore "banks." In southern waters coral reefs are favorite hangouts for various kinds of bottom fish. And in all waters if you can locate a sunken ship or wreck you'll have a choice fishing spot.

Nowadays, with salt-water fishing becoming so popular, it is common to see whole fleets of party boats, private boats, and charter boats congregated over good bottom-fishing spots, especially on weekends. Then all you have to do is join them and drop anchor nearby. In many areas such offshore bottom-fishing grounds are being created by dumping old autos, concrete, rocks, weighted boxes, and other kinds of rubble and junk. In time these are covered by mussels, barnacles, seaweed, and attract crabs, small fish, and other marine life. Then the larger fish move in and you have a good bottom-fishing spot. In some areas such bottom-fishing spots are well-marked with buoys so that they can be easily located.

Let's say we're fishing from a crowded party boat and here you are taken to the best spot by the captain. Most of the party boat regulars prefer to fish from the stern of the boat if they can get that spot. You have to come early to get a spot at the stern because there is room for only a handful of anglers there. The rest have to line up along the sides of the boat. The stern of the boat is the best spot if you will be fishing at anchor. Then the fish moving up against the tide or current will come up to the baited hooks of the anglers fishing the stern first. If you are drifting then it doesn't make so much difference. Here you should be on the side where the lines move away from the boat.

But no matter where you stand on a party boat there are a few tricks which will put more fish in your bag. Have your hooks baited and ready to go over the side the second the boat stops and the captain signals to start fishing. The first rigs to hit the bottom stand a better chance to be seen and approached by the fish than later on when everyone has his bait overboard.

When your sinker hits bottom see how it holds. It should stay in one spot until you raise your rod. Then it should move a short distance, and then hit bottom again and remain in one spot. If you find that you cannot feel bottom or that the sinker and bait are being carried too far away from the boat change to a heavier sinker. You should have a big loop or a snap to hold the sinker and to permit you to change to different weights. If, on the other hand, you find that the sinker remains in one spot all the time, even when you lift the rod tip, then its time to change to a lighter one.

Four bottom fishermen trying their luck. Who will catch the most and biggest fish? Despite popular belief, bottom fishing isn't always easy and the angler who knows his stuff usually winds up with the best catch.

Even though a sinker may hold bottom when the tide is weak it may not be able to do so when the tide starts running strong. Then you have to change to a heavier one. Likewise if the tide is strong when you start fishing and you need a heavy sinker this doesn't mean you'll use that weight all day long. Later on when the tide slows down you should change to a lighter sinker.

The main secret in bottom fishing is to "feel" bottom at all times. Then you know your bait is down where the fish can see it. One way to make sure of this is to lift and lower your rod tip at regular intervals. This bottom bouncing is done by raising your rod slowly and then dropping it quickly. When the sinker hits bottom you should feel the bump.

This serves another purpose also—when the bait rises and then falls, the movement catches the attention of any fish in the vicinity. And the sinker emerging from the sand or mud and then dropping back raises a puff which also helps attract fish.

When the tide is running fairly strong, raising and lowering your rod tip will also move your rig and bait away from the boat. This not only places your bait in a new spot but also takes your rig away from the rest of the lines directly under the boat. The farther away your bait is from the rest of the lines the less competition you have. Thus any fish moving into that area will see your bait only. Some anglers get the same result by casting their lines out away from the boat as far as they can. This can often be done with an underhand cast by flipping your rig out. Casting overhead is dangerous on a crowded party boat and should be avoided. Unless, of course, the boat isn't crowded and you happen to be the only one up at the bow, where there is no danger of hooking anyone or hitting someone with the sinker.

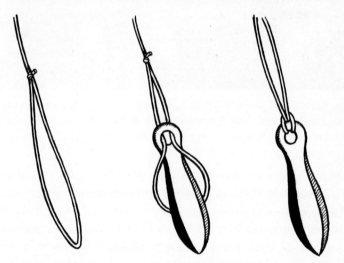

Large loop on end of line for holding and changing sinkers

If you really want to increase your chances of catching bottom fish don't overlook chumming. Most species of bottom fish will respond to such free handouts and will come swarming to the scene. Chumming for bottom fish may be as simple as bringing along a supply of clams, mussels, oysters, crabs, etc., and cracking them and then throwing them all around the boat. This can be done when the tide isn't too strong. Then the stuff will sink directly under the boat. When the tide is running strong you have to use a mesh bag or chum pot and put the mussels or clams inside and lower it to the bottom with a weight. Chumming can also be done for many bottom fish by cutting up fish into small pieces and scattering them around the boat.

Another so-called "secret" of bottom fishing is detecting a bite and knowing when to set the hook. The most expert bottom fishermen seem to develop a delicate sense of feel which enables them to hook a fish at the right moment. Too many beginners are impatient and try to set the hook as soon as they feel the first nibble. Usually it pays to wait until you feel a solid tug or pull, then raise the rod tip quickly to set the hook. With some fish it's a good idea to lower your rod tip and allow slack line when you first feel a nibble. This gives them a better chance to swallow the bait and also doesn't make the fish as suspicious as when it feels the pull of the line. With other fish you keep a tight line at all times so you can feel every nibble and the first solid tug or pull, indicating the fish has taken the bait.

If you feel a few nibbles and then they stop, wait a minute or two. If there are no more bites reel in your bait to see if it is still there. Most of the time the hook will be cleaned or only a small piece of bait will remain. Then you should put on some fresh bait.

Some kinds of bottom fishing are best done at anchor with the boat in one spot. In fact, when fishing wrecks or small patches of rocky bottom you may have to use two anchors to keep the boat from moving off. For example, when you fish for blackfish or tautog you often have to lower your bait into a small area to get results. If you are a few yards away from the wreck or hole where these fish gather you may not get any bites.

But there are other times, when fishing certain areas, when drift fishing from a boat is more productive. When fishing for species that are scattered or when fishing over banks, sand or rock bars, reefs, mussel, clam, and oyster beds which cover wide areas you'll often find drift fishing is worthwhile. The list of fish taken drift fishing includes such species as fluke or summer flounders,

In many areas boats congregate over the best bottom-fishing spots. When there are no other boats to guide you, look for rocky bottoms, shellfish beds, wrecks, and reefs.

halibut, cod, haddock, sea bass, porgies, snappers, groupers, and croakers.

Drift fishing means that a boat is moving with the tide or wind and anglers let out their lines so that the sinker bounces on the bottom as the boat moves along. Drift fishing is best when there is enough wind or tide to move the boat along steadily but not too fast. When there is little or no wind, drift fishing is not too good. On the other hand, when the wind is too strong it is difficult to keep the sinker and bait near the bottom.

When drifting you cover more territory, keep the bait moving, and show it to new fish. Drifting is also a good way to locate rocks, wrecks, kelp and seaweed beds, coral reefs, and other spots where bottom fish hang out. This usually happens when your rig gets hung-up on the bottom. Then it's often a good idea to drop anchor and fish that spot.

When drift fishing tie your leader and hook a bit higher than when fishing at anchor. Especially when drifting over a rocky bottom. Then there is less chance that the hook will get caught. Another trick is to tie your sinker on a lighter line than your main fishing line. Then if the sinker gets caught it will break off, but you'll save the rest of the rig. Bring along plenty of different size sinkers when drift fishing. You'll need light sinkers when the wind or tide is weak and the boat is barely moving. But when the wind or tide is strong you'll need heavy sinkers in order to reach and bounce them along on the bottom.

As the boat moves along you should raise and lower your rod tip at regular intervals and feel bottom. If you don't bounce on the bottom with the sinker let out line until you do. Keep letting out line until the sinker stays on the bottom. In deep water and on windy days you'll often have to let out most of the line on your spool to stay on the bottom.

In the beginning it is often difficult to tell when you have a bite when drift fishing. The sinker bouncing on the bottom feels like a fish fooling around with the bait. You'll get fooled often in this way. Later on, when you develop a sensitive touch you'll be able to tell a real bite from a phony one. Even so, you'll get fooled on many occasions when the sinker bounces off a rock or gets caught.

If you think you have a bite it's a good idea to let out slack line to give the fish a chance to swallow the bait and hook. Then reel in your slack until the line tightens and set the hook. On many other occasions the fish will gulp the bait and then you'll feel his weight or pull.

When bottom fishing from a pier, bridge, or shore you are limited to the number of different spots you can fish unless you move around from one location to another. But many such spots are crowded and you may be stuck in one spot. If you are over a pile or bridge support you can lower your baited rig right next to such supports. The fish often gather to feed on the barnacles, mussels, and crabs found here.

If there's a deep hole or channel within casting distance you can try to reach such a spot. You can cover more territory if you cast your rig out as far as you can, then slowly reel it in. The bait should be left in each new spot for a few minutes before reeling it in a few feet to a new spot. When fishing from a bridge or pier and the tide is running strong you can do the same thing in reverse. Here you use a heavy enough sinker to hold bottom, but light enough to move when you raise your rod tip. Then by raising and lowering your rod tip at regular intervals you can let the bait move out with the tide or current.

The bait you use for bottom fishing will depend on the fish you are seeking and what's available from the local bait dealer or tackle store. If live bait is called for make sure that it is kept alive. If you use dead bait make sure it's fresh. And bring along plenty of bait. There's nothing more frustrating and exasperating than to run out of bait when the fish are biting like crazy.

Bottom fishing can be just as much fun and sport as any other kind of salt-water fishing. If you use light tackle and experiment with rigs, baits, and different methods and techniques. Once you have learned how to catch a certain species you can always turn your attention to a new kind of bottom fish. In this way you'll find bottom fishing challenging and satisfying. And before you know it you'll join the ranks of the regulars who catch most of the fish.

*Chapter Fourteen*

# BOAT FISHING FOR STRIPED BASS

## *by* FRANK WOOLNER

FRANK WOOLNER, of Shrewsbury, Massachusetts, is the editor of *Salt Water Sportsman*, Boston, and for many years has written daily columns on fishing, boating, and hunting for the Worcester *Evening Gazette*, Worcester, Massachusetts. Frank has sampled a wide variety of fresh- and salt-water game fish, but devotes a lot of time to the pursuit of the wily striped bass, both in the surf and from boats. He is coauthor with Henry Lyman of *The Complete Book of Striped Bass Fishing* and *The Complete Book of Weakfishing*.

SURF fishing for striped bass is one of the most exciting sports in this seagirt world, but the man who is looking for a record striper had best take to the boats. Check any accurate list of the heaviest linesides ever landed on sporting tackle and you'll find ample verification. Boats and big bass go together, like Scotch and soda.

Come to think of it, boats and small bass are equally compatible. The pan rock of the Chesapeake and the school striper of New England have much in common. Together with their blood brothers of the Pacific Coast, they rattle aboard fishing boats!

For a few paragraphs, though, let's examine the three largest stripers ever brought to a waiting scales via rod and line.

Every red-eyed and brine-soaked striper addict on the Atlantic and Pacific coasts knows that the late Charles B. Church hooked his world record 73-pounder from "a rowing boat" near Nashawena Island, one of Massachusetts' famed Cuttyhunk chain, back in 1913.

Forty-five years later, in 1958, Ralph Gray approached

Church's mark when he whipped a 68½-pounder at North Truro, Massachusetts. Ralph hooked this one from a 14-foot aluminum skiff; I know, because I was there to lend a hand with the gaff!

Third among the great stripers of all time was Frank Mularczyk's 66-pound, 4-ounce trophy, fought from the cockpit of Capt. Bob Smith's *Susan B*, a 26-foot MacKenzie Cuttyhunk bass boat, at Devil's Bridge off Martha's Vineyard in 1954.

The lesson to be learned from this recital is not that all trophy bass are taken in Massachusetts waters—for huge linesides are boated from North Carolina to the Maritime Provinces on the Atlantic Coast, and from central California through Oregon on the Pacific seaboard—but that each was hooked from and subsequently brought aboard a different type of craft.

I have a sneaking suspicion that there is no all-round bass boat. At the same time, I am sure that specific types are ideal under certain conditions. How does one go about choosing a boat for striped bass fishing?

Well, stripers have been hooked and landed from kayaks and Indian canoes. Livery rowboats bring back a tremendous poundage each season, and sea skiffs are classic in many of the famed fishing locations. The so-called Prince of the Unpredictables has been wrestled aboard everything from rubber rafts to luxurious offshore cruisers—and each of these, with the possible exception of the chrome and high-luster job, is effective in its own sphere of operations.

I'd break it down this way: small craft are most effective in the sheltered waters of rivers and bays, and for one specialized use to be discussed further along. Outside, where wave action may be severe and where changeable weather poses a problem, go to larger, more seaworthy hulls.

By small craft, I mean outboard skiffs in the 12- to 16-foot class, featuring ample beam for stability when it's necessary to "stand up and fight." These may be constructed of wood, metal, Fiberglas, or any of the new plastics, and they may be auto-top or trailer models. Canoes and kayaks, rubber life rafts and the various folding boats may suffice in sheltered, inland waters, but they are never as practical as the rowboat, half-dory, or planing outboard for the work involved.

Frank Woolner     189

The *Susan B*, a MacKenzie Cuttyhunk bass boat, skippered by Capt. Bob Smith, is typical of the type of craft used at Cuttyhunk and Martha's Vineyard, Massachusetts, when casting and trolling for striped bass.

My definition of "larger craft" would encompass the magnificent Cuttyhunk bass boat, which measures 20 to 26 feet in length, the various clinker-built Jersey sea skiffs, and, finally, any of the serviceable sport fishermen you find for charter along the coast.

Basically, a good striper boat should draw little water, for she'll work over reefs and rocks, around sand bars, and through the perilous juncture of blue water and surf. The craft should be open, or at least feature plenty of cockpit room for casting when this becomes necessary. Ample power and maneuverability are musts if the boat is to cope with typical bass water—which is best described as confused.

190

Before we touch on tackle and technique under varying conditions, it may be well to scuttle a few myths. Such as, for example, the squidder's time-honored cry that *Roccus saxatilis* is a surf running fish and is most often taken in the suds.

Or, the charge that boat fishing is less fun—and less sporting than surf casting.

True, the striper likes to feed in white water and may be found with his olivaceous snoot in the wash of breakers. However, for every bass in the surf, I'd wager that ten are lying on the offshore bars, in the rips, around the rocks and reefs beyond reach of the most efficient squidder.

The boatman who knows his business can fish almost anywhere. His horizons are unlimited because he can go to the bass and use the tackle which is most effective under any circumstances. He can troll, jig, cast artificial lures or live-line bait—and he can cover a tremendous amount of territory.

Less sporting? Say that again, pardner, after you've ridden a powerful little bass boat through the swirling rips and around the weed-draped rocks that trophy bass call home.

Less fun? Light-tackle a half-dozen terrible tempered schoolies in a coastal river or bay and you'll discard the notion!

Sportsmen tend to forget that old *Roccus* is a versatile cuss. He's a surf running gamester, sure enough, but he also delights in feeding around offshore rips and reefs. He ranges the length and breadth of coastal bays, chasing bait, or swims far up into coastal streams. The transition from salt to brackish to sweet water doesn't bother him a bit, and there's ample evidence that stripers sometimes winter over in rivers far north of the famed Chesapeake nursery. Indeed there is evidence of local races that rarely, if ever, migrate.

Depending on seasons, weather conditions, water temperatures, and the movement of bait, bass feed on night and day tides —and they gorge on a tremendous variety of sea creatures. One that I examined many years ago at the Cape Cod Canal had a common tern in its stomach. Terns are not recommended as bait, however!

In fact, no one bait may be recommended over another for boat fishing on a coast-wide scale: local abundance of forage fish and crustaceans always determine the choice. By the same token, no one tackle combination is all-purpose.

Generally speaking, light tackle is most efficient—and a lot more fun—on inland waters where bass are likely to run small, while big sticks and king-sized lures hit the jackpot outside.

Casting is often profitable. The small-boat angler who fishes rivers and sheltered bays will find one-handed spinning, bait casting, and fly casting outfits capable weapons. Stan Gibbs of Buzzards Bay, Massachusetts, uses fresh-water spinning tackle with lines testing 4 to 6 pounds—and he catches hundreds of schoolies in the 3- to 10-pound class. Morrie Upperman of Atlantic City has pioneered the same light bait-casting and spinning gear in the "Jersey Everglades," that wonderful back country of Great Egg and Little Egg bays.

Reconnaissance is half the battle in this game. The really successful angler is an explorer who discovers striper banquet tables—a hole at a river bend, a pile of rocks, a little rip that develops on a specific phase of the tide, the edge of a channel—and works these areas at optimum stages of the tide.

Details? You'll have to go and see for yourself, for each area presents special problems. Sometimes bass hit best on a flooding tide; at other spots the ebb is most productive. Almost always some current is necessary, for it is the flow of water that keeps bait moving.

On certain wild and wonderful occasions, bass show themselves by rushing small bait at the surface. Terns and gulls spot the commotion and hurry to this Roman holiday of the sea. Anglers see the birds—or the breaking fish—and rush to share the feast.

There is a generally accepted observation on inland waters that 10 per cent of the fishermen catch 60 per cent of the fish. I'm sure that the statement is just as apt on salt water. Skill and knowledge of the fish sought pays off in tight lines. For example, a few outboard-motor manufacturers blithely assert that fish aren't bothered by the roar of the kicker. This is proof positive that the manufacturers are not fishermen!

Motors often spook striped bass, especially where the water is shoal and the bottom rocky enough to serve as a sounding board. Even in deep water, a motorboat driven right through a school of breaking fish will often put them down.

Smart fishermen stalk their quarry. It pays to ease up to a spot where bass are expected to be feeding. Operate at half-throttle during the final approach, and then drift, if possible, the last few yards. If anchoring is called for, lower the hook gently.

In casting to a school of stripers on the surface, try to make the approach from the upwind side, and cut the motor well before you reach the edge of the school. It is far better to drift into this melee of stripers, bait, and frantic birds than to roar right into the center of it. Better, that is, if you want to catch fish.

Artificial lures that take a lion's share of bass in sheltered waters include the various bucktails, metal squids, and midget plugs. On a coast-wide basis, I'd guess that bucktails are most effective, but there are days when small, surface popping plugs and darters provide hair-raising action. Metal squids can be just as effective.

Wherever possible, it pays to cast a bucktail, plug, or squid up into and across the current flow. Try various speeds of retrieve, and experiment with depth. Sometimes stripers will tear the surface wide open to grab a top-water plug, and again you will find it necessary to dredge.

Live-lining fresh bait from an anchored boat is one of the time-honored and highly successful methods. This is done on night and day tides, depending on the season and the feeding habits of the stripers in attendance. The bait may be seaworms, shrimp, soft crabs, eels, sand launces, anchovies—or any of a host of other marine tidbits.

Strangely enough, in view of its effectiveness, chumming for stripers is now pretty well limited to the Chesapeake Bay area, where boatmen anchor their boats and send a steady stream of transparent little grass shrimp kicking down with the tide. Gradually, as bass find the bait, they move up toward the source of supply and discover that a few of the shrimp are spiked with hooks! Many years ago New Englanders employed the same general method, using ground menhaden, herring, and even lobsters!

Sand and blood worms are effective when trolled behind a small boat, usually in conjunction with a spinner. The willow leaf spinner is very popular, but good catches are made on other blade combinations. Wobbling spoons sometimes provide the attracting flash and rubber worms have proved themselves in recent years.

When natural worms are used for trolling they should be threaded well up on the shank of the hook so that they will stream out naturally. Bunching a worm on a hook is poor practice.

Small spoons are effective trolling lures and bucktails often work wonders when dragged (and jigged) behind a boat. Either lure may become a better fish-taker by the addition of a pork rind strip on the hook. Subsurface plugs regularly hit the jackpot.

Boat fishing for stripers encompasses all sorts of water and bottom conformation, but roughly speaking it is possible to divide the clan right down the middle—"inside" and "outside." Also generally speaking, the sportsman who fishes inside waters is likely to catch school bass, while he who probes offshore rips, reefs, and swirling outer bars comes up with trophy specimens.

There are many exceptions to this rule of thumb. Heavyweights are sometimes boated in the relatively landlocked "Jersey Everglades," and California anglers account for big ones far from the sea in the San Joaquin Delta. By the same token, offshore buffs often run into schools of small bass.

Putting aside, for the moment, the size of bass in attendance, it is worth noting that the offshore boat must be considerably larger and more seaworthy than the skiffs used inland. One spectacular exception is the aluminum "surf boat" used by beach-buggy anglers on Cape Cod. These beamy little outboards are launched in the surf and used to probe bass feeding and loafing grounds adjacent to sand bars which lie 100 to 200 yards off the beach.

The beach-buggy craft measures 12 to 14 feet, features 24 inches of freeboard and 56 to 58 inches of beam. In its size bracket, it is a fine little sea boat—but one must not assume that it is ever launched in heavy surf. The aluminum construction is favored because sloping sand beaches and lack of hardpan in remote areas makes manhandling a necessity. The skiffs weigh 120 to 150 pounds and are usually transported on rooftop racks.

In 1960 some of the largest bass taken from America's coastal waters fell to anglers who fished live mackerel baits from these small surf boats off the outermost tip of Cape Cod. The technique

A line-up of beach buggies and aluminum boats which are transported on rooftop racks and launched in the surf to catch striped bass on Cape Cod.

was used by Mrs. David Webb of Shrewsbury, Massachusetts, who set a new women's IGFA all-tackle record at North Truro by catching a 64½-pound striper.

Small boat surfing on the outer Cape is a combination of hunting and fishing! Anglers insist on extension operating handles on their outboard motors—so that they may stand while cruising just outside the breakers or close to the offshore bars. Polaroid glasses are another must; they diminish surface glare and permit the wearer to see bass lying in the holes and sloughs.

Striper concentrations are often spotted prior to any angling effort in this area. Thereafter, trolling, casting, or the live-lining of fresh bait is essayed.

This is not a game for beginners, and the sportsman who intends to experiment with surf fishing from a small boat should understand that launching is possible only when the surf is light. Even then, one must wait for the relatively gentle ground swell following the "third wave," before pushing off. A majority of experts use oars to pull out of the wash, and then turn to an outboard motor of at least 10 horsepower.

195

On the sand beaches of Cape Cod, a bow-landing at full throttle is the accepted landing procedure. The trick lies in possessing sufficient power to ride in on the crest of a wave. To overshoot, or to fall behind the inward racing comber, usually means a wetting.

Small-boat angling is spectacular, but I doubt that any striper fishing technique offers thrills comparable to surf casting from a powerful Cuttyhunk bass boat or Jersey sea skiff. Experienced skippers work these 20- to 26-foot craft right in among the rocks, and it's the angler's job to heave his plug, metal squid, or rigged eel into the boiling wash a few feet from shore.

Skippers who specialize in this type of fishing must know their coast—or take the consequences. Fortunately for striper addicts, dozens of fine captains are available at the hot spots. They leave an occasional smear of antifouling paint on the house-sized boulders that heave out of the tormented sea, but rarely buy real trouble.

Each section of the coast features specific areas which lend themselves to this type of sport. In New England—Cuttyhunk, Martha's Vineyard, and Rhode Island's rock-studded seaboard offer classic surroundings. New Jersey boasts jetties that are highly productive, and there are many locations where it is profitable to stand off some 40 or 50 yards from a boiling offshore bar or reef and drop artificials right into the clashing currents.

Try, always, to place the lure as close to rocks, rips, and jetties as your skill will permit. Stripers feed in a smother of white water and a maelstrom of currents because baitfish are washed into these turbulent areas, to be helplessly tumbled.

Trophy bass are fond of crashing waters, but they also feed in holes and sloughs adjacent to the rough spots. It is often possible to hang prize-winners on plugs and metal squids while cruising just outside the surf line, or between the outer bars and the shore. Offshore rips, reefs, and subsurface rock piles are favored locations: many are well known, and others have yet to be charted by canny skippers who employ modern electronic depth sounders.

Here, as in the sheltered bays, it is imperative to keep a sharp eye open for birds, bait, or other indications of a "blitz." The

One of the largest striped bass caught on rod and reel in recent years is this
68½-pounder. It was taken by Ralph Gray, left, with an assist at the gaff by
author Frank Woolner, right. Fish hit a trolled swimming plug at North Truro,
Cape Cod, on October 1, 1958.

most effective lures for casting are surface and subsurface plugs,
metal squids, and rigged eels. Eels, incidentally, are most successful at night.

Among the surface plugs—lures that provide some of the most

197

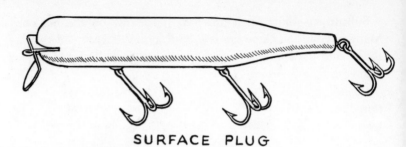

**SURFACE PLUG**

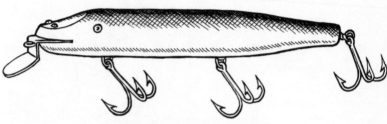

**UNDERWATER PLUG**

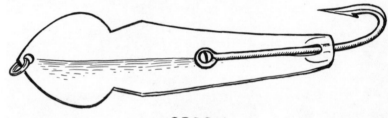

**SPOON**

**NYLON EEL**

Lures used for striped bass from boat

spectacular strikes in the world of bass fishing—swimmers, flap-tails, poppers, and darters are the major killers. All are effective during daylight hours, but the swimmer reigns supreme at night. One tip which will mean more fish in the box: slow the retrieve to half normal speed at night.

Subsurface plugs often prove to be deadly on the big ones. Many pay off, but there are few basic types. Highly effective are those with a swimming action and those that dart, rather than swim.

While any tackle combination is "right" under certain conditions, smart fishermen load for the game sought, and for the technique that must be used. For surf casting from a bass boat, tackle should be rugged enough to heave a 3-ounce plug or a 5-ounce eel, and then control an infuriated bull bass—who is always determined to cut the line on the nearest barnacle-covered rock.

Where stripers are king-sized, two basic outfits get the nod. One is the standard, high-surf, squidding rig, and the other a heavy spinning combination. Boat fishermen usually prefer a variant of the true surf rod, a stick designed for this one purpose —the business of casting from a boat.

Such rods are short, 8 to 9 feet over-all, and feature 16- to 20-inch butts instead of the 28- to 30-inch butt of the high-surf outfit. Standard, wide-spooled squidding reels are used, and lines are nylon or dacron braids in the 25- to 45-pound test class, or monofilament testing 25 to 36. The new flattened monofilaments are my choice on a revolving spool reel.

Beefed-up spinning outfits have become popular in many areas of both coasts. They are entirely adequate under normal conditions, but due to the fact that lines are lighter (15- to 20-pound test) and rods more resilient, the spinning rig may handicap an angler who must turn a very large fish away from barnacle-covered rocks.

Trolling accounts for thousands of trophy stripers during the course of each year, and the brother who thinks that trolling is defined as "dragging a lure" has much to learn. This method has become a fine art, invariably demanding finely matched tackle and often calling for exceptional skill in handling.

For large bass, select a 5- to 5½-foot tip matched to an 18-inch butt. The rod must have enough backbone to handle lures scaling 5 ounces, yet should be fairly resilient in order to turn big fish without popping the 36- to 45-pound test lines used. Reels in the 3/0 to 4/0 bracket are well chosen for this fishing.

Experts who specialize in big stripers often employ two or
three trolling combinations. Nylon braid, dacron or nylon monofilament lines are used for trolling close to, or on, the surface.
Lead core or wire line is the ticket when a lure must be presented
in the depths. In this connection, note that lead core is the easiest
of the weighted lines to handle, while wire slices deeper. By
that token, lead core is best for combing the intermediate depths
while wire is a better dredger's tool.

In many cases it is sufficient to splice 100 feet of wire or lead
core to 150 yards of braided backing. Trolling sinkers can be used
to take monofilament or braided lines into the depths. In some
areas the quick-release snap and cannon-ball sinker used on the
West Coast has merit.

Nobody can tell you exactly how much lead core or wire to
troll, for requirements vary. On some grounds 100 feet of the
stuff is more than sufficient: elsewhere, you'll find it necessary to
strip off twice that much to plumb the strike zone. Charter skippers usually know, to the foot, how much line should be trolled
with a particular lure on a specific ground, and private boat owners may reach the same conclusions through trial and error. There
is no royal road to success: good catches indicate preliminary
study of bottom conformation, depth, lure action, and trolling
speed. This is one of the reasons why some charter skippers are
booked solid, while others go hungry.

What to troll? We'd need another chapter to go into all of the
baits and lures that pay off. Plugs are effective: they may be
worked right on the surface or at various depths. Spoons have
accounted for thousands of linesides, and these tempters range
from standard-sized creations on up to the huge pie plate-
sized "bunker spoon" first used off Long Island and New Jersey.

Eelskin rigs are killers wherever big stripers are found. Both
the high riding trollers and heavier bottom-bouncing rigs are
effective. Whole eels usually produce best at night, as do the
skins.

Among the artificials used successfully on big bass, one must
include such offerings as the nylon eel, which is often improved
by the addition of a large pork-rind strip, and the so-called "junk"
lure, which is a conglomeration of plastic skirts, beads, and

All striped bass caught from boats aren't big ones. In fact, the largest percentage are smaller ones like this one held by Stan Gibbs of Buzzards Bay, Massachusetts.

Japanese feathers. It is said to resemble a school of small bait, and perhaps it does. Bass find it interesting, and that's testimonial enough!

As you troll over the striper grounds with one of these tempters, it is necessary to jig the rod back and forth. Try to impart a darting, up and down, undulating action to the lure. Rigged eels and eelskins, bucktails, and Japanese feathers may also catch more fish when they are jigged.

In addition to a host of artificial lures and borderline baits which make use of eelskins or whole, dead eels strung with two or three hooks, the knowing boatman may employ various combinations. Twin bucktails on a spreader rig may be productive. A subsurface swimming plug, above, and a bucktail, below, often collect stripers.

Whole natural squids can be eyebrow raisers for trolling right on the surface. Use two or three hooks, connected by a line, or prepare a rig by stringing three hooks together, point through eye. The baits must be strung so that it will not double up, but will skip cleanly when it is trolled.

Whether the offering is an artificial lure or a fresh bait, the experienced troller will refrain from driving his boat through a school of bass feeding on the surface. Always work the edges of such a school, so that the individuals will not be alarmed by the motor sound or the antics of a hooked companion.

Live-lining has always been a deadly technique in striped bass fishing, and the list of successful baits is impressive. Included and sea worms, crabs, herring, mullet, mackerel, eels, anchovies, bullheads, squids, and shrimp—and a host of other striper delicacies.

Without any doubt, monofilament line is best suited to this technique, and it pays to use the lightest mono that is practical. Object is to present the bait in a natural manner, utilizing tidal currents to float or "swim" the tempter into a striper's banquet hall.

Seaworms should be secured well up on the shank of the hook so that they will stream out in the current. A bunched-up worm may produce when live-lined, as it will in trolling with a spinner, but the odds favor more natural presentation.

Live eels are easy to keep alive and they make wonderful baits for trophy stripers on night tides. "Snakes" may be fished under a float to regulate depth or on a live line. When a striper hits one of them, you feel the solid impact of the strike and should then permit the fish to run off line, pause, and swallow the eel.

In some cases skippers feel the necessity to stun an eel before hooking it through the lips and tossing it overboard. The critter will revive shortly, but will not have sufficient strength to produce the usual gosh-awful terminal line tangle.

At North Truro, Massachusetts, where anglers caught an astonishing number of large bass in 1960, live mackerel were the killing baits. Note, however, that herring also turned the trick, and on at least one occasion a large striper was hooked on a 4-pound (weight estimated) pollock!

"Big bait for big fish" was the theory at North Truro. Boatmen wanted mackerel in the 2-pound class, and caught them on diamond jigs fished well offshore. The mackerel had to be kept alive on the run back to striper hot spots, close inshore, so most of the small-boat fishermen transported them in old-fashioned galvanized wash tubs. A few chartermen made use of larger aerated tanks.

Trial and error proved the worth of monofilament line and single 8/o O'Shaughnessy hooks. The mackerel was hooked lightly through the skin just ahead of the dorsal fin, and allowed to swim in the current. Occasionally, when it was deemed necessary to keep the bait off the bottom, floats were used.

Look for a sudden increase of action on the part of a mackerel bait—or an eel, for that matter—just before a strike. The actual pick-up is usually felt as a solid bump, and is followed by line peeling off the reel spool at a steadily accelerated rate of speed. Often the bass will chase a hooked bait to the surface and there engulf it in the characteristic cartwheeling smash of the striper.

Generally, it is wise to permit the line to flow off on free spool during the initial run, and to set the hook after the striper has paused and then uncorked a second run—theory being that the fish pauses to turn the bait and swallow it. Often, though, it is possible to see the strike and ascertain whether the bait has been engulfed. In this case an immediate hookup may be assured.

Striped bass fishing is a rough, tough—and wonderful game. Fighting chairs provide comfort on a bass boat, but they are unnecessary. Outriggers permit the trolling of four or more lines, yet a drop-back is uncalled for when artificial lures are used. One item you *must* have aboard—a sharp pick gaff with a handle long enough to reach the whipped fish. Substitute a wide-mouthed landing net if the bass are school sized and/or will be taken on light tackle. A hardwood billy should be used to quiet the thrashing of a bull bass before an angler attempts to remove the hooks.

Finally, on a boat as in the surf, remember that *Roccus saxatilis* is a fish of many moods; occasionally savage in his feeding, usually selective, always unpredictable. In addition to a wise choice of tackle, your most important weapon is an open mind. Be prepared for the unexpected. Take advantage of every opportunity—and you'll catch bass!

## Chapter Fifteen

# CHANNEL-BASS FISHING

## *by* CLAUDE ROGERS

CLAUDE ROGERS is the executive secretary of The Salt Water Sport Fishing Association of Virginia. He has played a big part in the development of new fishing methods and techniques and areas in his home state of Virginia. He is a top-notch surf caster and has won many casting tournaments. He fishes in both fresh and salt water, but particularly enjoys catching channel bass from the surf. His article in this book provides some helpful tips and pointers gleaned from experience in catching channel bass in Virginia and North Carolina waters.

THE channel bass is king of the Southern surf and one of the great blessings for the East Coast angler. His size, his range, his co-operative feeding habits, the manner in which he may be taken make him available to the expert and amateur angler alike.

He comes in all sizes from the small silvery-finished "puppy" drum, to the world's record red drum of 83 pounds boated off Cape Charles, Virginia, by Zack Waters in 1949. Surf records are almost as high with a 74-pounder beached at Chincoteague, Virginia, by Charles D. Beckmann in 1929 and a 75½-pounder hauled from the Hatteras surf by Captain Bernice Ballance in 1941. And, lest we forget the "old days," a 65-pounder was taken at New Inlet, New Jersey, in 1919 when channel bass were plentiful along the Jersey beaches. Regrettably the appearance of channel bass now in the New Jersey area is considered unusual.

He may be taken at different seasons from piers, surf, and boat. He accepts bait, cut and live, lures, cast or trolled, and all in all, he is most co-operative, if given a chance.

But the sportiest way to take old *Sciaenops ocellatus* is from the surf and no dyed-in-the-wool surf caster considers his life complete if he has not had the opportunity to catch both channel bass and striped bass and compare the relative fighting qualities of each.

Channel bass reach giant size in the Virginia–North Carolina area and for the past ten years these two states have divided honors in the "top ten division" for this species in the national contest. His importance to the sport fishing industry is now recognized by both North Carolina and Virginia, and in each state there is a limit of two per day, per person, over 32 inches in length. Channel-bass fishing in these two states is not a sport where the man with the most money has the best chance to catch the biggest fish. For with the exception of "guide boat fishing" the channel bass is available from piers, small boats, and surf for the same price you pay when seeking any of the smaller fishes. Even channel-bass charter trips are inexpensive when compared to the offshore blue-water charters.

He arrives in the fishpound nets off Hatteras in mid-March and from this time on he is in evidence in North Carolina or Virginia waters through late November or mid-December, depending on the severity of the weather. During his short absence from the local scene in the coldest months of January and February, he is picked up by commercial fishermen from the Diamond Shoals area off Hatteras to the inner edge of the Gulf Stream. Many old-timers believe the jumbo channel bass winter in the Hatteras Bight area off Cape Hatteras, North Carolina.

Although channel bass are picked up in pound nets in Hatteras Inlet around mid-March, these are only sign posts, and the best spring month to try for him in the Hatteras Inlet area is April. Boat anglers fishing Hatteras Inlet enjoy the most activity during the spring run and surf casters score on a catch-as-catch-can basis with success and length of the season varying each year.

Usually by mid-April the scene of activity shifts from Hatteras to Oregon Inlet, and with the shift a change of emphasis from bottom baits to trolling lures. The spring run at Oregon Inlet may carry over into May (as it has in 1961), but April is usually the best month. All the while, the surf casters continue picking up a few on the beach in the Cape Hatteras area.

The first schools appear at the Capes of Chesapeake Bay around the third week in April, and for the past three years rod

Claude Rogers

and reel success for this species has been reported by the last week in April. These first Virginia catches have always occurred in the Fisherman's Island–Magothy Bay area of Eastern Shore Virginia.

Channel-bass fishing in this area is a fairly recent development, the first concentration being discovered in the Magothy Bay in April 1959. Here in the shelter of Fisherman's and Smith islands the outboarder can get into the act along with the larger charter craft. Most of the fish here are taken by trollers using large spoons, but when the schools are sighted on top you may enjoy the additional pleasure of casting to the quarry with stainless jigs or large spoons. This type of fishing very closely approaches the thrill of snagging Big Red on artificials from the surf. You will not have the gulls pin-pointing the schools in this area as you do off Cape Hatteras in November or early December. Whether you are casting to a school of channel bass from a charter boat off Oregon or Hatteras Inlet or from a small boat in Magothy Bay, it is important not to approach any closer than casting distance. Cast ahead and a little beyond the leading edge of this school. Channel bass are not as shy as tarpon, but if you can see him, he can see you.

The spring run of channel bass for the trollers in Virginia waters peaks about mid-May, and then the schools will begin to scatter along the Barrier Islands of Eastern Shore. At this time it is possible to pick up both channel bass and black drum from the surf. I might say here that if you think, from what you have been reading, that you can tell the difference in the color or the fight of a black drum from the surf—you are in for a surprise. The black drum over 30 pounds, when first sighted from the air or boat, looks more like a red drum is supposed to look than the red drum does himself. Black drum are not as streamlined or as racy as the red drum, but he puts up a creditable performance, especially in the surf. Any fish that averages 40 pounds cannot be horsed in.

Like North Carolina, although not as well known, there are two main periods of channel-bass fishing from the surf along the Virginia Barrier Islands beaches. One, during the spring run from May through June and in the fall from September through Octo-

Two handsome copper warriors or channel bass taken from the surf by Fred
Edwards at Cobbs Island, Virginia. One weighed 48 pounds and the other 53.
Caught in the fall of the year, a good time for big fish.

ber. These islands, unlike Carolina's Outer Banks, are accessible
only by boat or plane, although a bridge now under construction
will soon link Assateague Beach with Chincoteague, Virginia.

Not all channel bass migrate northward from Carolina to Virginia each spring, as schools are sighted or in evidence in the
North Carolina sounds all summer. Also, a few are taken all summer long in the Hatteras Inlet area, mostly by the boat fishermen.
The channel bass cycle seems to be on the upswing, but we certainly cannot say summertime surf channel-bass fishing is anything like the good old days. Spring and fall are still the best in
both states.

During the warmer months of July and August the channel
bass seeker has a much better chance of success if he fishes late
afternoon and early night hours, depending on the tide. This
type of late evening fishing is practiced rather extensively by
charter boats fishing out of Wachapreague, Virginia, and to a
lesser degree by boats operating out of Cape Charles, Quinby,
and Chincoteague. Also to some extent by Hatteras skippers, but
blue marlin and other offshore species off Hatteras at this time
receive most of the attention. In practice, the boats sail early
enough in the evening to be on location before dark. The boat is
anchored just beyond the breakers off some favored spot in the
surf, if the tide is rising, and off the middle-ground shoals of
one of the inlets if the tide is falling. Unless you are personally
familiar with the area, the best time of tide and best location
must be left to your skipper's judgment, or local professional
advice. For the surf-fishing-or-nothing angler, I hasten to add that
I have been with successful "high-noon" surf fishermen in both
July and August, but I still do not consider midday surf fishing
the ideal time in hot weather.

Cobia fishermen in the Cape Charles area are apt to boat channel bass any time during the summer months and the all-tackle
record for this species was captured off Cape Charles in early
August. Schools of channel bass are present in Chesapeake Bay
all summer.

The best fishing from the Virginia Beach and Nags Head piers
generally occurs after the fifteenth of September and during or
immediately following a northeaster. The northeaster and the

Pier fishing for channel bass is mostly a waiting game. You wait for the right weather and water conditions, tide, and the appearance of the big redfish themselves. *(Photo by Vernon E. Stevens)*

cooling fall waters generally shake up the schools and sends them on their way to their wintering grounds. The bait heavers don foul-weather gear, rig heavy sinkers to combat the strong currents, and form a picket line on the end of the nearest pier. When an obliging school, or a straggler, swings around the end of the pier all enjoy the excitement. This is the one occasion that a surf caster will humble himself enough to leave the beach and join the fun and conversation or brood and curse the "foul" northeasters.

211

These fall northeasters not only move the channel bass south-ward from Virginia waters, but bring the fish out of the Carolina sounds and back to the beaches to provide the October and November fishing thrills for the multitudes who seek *Sciaenops* from the surf.

I have briefly outlined the present migratory pattern of the jumbo channel bass in the Virginia–North Carolina area, but I wish to emphasize that this should serve only as a general guide. If you have a limited amount of time you should either call or establish a local contact that will keep you posted on the first arrival. Pattern predictions and fishing forecasts are never more than a guide and we all agree it is impossible to recapture yesterday's or last year's fish.

On those days, which are often in the channel bass angler's life, when the water just does not run red with his arrival, it is necessary that the angler know just a little bit more than where they caught 'em yesterday.

It has been my good fortune and pleasure to meet most of the present day "regulars" and a good many of the old-timers who fish for, or guide, parties seeking channel bass in the Virginia–North Carolina area. I have personally taken channel bass in Hatteras Inlet on bait as early as March 31 and as late as December 17 from the Cape Hatteras surf on artificials. Between these extremes I have boated him on spoons at Oregon Inlet in April, in Magothy Bay in May, and from Virginia's Eastern Shore surf on cut bait all of the summer months as well as the fall months of September and October.

I am still learning much of the lore of lures and baits and techniques employed that make the difference between skill and good luck—for a skilled fisherman helps make his own luck; while an unskilled amateur must rely on luck and professional assistance. Luck helps, but not the angler who is unable to select, or is improperly equipped to fish, the areas of opportunity. Fishing tips gleaned from experience and contacts are of value only to those anglers properly equipped to utilize and not nullify any luck that may present itself.

There is always a question of taste when it comes to "best baits" from both the angler's and fish's point of view. I wish to emphasize that channel bass feed on whatever is available and not necessarily what he prefers, and I operate accordingly. For trolling I have successfully used rigged eels as well as spoons and bucktails, and for bait fishing an even wider variety of cut and natural bait such as squid heads, hickory shad, menhaden, spot, mullet, and peeler crab.

Although I believe that most game fish feed on whatever is available, I pay due homage to what the locals recommend as the favorite bait for that particular species in that particular location. The expert angler should be able to sift all of the local information and reduce it to a practical application for the tools he employs and the conditions under which he is fishing.

Here we come to one of the most important elements of the angling game: Conditions very often dictate the type of lure or choice of bait.

To illustrate this point, for the warm summer months while fishing the barrier islands of Eastern Shore Virginia, I use cut pieces of the small fish called spot. Menhaden or mullet being more oily have a better "chumming" quality, and shedder crab may be more tasty, but other conditions must be considered. One: Spot are easily obtainable from the local commercial fish houses and many times fresh spot may be obtained from small-haul seiners right on the grounds. Two: It keeps much better in warm weather than menhaden. Three: And most important, the shape of the spot lends itself to my particular method of rigging for surf casting.

Now I wish to emphasize another "condition" that dictates the choice of bait for channel bass and that is durability. There are times when a strong current makes it difficult for the surf caster or pier fisherman to hold bottom regardless of what size and shape of sinker he employs. At such times it is necessary, once the sinker does take hold, that the bait be durable enough to resist the chewing efforts of all the little crabs in the area for a reasonable length of time and maintain an attractive appearance to the first jumbo channel bass that appears.

Actually, these little animated chum grinders are one of the anglers mixed blessings, for while a little calico crab is busily chewing away at the fish head, he is also creating a small and attractive "slick" for the game fish the angler seeks. On the other hand, a big blue crab can chew away a slab of cut bait so rapidly that the angler is forced to waste precious time with frequent bait changes and reanchoring the sinker in the fast currents. The most durable bait available locally, and sufficiently oily to be attractive to fish in thick (sandy) water, is the head with a portion of the body trimmed from a 6-inch mullet or spot.

To rig this type of bait, simply force the hook up through the lower jaw and out through the nose, exposing the entire point of the hook. (See illustration). The hard, bony blue crab is a principal item of food for the channel bass, so the bass is not apt to spit the hook simply because a portion of the barb is exposed.

Menhaden, although quite oily and ideal for cut bait, is unsuited for this chore as the fragile bony head contains little flesh and tears from the hook quite easily. Some of my angler friends say that fish heads are also more attractive to shark and other pests, but as long as the bait is "attractive" I will put up with the inconvenience of a few sharks. I use hooks snelled with a 60-pound monofilament since the monofilament acts as a "releasing link" and you do not waste valuable fishing time fighting sharks.

Author's favorite method of hooking head section of a spot for channel bass

The use of fish heads for bait, although desirable under the conditions just described, makes casting somewhat bulky and difficult. There are times when maximum distance is the condition essential to success. Quite often this is the case when fishing that area of Cape Hatteras known as the "Point." Here, during

Many channel bass are caught by casting from a boat to a school of fish on or near the surface.

the fall months, channel bass will congregate off this little underwater peninsula, formed by opposing currents, where the seas toss together in a peculiar manner that provides a marine banquet table for Mr. Red Drum. Only those anglers who can cast to the outer edge of this little underwater spit are successful. Here it is necessary that anglers cut, trim, and rig a streamlined bait of minimum wind resistance so that the sinker may carry the bait out to maximum distance. A bait cut in a triangular or pennant shape may be folded at the blunt end and impaled on the hook in such a manner that it is of little bulk and the streamer shape offers little resistance when cast.

Method is the result of trial and error in the area that it is practiced. The presence of both channel bass and black drum in the same area at the same time has resulted in the development of the famous "sandwich" of peeler crab and clam by Eastern Shore Virginia anglers. The black drum seems to prefer clam, but will take both peeler crab and clam; the channel bass accept crab readily, but only rarely will he touch clam. Other combinations which include fish do not work as well, so here again we have local conditions controlling the selection of bait.

It is not only my opinion but that of the regulars who fish for the jumbo channel bass that tackle should be conventional and rugged. The best advice to follow is to use the lightest practical tackle. It must be practical before it can be sporty. Except for boat fishing, some distance is always necessary and distance requires a relatively stiff rod. It takes a good-size sinker to carry out a whole peeler crab or an attractive size slab of cut bait. This is not the job for light tackle. Red drum are rugged, powerful fighters who live in strong currents and crashing surf and do not exhaust themselves as quickly as some of the more acrobatic varieties. The light-tackle stunt fisherman, who insist on taking fish just to make headlines, is never popular on a crowded beach, boat, or pier that is not exclusively his. And the longer he imposes on the other anglers' time, the longer they have to reflect on his idea of sportsmanship. Stick to conventional tackle with 25- to 36-pound test for surf fishing and 36 to 50 pounds for trolling or bottom fishing. On this tackle, Mister Channel Bass will give you all the fight you seek and don't kid yourself about taking the fight out of him or horsing him in. If you cannot cast a conventional reel, use at least 15-pound test on the spinning reel. Remember that most casters who use conventional tackle are not too impressed about the superiority of spinning if the advocate is not able to turn in a creditable performance with conventional revolving-spool reels.

When the channel bass are schooled off Cape Hatteras in late fall, the natives believe that a fish hooked on a line so light that the angler has no control of the fight will result in the entire school following the hooked fish as he rushes out to sea. Whether this can be proved or not is of no consequence as this is the code and the visiting sportsman angler should respect it if he expects to be popular.

When fall northeasters are pushing channel bass past the piers, sometimes as many as 20 rods are fanned out along the end of a single pier. At the word "strike" all anglers, other than the lucky guy, reel in until the fish is either netted or lost. The time required to land the fish is given with grudging good humor and it is not easy for the light-line "sport" to endure jibes. Even with what should be considered adequate tackle you are going to have to endure a few jibes from the crowd. In other words use tackle to match the condition, not what someone wishes to sell you as adequate.

Recommending the proper surf rod to do the job for North Carolina and Virginia could be tossed off lightly by saying, "Any over the counter rod between ten and eleven feet in length and just as stiff as you can buy." This sounds like a broad generality, but it is doubtful if, at the present time, you could purchase a surf rod in the prescribed length that would be too stiff. The local surfmen, influenced by the success of the 10½-foot handmade surf sticks developed by the five-time champion Virginia Tidewater Angler's Club surf casting team, have a good market going in custom-made calcutta and hollow-glass rods. These rods were developed as the results of experiments to obtain absolute maximum distance with a minimum of backlashes using a 4-ounce pyramid lead and 36-pound test line. A 5-pound weight rigged to the tip of one of these 10½-foot rods will cause a deflection of 18 to 26 inches. There is a shortened version of this distance stick designed for pier fishing that is approximately 8 feet long and just as stiff in proportion. As Mr. Channel Bass is always on the long end of the lever this leaves the angler on the short end of the stick, so don't worry about bludgeoning him.

It is not easy to recommend lines as development occurs so rapidly with this item of tackle that your advice could be "dated"

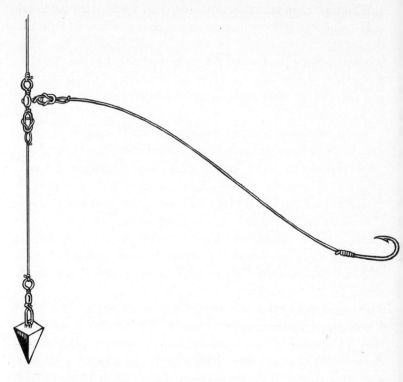

Rig for bottom fishing for channel bass

before it goes to press. Practically all changes in line construction
are designed to improve the angler's fish-taking potential, although some are designed for a specific type of fishing for a
special fish. As far as channel-bass fishing is concerned it is important to note that round lines offer less resistance to tide or
current than flat lines of equal strength. This is relatively unimportant, and in most instances a 4- to 6-ounce pyramid will
hold in practically any surf that can be fished. For those occasions when a strong current running parallel with the beach
makes it difficult to hold bottom, a 4-ounce pyramid rigged with
a short leader to another 2- or 4-ounce pyramid will hold better
than a single sinker of the combined weights. In effect, one sinker
acts as a back anchor for the other. Pier fishermen are sometimes
forced to use as much as 16 ounces of lead as channel bass come

breezing by with the strong currents that accompany the northeast winds.

Sometimes it is not the size of the fish but the bottom conditions that dictates the size of a line. Sections of several of the barrier beaches of the Eastern Shore Virginia Islands are sod banks that were once marshy areas protected from the eroding surf by sand hills. As these sand hills drift westward, they cover more marshy areas and expose the sod on the easterly side to the surf. These sod banks, now underwater, frequently foul the angler's pyramid sinkers and a 36-pound test line is just about the minimum required to pull the line free. Fortunately, this is not true of most of the Barrier Islands, but the visiting angler should be prepared for the eventuality if he plans to visit these beaches.

Successful surf fishing for channel bass in Virginia and North Carolina generally hinges on the selection of the right slough. These deep water indentations along the shore line can be recognized by the darker color of the water, if the water is clear. If the slough cannot be identified by the darker shade of the water, then look for an area where incoming waves are not as high as in the surrounding area. Seas tend to build up over shallow areas and level off over the deeper holes. And if the sea is dead calm, and sandy, which is rare, look for a telltale eddy that seems to be running directly offshore. Local commercial fishermen call these eddies "out sucks," which is pretty descriptive as they not only carry water out, but any helpless baitfish that are caught up in them. If you are fortunate enough to find a deep slough up against the beach with one of these so-called "out sucks" running through a bar that parallels the beach within casting distance—you have it made.

It is not difficult to select the good sloughs along the Carolina coast south to Hatteras Inlet as most of these are spotted and sometimes even marked by the locals who have easy access to them either from the highway or by beach buggy. Such is not the case of Eastern Shore Virginia Barrier Islands and here you are out on your own.

So when you are slough sleuthing at Eastern Shore it is well to remember that the rise and fall of tide is approximately 5 feet, and a good slough that is quite noticeable and easy to locate at low tide will completely lose its identity at high water, and most important with this loss of identity its attractiveness to the fish. For once the slough takes on the appearance of the surrounding area, bait disperses, currents and eddies cease, and there is nothing to uncover, direct, or concentrate marine life attractive to the feeding fish. If this is your first trip to a new beach, plan to arrive just one hour before the last of the ebb tide. Try to find a slough that has 2 or 3 feet of water in it even at dead low water. Also, study the exposed bars or any other features that would be noticeable only at low water. If necessary, line up what you consider the best entrance to the slough by placing a couple of stakes above the high-water line, pointing out where you should cast when the tide rises. Most sloughs that have as much as 2 or 3 feet of water at low tide will produce just as well on ebb tide as flood tide. It is the depth of the water and the direction of the current that is important. Actually, there is a greater concentration of bait in the sloughs as the tide ebbs. Ebb tide concentrates the bait in the sloughs and deeper channels; as the tide rises the bait scatters.

Once you have located the slough or any other fishy-looking area, you can rig up, cast out, and wait or really "fish" the slough. If there is a channel bass working the slough there is a good chance he will locate you in short order. I prefer to give him all the help I can to find what he is seeking. Cast out, take up the slack, sweep the rod tip up sharply, bumping the sinker along the bottom. Now let it rest for a few minutes and then repeat the same action. Reel in the sinker a few feet each time until you reach the shallows. This bottom-bumping technique is heard or sensed by the channel bass and will take far more fish than when the bait is lying dead still on the bottom. I have had channel bass take my bait when I was reeling it in to give a fellow angler free rein to fight his fish. I use this technique of working a slough until I have covered the entire slough, then if nothing happens I leave the bait in what I consider the most fishy-looking spot, "fishing" it back to the beach about every twenty minutes to check the bait.

You cannot use this technique when there is a strong current

Claude Rogers prepares to cast to an offshore wreck. When channel-bass fishing in the surf, long casts are often required and tackle is usually on the heavy side.

paralleling the beach, for on these occasions you do everything possible to keep the sinker and bait in position. When a strong current is running, making it difficult to hold, you can "walk out" the slough by casting out across the up-tide end of the slough and then walking down the beach, keeping pace with the current and swinging the line and bait along. This is a more effective method than standing flat-footed as the drift swings your bait down current and back up on the beach. Unfortunately, when you have these strong currents you usually have a lot of trash and grass to collect on the line and it is almost impossible to hold bottom with any sort of rig, regardless of the line diameter. These adverse conditions for the angler do not necessarily affect the channel bass and many are taken in rough water—it just takes a little more effort. The walking technique is also quite effective at the "Point" of Cape Hatteras, where you may cast to either side of the "Point," depending on the direction of the tide, and let the current swing your bait over the end of the underwater spit and possibly into the waiting maw of a hungry bass. When I find such a current between the beach and unbroken offshore bar, I generally select a spot on the down-tide terminus where Mr. Channel Bass would expect his marine dumb-waiter to deliver his dinner.

The best advice I can offer the angler who seeks channel bass from a charter boat is to listen to your skipper, for no matter how skilled the angler thinks he is in the surf, he should rely on the local professional skipper's judgment as to the best time of day, tide, and fishing location. This is the charter boat skipper's business—to give the angler the best opportunity—and your casting, rigging, lure selection, and presentation techniques are of no avail if your skipper does not put you in the fish.

The best thing you can do while exposed to this wealth of local lore is to ask questions: Peak season? Optimum tides? Winds? And with a chart, pin-point the location and try to determine what bottom condition or conformation accounts for the skipper's selection of that location at that particular time and season. If the captain makes a mistake it will be an honest one, but remember you would be starting from scratch.

I will take Big Red anyway I can get him, but I always have greater personal satisfaction if I can take him from the beach. What more could a sportsman wish than the opportunity to be present at his favorite slough at early dawn, facing a freshening fall breeze from the ceaseless surf and listening to the gentle swish of sea oats as they mildly protest the same salty zephyrs that keep the terns and striker gulls hovering effortlessly over small bait or even the red warrior the angler seeks.

This is the nostalgic atmosphere of channel-bass fishing and the lovable old lunker is waiting to serve you with moments of heart-skipping excitement and memories to last a lifetime.

*Chapter Sixteen*

# HOW TO CATCH WEAKFISH AND SEA TROUT

*by* HENRY LYMAN

HENRY LYMAN, known as "Hal" to a host of marine anglers throughout the nation, is publisher of *The Salt Water Sportsman*, the only magazine in the world devoted entirely to salt-water sport fishing. His job carries him to every coastal area, where he goes to work—fishing. A specialist in the use of light tackle from beach and boat, he has taken members of the weakfish family from all the famous grounds along the coasts. He is coauthor with Frank Woolner of *The Complete Book of Weakfishing*.

THINK of old Izaak Walton and his conversations with the milkmaids, his slow-moving English rivers, and his endless contemplation of the countryside. Dream of the fish you want to catch and of the monsters you have missed. Relax, slow down, and set your pace to that of a hundred or more years ago rather than to the rocket speed of the present space age. Follow these instructions and you will be prepared mentally to fish for the common weakfish and its close cousin, the speckled sea trout.

Once mentally prepared, you will be able to follow up the same slow-moving plan physically—without haste, without frantic rushing about, without shouts and stompings. And you will discover one of the major secrets of the successful weakfisherman. These anglers learned long ago that a leisurely approach to their quarry, whether it be in the presentation of the bait and lure or in the actual approach to the fishing grounds, brings results. It makes no difference whether you call these species squeteague, chickwit, weakfish, or sea trout, whether you are after the common, speckled, sand, or silver varieties, the rules of care and patience apply. Crashing surf in a howling northeaster and flying scud around a tossing boat are not part of the weakfishing pic-

223

ture. This angling is a more gentle sport—gentle until the strike, which may strip an amazing amount of line off the reel in the fish's first dash for freedom.

Tackle for the sea trout family has changed considerably in the past decade. Instead of the stiff, two-piece "weakfish" rod with bay reel and heavy line once common in the Northeast or the "popping" rod and service reel of the South, the trend now is to lighter outfits, which are more versatile and which give more sport when the quarry is hooked. Ideally suited to the task at hand is the spinning rig with a rod 6 or 7 feet over-all, mounting a small- to medium-sized reel filled with 6-pound test monofilament and calibrated to handle lures or natural baits in the ½- to 1-ounce brackets. Favorite in many southern waters is the sea-going bait-casting outfit—a rod not in excess of 6 feet, a free-spool reel equipped with a star drag, and nylon braid or flat monofilament testing between 9 and 12 pounds. This last-named tackle is to be preferred for trolling, but either outfit can be used for all methods of weakfishing.

There are dozens of other combinations that take sea trout successfully every season and they range from the heavy surf stick to the light fly rod. However, the spinning and bait-casting outfits are the choices of anglers who seek these species primarily. It is, therefore, with their use as basic weapons that this article will deal. The methods and techniques described can be adapted readily to other tackle combinations.

Before launching into the various ways of presenting a hook to a weakfish, a few facts about this tribe should be made clear. First, all members of the family are fundamentally coastal or estuarine species. Although they may be found in deep waters well offshore during cold weather, and although they may cover considerable distances in their migrations, their favorite haunts are around bays and inlets, at the mouths of tidal rivers, and around the channels and flats inshore. They will venture into brackish waters often, but rarely, if ever, will they swim in waters which are entirely fresh. Note particularly that muddy or dirty water conditions do not bother them. In fact, chances are better than even that if there is a clash where turbid currents mingle with clear, the fish will be found on the muddy side of the rip.

Fishing Secrets
of the Experts

Henry Lyman

A mess of common or northern weakfish taken on a fly rod and fly. Note the special short-winged, double-hooked fly.

A second factor of which successful weakfishermen are fully aware is that these species favor as feeding grounds an area where there is a sharp drop from shallow water to deep. Granted, sea trout may often cruise the flats in what appears to be an aimless fashion, but even under these circumstances, best catches are made at points where channels or holes are close to the shoal water. Note particularly that the drops may change as the stages of the tide change. A hot spot on a low, outgoing tide may be worthless when the current turns. Anglers keep such drops closely guarded secrets and it is only by observing them and the fish themselves that you reach the point where you are finding secret spots of your own.

The third point to remember as far as the fish are concerned is their sensitivity to change in water and air temperatures. A sudden cold snap in the late autumn has been known to kill thousands of sea trout in a single small bay. If fishing in either the late fall or the early spring, watch the thermometer carefully. When the mercury drops, the fish tend to hug bottom in deep holes and channels, stop feeding, and generally ignore any lures or baits. On the other hand, if the weather warms up suddenly, speckled sea trout in particular may be caught even in midwinter as many anglers in the Carolinas and Georgia have discovered to their pleasure.

Noise is the final point to keep in mind as far as weakfish of all species are concerned. The splashing of a surface plug or similar attractor does not alarm the fish; sound from some unusual source does. An oar dropped on the bottom of a boat, hammering on a pier or any other structure built out over the water, the rolling of rocks off a jetty will all scare fish. When the water is shallow, this fright may last for a considerable time and it is wise to move elsewhere if the noise has been loud and prolonged. Some claim that even loud talking will spook a school of weaks feeding on the surface, but conclusive proof of this is lacking. Because of this sensitivity to noise, it is wise to troll for weaks using oars rather than a motor when fishing in shallow water. When it is deep, use a long line and change speeds only when a given speed fails to produce.

Despite the fact that unusual noise frightens these species, a surface commotion often will attract them. Always on the prowl for a free meal, weaks will hurry to investigate what they consider may be a school of bait in trouble. If it is indeed such a

SURFACE

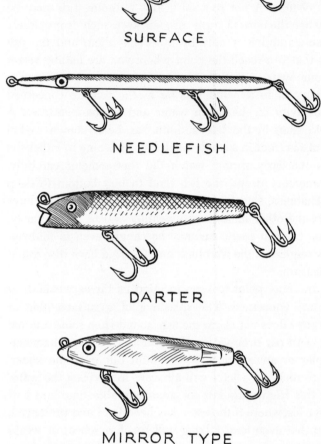

NEEDLEFISH

DARTER

MIRROR TYPE

Plugs used for sea trout

school, the game fish will slash into it in a series of individual attacks, not in a mass onslaught such as that typical of feeding bluefish. It is under these conditions that the angler should remember the calm and relaxed approach. A fast retrieve that speeds the lure through the water is almost instinctive when reel-

228

ing under exciting conditions of this sort. Relax, reel slowly, whip the rod sharply if you wish, but keep the pace down. Your catches will be doubled or trebled.

At certain times sea trout will gobble down a surface lure when they are feeding in this manner. At others, they will ignore such a lure completely. When the ignoring process starts, many fishermen will shift frantically from plug to plug in an attempt to entice a weak into striking. It seems obvious that the fish are hitting at or near the surface, and, therefore, that a lure swimming at or near the same surface will get results.

Stop right there! It is obvious to the angler, but it may not be at all obvious to the weakfish. Shift to a bugeye-type lure—a hook with a weighted head dressed with bucktail, nylon, Saran, or any other material—to a metal spoon or jig, cast to the edge of the school and retrieve slowly. If this does not produce a strike—chances are that it will—use the whip retrieve described below. Remember that, for every sea trout seen breaking the surface, there are probably half a dozen feeding deep. These are less suspicious than their surfaced brothers and they will grab a deep-running lure.

The whip retrieve for underwater lures is one of the major tricks used by the successful weakfisherman. In some areas, it is the only type of retrieve ever employed, but these whip purists would do well if they changed their style from time to time. The technique is simple enough. Make the cast. Allow the lure to sink while you think fondly of old Izaak and his milkmaids. Start reeling and, after all slack has been taken out of the line, jerk the rod smartly. Unless circumstances prevent it, as when fishing in a fairly heavy surf from the beach, this whipping of the rod tip should be made approximately parallel to the surface of the water. In other words, keep the tip low and jerk sideways rather than upwards. Give the reel handle another three or four turns and repeat the process. The strike is apt to come as the lure reaches the top of its arc of movement. For this reason, do not bring the rod so far back that it can come back no further. If this is done, it is impossible to move the rod tip sufficiently to set the hook. When using the whip retrieve, do *not* reel fast. Often the best success comes while just ghosting the lure near the bottom with only sufficient speed to keep slack out of the line. The whip action will do the rest.

What might be considered a modification of a whip retrieve may also be used by the troller. When a lure is being towed astern, obviously no actual retrieve is involved. However, if the lure used is of the bugeye type, sharp jerks of the rod tip at 5-second intervals will greatly increase its fish-catching powers. When using a spoon, or a spinner rigged ahead of a bait strip—an old-time weakfish favorite, incidentally—move the rod tip more gradually through a 30° arc, then let it drop back quickly. This not only varies the speed at which the lure will travel, but also varies the depth. Here again, as is the case with the whip retrieve, watch out for a strike as the lure reaches its highest point of travel.

A refinement of this technique is highly successful when trolling in shallow waters that are intersected by deeper channels, in bays or tidal rivers where sand bars are encountered—in fact, in any areas where depth conditions vary abruptly. Troll slowly and steadily over the shoal sections. Often it is necessary to hold the rod tip high overhead to keep the hook from fouling bottom under these conditions. A short time after the boat reaches deeper water, the hook will do the same. Drop the rod tip smartly so that the lure will plunge sharply from the shallows to the deeps: Weaks of all species favor such drop-offs as feeding grounds, and the sight of a diving lure right at the edge of their dinner table is almost irresistible.

Trolling and casting will take weakfish, but there are other methods which cannot be ignored. The first of these, brought to a fine art in the waters of southern New England, New York, and New Jersey, is chumming. By dropping a weakfish's favorite meal, such as grass shrimp, over the side of a boat, a free lunch line is set up down current. Mixed with the lunch is an offering with a hook in it.

The secret of successful chumming depends upon the amount of chum used. Without question, live grass shrimp make the best attractors. These are usually packed in sawdust and the sawdust itself is a visual drawing card for weaks. The shrimp supply can be "stretched" by adding a box of dry rolled oats to the packing.

A steady chumline made up of small quantities of shrimp and packing is far superior to one established by tossing great scoops of chum over the side at infrequent intervals. Small and steady is the rule for building up a slick. Some anglers add ground-up oily fish such as the menhaden to the chumline when the supply of shrimp is scant.

When fishing by this method, a shrimp itself may be used as bait. However, better results will be forthcoming if an entirely different lure or bait is offered. A sea worm, rigged so that it lies along the shank of a hook and swims in a natural manner; a live minnow of any sort; a strip of squid, cut so that it flutters in the current, all are to be preferred to the chum. Artificials, either cast or jigged in the slick, will also do well.

Boat drifting, with or without the use of a chumline, is another way of taking sea trout and is used wherever these species are found. Because of the lack of noise and because of the natural appearance of the bait or lure presented by this method, it will often get results when other attempts fail. The angler must first determine whether the wind or the current is the more powerful and whether the effects of both cause the craft to drift in some unusual direction. Once this direction has been found, run the boat so that the drift starts in shallow water and is carried to deeper. It is better to make the initial run under oar power than by motor. If a motor is used, stick to slow speeds, then kill the power entirely. Using either natural or artificial baits, let out line until bottom is reached, then reel in a couple of feet. If more than one angler is fishing, have the lures ride at different depths. As the boat moves with wind and current, keep the baits moving and sound for bottom from time to time. Once weakfish are located, it is better to keep drifting until strikes cease. Then give the payoff area wide berth, head to a point well above the school, and repeat the drift. Although anchoring where the fish are located may result in a few catches, chances are that the school will spook after several of its members have been hoisted skyward. If currents are such that anchoring is a necessity, be sure to lower the anchor gently rather than to toss it with a great splash.

A refinement of this drifting technique produces well for the

Charlie Whitney looks over a sea trout or spotted weakfish taken off Cocoa, Florida, a spot noted for the big size of these fish.

caster. Using currents and winds as described above, the cast is made *toward* the direction in which the boat is moving. The lure is allowed to settle on bottom, slack line is reeled in, and a slow whip retrieve follows. Often weaks will follow a bugeye presented in this manner right up to the side of the boat and will hit just as the lure is about to be lifted clear of the surface. For this reason, be sure to fish out the entire cast. A swirl at the gunwale can be highly provoking and is slim eating in the pan.

When using this method for fishing over flats, floating grass can be a headache. The grass hits the line, slides down it, and

Both the northern and southern species of weakfish can often be caught in the surf from the beaches and jetties.

mats around the lure almost immediately. There is no complete answer to this problem, but some of the trouble can be corrected by tying an ordinary small button about 18 inches ahead of the lure. Grass will be checked by the button and the lure will be effective for a short time until fouled itself. In a pinch, a large swivel will act in the same way, but the larger surface of the button is more efficient.

The final method of taking sea trout, which probably accounts for as many of this family being caught as any other, is still fishing. This may be done from boats, from shore and from piers, bridges, or similar structures built over the water. The techniques vary widely and may include some of those described in casting, drifting, trolling, and chumming. The still fisherman fundamentally presents a natural bait in an area where he expects to find weakfish and waits for the fish to come and find the offer-

233

ing. Much depends upon making the bait presented appear natural. If live bait is used, it should be hooked so that it remains alive as long as possible. If dead bait is used, it should be given lively action by gently raising and lowering the rod tip at regular intervals.

The still fisherman should remember at all times that the depth of the bait is vitally important. In deep water, weaks often will cruise at a definite level and will not look at anything above or below that level. By using several hooks on the same line above the sinker, various depths may be investigated simultaneously. Once the feeding schools or individuals have been located, the angler is in business. When fishing flats or shallows, a float is desirable for the same purpose. A couple of split shot will hold the bait down and variation in the length of line or leader below the float will mean a similar variation in the depth at which the hook rides.

Florida and Gulf of Mexico sea trout fishermen put their floats to work in another manner. The head of the float is hollow and by lifting the rod tip smartly, the bobber is made to pop and gurgle on the surface. This attracts the quarry so that, when a weak comes to investigate the cause of the disturbance, it finds a tempting morsel close at hand. Small floats may even be used when fishing in deep water. By placing such a device between the leader and the hook or between the line and leader, the bait will be kept off the bottom and away from scavengers. In addition, the float moves with the current and gives a natural action to a dead bait.

No matter what method is used for taking members of the weakfish family, someone will dream up an improvement upon it. By watching both fish and fishermen, the average angler can learn a great deal, and, if he is willing to experiment, will soon be rated as one of those mythical creatures of the Waltonian world—an expert. When he reaches that height, he will realize how little he really knows!

*Chapter Seventeen*

# THREE WAYS TO CATCH TARPON

## *by* CHARLES F. WATERMAN

CHARLES F. WATERMAN of Deland, Florida, is a former newspaperman
and photographer who is at present fishing editor of the magazine
*Florida Wildlife.* He also writes magazine articles for many publications
on fishing in Florida and adjacent areas. He should never run out of
material since he claims he fishes two hundred days of the year! He has
caught a great variety of species in southern waters, but prefers fly fishing in salt water. He has taken tarpon on very light tackle and in this
book tells how to catch these fish by various methods.

D ESPITE his "Silver King" nickname, the tarpon is pretty
democratic. On occasion, he can be hooked in strange places by
strange fishermen. Take the tourist lady I saw fishing with a
dime-store outfit down near Marco, Florida, some years back.
She had baited her hook with some picnic lunch leftover and
had hurled her tidbit some 20 feet into Marco Pass while she su-
pervised her children's sunbathing.

She had a nibble and a 100-pound tarpon blew up in her face.
Since she had hoped for nothing more than a 10-inch salt-water
catfish, her reaction was well worth watching.

Tarpon aren't usually that easy to hook, but they're often
*almost* that easy. They can be hooked casting, trolling, or bait
fishing and even though the fish may be outsized and the battle
violent, light tackle has a good chance because of some tarpon
peculiarities we're going into right now.

Tarpon are primarily inshore residents and primarily lovers
of shallow water, and these characteristics make them accessible
to small craft or even to shore fishermen. It is true that I've seen

them well out at sea and that some of the finest tarpon fishing in the world is at Boca Grande, Florida, in nearly 100 feet of water, but most tarpon wrestling is done close in where it's pretty shallow.

You see I've already backed water a little on one statement. Rigid rules about tarpon fishing are pretty silly and because a tarpon has no commercial value there hasn't been much money spent in learning about him. Vast migrations are routine in tarpon country, but just where they come from and go is open to question.

There is year-round tarpon fishing among many of the Caribbean Islands, along the coasts of Central America and the mangrove coast of southwest Florida, and occasionally on Florida's east coast, but it is in the spring and summer months that the big fish show themselves all along the Florida shore, up along the Carolinas, and in the upper reaches of the Gulf of Mexico. There are resident tarpon in the Keys, but the best fishing there is in the late winter, spring, and summer. May is about tops. That's when the passes fill up with the big ones and when the bridge fishermen go home with far-away looks and broken tackle.

Perhaps the easiest way to catch a big tarpon is by trolling—unless you have a concentration of them already located. Big spoons, feathers, strip bait, or plugs will do the job and you keep your craft putting along until you either get a strike or sight fish rolling. If you see a school rolling, you check their course and try to cut them off. They'll go down if your boat comes too close, but one may come right up out of the wake and powder the lure anyway.

Now this kind of trolling is done in relatively open water—such as they have at Cape Coral near Fort Myers, Florida. Most of the boats used there are inboards and some of them are open "tarpon boats."

The strike is seldom very fast. I know this is a contradiction of what is commonly said about tarpon, but I have watched a lot of them taken in clear water and most of them swim fairly slowly until hooked. Once "Old Shiny" learns the lure wasn't good to eat after all, he's likely to take to the surface in a writhing, slashing, crashing series of leaps that often erases memory of the

Charles F. Waterman

strike itself—hence the frequent statements about the "lightning strike." Even a foot-long tarpon doesn't take with the speed he's generally given credit for. Many game fish hit at a much higher speed.

The first five seconds are often so violent the faint-hearted fisherman feels he hasn't a chance—and since the lure is frequently thrown during that period many a fisherman doesn't know that the fight settles down a little after a minute or so. Remember we're talking now about open water trolling. Sometimes

237

Most tarpon, especially those hooked in shallow water, will leap high out of the water. This often enables them to throw the hook or lure and escape.

tarpon will jump only two or three times if hooked in water over 20 feet deep. Occasionally he won't jump at all.

It is a different story when you hook one in water of less than 10 feet. In that kind of spot I have caught only one tarpon that didn't jump at least once.

Playing a tarpon with a star-drag reel or heavy spinning tackle involves keeping a heavy strain on him but "bowing to him" when he jumps close in—that is, let him have a little slack to keep him from wrecking things. He shouldn't have enough loose line to get tangled in. Many tarpon break-offs occur when the fish swats loose line with his tail or becomes entangled. I once saw one break a rod, bust a line, and throw a plug on the same jump close to the boat. These are strong fish and if they had sense enough to run and keep running, you couldn't land 100-pounders on 20-pound test or less.

The jumping fight is spectacular and it tires the fish; the higher he hops the better. Many of the experienced tarpon fishermen who have landed big ones on fairly light tackle would just as soon the fish got off after the acrobatics, because from then on a tarpon is just another fish and it's crank and pump, crank and pump.

Tarpon should not be gaffed until thoroughly played-out, because a green tarpon will rearrange the cockpit to suit himself. Once the gaffing operation is started it should be handled smoothly. Most tarpon are gaffed through the lower jaw and then released, but where a fish is needed, some guides or captains kill them with the gaff. Easiest way to release a plug-hooked tarpon is to yank the hooks out with pliers. He'll be less hurt by the jerking than by a lot of hacking and wrestling.

I have seen tarpon come to life after a bungled gaffing operation and start to fight all over again. Suppose he's on his side, moving his tail feebly and apparently all in. You gaff him neatly, haul him aboard, slip a rope through his gills or release him and he won't make too much fuss—but, by gosh, you can bat him clumsily with the gaff and bring forth some hidden form of energy that starts the ruckus with new enthusiasm.

Finding a good tarpon spot by trolling is a long job unless you have a pretty good idea of where they might be and the stranger usually hasn't this information. There are spots that are good year after year—often for unknown reasons. Generally the fish lie in or near channels, but they also forage on muddy flats. In "small" water, fish are often found along the shore line out of the sun and shallow-draft trolling boats can "scrape the edge."

Bait fishing is usually carried out in two ways—drifting and still fishing. I have seen the drifting method used only over fairly deep water and it is extremely popular in Boca Grande Pass. Usually the bait is fairly small and alive. Depth is extremely important and Boca Grande captains have their lines carefully marked so that once the fish are located they can continue fishing at the proper level. They know the depths almost to the inch. As they drift, they leave their engines idling for aid in playing the fish and to avoid other boats. Sometimes traffic gets pretty thick in that pass—day or night.

The usual outfit involves a husky boat rod and star-drag reel and this is no place for ultralight tackle—too hard to get a tired fish off the bottom. If you connect with a big one on ultralight tackle the chances are a big shark will beat you to him during a protracted battle.

Pinfish, small crabs, squirrel fish, and mutton minnows or sand bream are favorite choices for drift fishing. For the most part, they are handled with care and fished with as little weight as possible.

Now when it comes to still fishing, a foot-long mullet with its head removed is first choice. Carefully threaded, the bait is cast well out from the boat, usually in shallow water where the fish are working. The tackle is generally fairly heavy and the bait is left lying on the bottom. Slack line is given and the boat is staked or anchored to prevent swinging. This method is generally used for big fish.

Tarpon bottoms are frequently crab bottoms and many a big fish is lost because crabs have chewed up the line. Old hands are careful to keep fish slime or odors from their lines and they use heavy wire leaders.

When the bait is picked up, the reel is free-spooled and many fishermen have some loose line coiled in the boat to offer a minimum of resistance.

Once the fish moves away with the bait, most experts give him a free hand and don't set the hook until he jumps. A tarpon that finds he has swallowed a bait with line attached almost invariably comes out in an effort to throw it. The bait is generally swallowed or, at least, taken very deeply. That's the most frequent criticism of still fishing. Playing a fish on a swallowed bait is likely to kill him, whereas the fish caught drifting are likely to be hooked superficially.

Still fishing results in many hooked sharks. Sometimes they're

For still-fishing for tarpon, a mullet with its head removed is first choice. The hook and leader is run through the body of the bait after a hole has been made with the long needle.

persistent enough to drive tarpon fishermen out of good spots. Salt-water catfish love to tug away at big tarpon baits, giving fishermen occasional thrills when the real thing is lacking.

Casting for tarpon is the sportiest method of all. Heavy tackle and big plugs are best if you want a big one to keep, but most tarpon old-timers finally get to the point where they use light tackle and don't care if they land many fish or not.

Regardless of size, probably the best single type of plug for tarpon is one that floats at rest and can be reeled under on the retrieve. It's better if it will pop loudly on top. I have seen times when only the loudest plugs were effective.

For bait-casting tackle with 15- or 20-pound test line, darter-type plugs weighing around ⅝-ounce are popular, generally in yellow or silver finish. Ordinary, high-grade fresh-water bait-casting reels with the addition of slip clutch handles are satisfactory, and some of the newer, free-spooling lightweights with star drags are fine. Some sort of slip clutch or drag is a near-necessity unless the fisherman uses a thumbstall.

I used ordinary bass-type fresh-water bait-casting rods for years, but I've recently gone to something a little stiffer for tarpon. It takes backbone to make a big plug perform and set a hook in a concrete jaw.

Spinning tackle is probably used more than bait-casting stuff for casting at tarpon, but many of the spinning rods employed are a little too soft for proper manipulation of lures and hook-setting. In spinning, a fairly strong reel is necessary for the heavy work of the final stages of tarpon landing. The use of 4- or 6-pound line on heavy tarpon is in the nature of a stunt, even though you may eventually boat one with it. I'd say 10-pound monofilament is about as light as should be used with a practical tarpon outfit.

Except on those occasions when he clobbers everything that moves, tarpon seem to be scaly bundles of indecision. In casting over a likely spot, your lure may provoke horrendous boils, frightening splashes, and washtub swirls—and never be touched. I once looked down into some clear water when the light was just right and saw five big tarpon squirting back and forth under my plug. None of them struck.

At such times, it takes a bit of self-control to keep from yanking the lure away. When you have a fish working under it or behind it, change the speed of your retrieve and keep cranking. Likely as not your fish will follow until the last instant and decide to strike so near the boat his tail will whack it.

Sometimes tarpon are caught by bumping a feather jig or plug along the bottom. These strikes are gentle and in shallow water you often see a good-sized fish stick his tail clear out of the water as he appears to pin such a bait to the bottom.

A successful angler sees his tarpon gaffed at Cape Coral, Florida. It was hooked on a trolled spoon. Unless the fish is of unusual size or wanted for mounting, most tarpon are released alive to fight another day.

Best for use with the fly rod is a big streamer. Popping bugs get the strikes but are so light that hooking is often a difficult problem, chiefly because the fish pushes the bug away with his bow wave. A hard splashing strike on a bug generally fails to

243

connect and the same is often true of high-floating plugs.

Tarpon don't have much in the way of teeth but their mouths are extremely abrasive and soon wear through braided line or light mono. Casters should use leaders of wire or heavy monofilament about 10 inches long.

Casting for tarpon in open water usually involves drifting along in a small boat and either fishing "blind" or throwing to rolling fish. There are a number of fables regarding rolling fish. One of the most common is that "rolling tarpon won't strike." Occasionally they won't, but ordinarily I like to see them roll. There are some times when you have to cast right on a rolling fish to get results. On other occasions, fishing a shore line near surfacing fish may produce, although the ones that show themselves won't hit.

I have frequently had plenty of tarpon action at the mouth of a tributary canal on a small tidal river in south Florida. The fish usually come up on a rising tide and you could see them rolling on the way. However, they wouldn't strike until they reached the mouth of the canal. Repeatedly, I've tried to intercept them in a downstream bend with no success, but if I watched for them to show in the bend and then gave them time to reach the canal mouth I usually had action. It appeared to be a simple case of fish heading toward a feeding rendezvous and showing no interest in lures until they got there.

I've often found tarpon lying like logs on shallow mud banks in calm weather. Although they weren't interested in any lure that kicked up much fuss they would slowly take a streamer fly, sinking plug, or jig if it came close enough. When resting on the bottom, a tarpon lies with his undershot jaw parallel to the mud. That places his tail higher than his head. Generally, he's visible only as a vague shadow. At such times you will spook him if you make any boat noises and you'll generally have to make a pretty long cast.

In fishing flats such as in the Florida Keys or in some of the Bahamas, the fish can sometimes be seen lying in the deeper holes at low tide. Off Cuba's Isle of Pines I have seen a whole school of tarpon lying in a "blue hole" no more than 50 feet across. A properly presented plug would get immediate action. Of course, such fish are generally easily scared and the fun probably won't last long.

Occasionally a school of tarpon throws caution to the wind and will hit anything and everything and you can't scare them away. You explain it; I can't.

When it comes to phases of the moon and solunar tables, rigid rules are tough to make. In the first place, the tidal areas most frequently occupied by concentrations of fish probably fluctuate in depth, salinity, and movement more than any other fishing waters. A change of wind and low tide may transform a good tarpon area into a bare mud flat. One careful follower of solunar tables put it this way: "According to the book, high tide on this coast would be at noon. With a wind holding the tide back, it may be two hours late and the spot where I expect to fish is an hour later yet, simply because of intervening islands and narrow channels. Now, should I go by the time we should have the effects of a given tide according to the book, by the time the given tide should reach my fishing spot under normal conditions, or by the time it actually gets there?"

A real student of tide and other conditions on the Florida Keys bridges is so far ahead of other fishermen it's no contest. Since my experience there had been spotty, I asked Roy Martin about it. Martin, who has a house full of big fish trophies, is spectacularly successful on the Keys bridges. Roy has this to say:

"The first two hours of the incoming tide (moving from the Atlantic side to the Gulf side) is best. Night fishing is much more reliable than day fishing as the fish tend to roll at plugs but not take them in daylight. At night, they gobble them."

Martin says you should use as large a plug as your outfit will throw and he has counted as many as seven different fish striking on a single cast. He'd let the line go slack so each fish could throw the lure, and then resume his retrieve. He sets May 1 to June 15 as the best time in the Keys.

I've had some of that night fishing off those bridges and it was so much better than what I had during the daytime that I wonder why I haven't done night fishing more in other areas.

Tarpon don't like cold weather and they seldom like wind. A brief blow may put them down for days in some areas. I'm probably sticking my neck out on this but it seems to me that a little wind has more effect on small fish than on large ones.

Near Everglades, Florida, several years ago there were literally thousands of miniature tarpon, many less than a foot long. We caught them on fresh-water trout flies by the dozen. This lasted for only one season, and, usually, a tarpon less than 20 inches long is something of a rarity there. All this time, the supply of big fish remained fairly constant.

I have been in many an argument about the effects of boat movements on tarpon. I'm getting pretty pigheaded about it and these are my views: If the water is deep, navigation may have little or no effect. If it's shallow, constant traffic will drive them out.

Several tidal rivers that used to be prime tarpon fishing spots are no good any more since boat traffic has increased. You can "drive" a school of tarpon with a 3-horse outboard, just letting it idle, if the water is shallow. I've seen an old hand herd tarpon toward a deep hole where he expected them to stop. You could see them rolling ahead of his outboard as he idled along. Then, 100 yards from where he wanted to fish, he'd stop the motor, row up to the deep hole, and start hooking fish. Don't tell me they like engines they can get away from.

In shallow water, schools of big tarpon are sometimes located by "bumps." As you plane along in a fast outboard you can feel the "lift" as you go over a big fish. If you feel several such bumps you're probably in the midst of some outsized tarpon.

One other thing about tarpon. Residents of tarpon areas aren't nearly as eager for the big bruisers as you might expect. It probably comes from the fact that they're not much good to eat, but it is considered fashionable in Florida to say you'd rather not fool with tarpon and that the Silver King is really for tourists only. This is an attitude I can't seem to acquire after ten years of Florida residence. I'm still a tourist where tarpon are concerned.

How is the tarpon population holding up? Far as I know they're as plentiful as ever.

## Chapter Eighteen

# SALT-WATER FLY FISHING

## *by* JOE BROOKS

JOE BROOKS is well known for his angling exploits and for the populariz-
ing of fly fishing in salt water. Think of any worthwhile salt-water game
fish found in inshore waters and chances are good that Joe has caught it
on the fly rod. He has also caught some monster trout and bass on flies
or bugs, in fresh water. He travels all over the world seeking new species
to conquer, but returns regularly to his early favorites—the bonefish, the
tarpon, and the striped bass. A frequent contributor to the leading outdoor magazines, Joe Brooks is also the author of five books on fishing.
His *Salt-Water Fly Fishing* is the only book devoted entirely to this subject.

NOT many years ago the angler who took a fly rod into the
salt was regarded as something of an oddity, but in the past fifteen years the light wand has proven such an effective weapon
for so many kinds of ocean swimmers that today's roster of fish the
fly man may expect to take includes almost everything that swims
close enough to the surface that a fly can be put in front of it.
Because of certain peculiarities of habitat, feeding, or nature, the
bonefish, tarpon, striped bass, and snook top the list, but numerous others crowd them for popularity. The barracuda, ladyfish,
snappers, sea trout, and, over the deeps, such surface cruisers as
the dolphin, bonito, and small yellowfin tuna are ready hitters
to flies.

The bonefish is justly the most publicized of these salt-water
species. Fly fishermen go for them in water from 5 inches to 4
feet in depth. Where the bottom is sandy or hard, it is possible
to get them by wading, moving slowly with the tide or the wind,
because bonefish feed by smell and will usually be found work-

247

ing into the push of the water in order to pick up scents. The fly caster's aim is to put the fly in front of the fish. The sound of a fly falling behind it will send a bonefish flying for the deep without a backward look to see what caused that peculiar noise.

If you are fishing from a skiff, with a guide or a friend who is able to pole a boat quietly, then the operation is the same; you move with the water, meeting the bonefish as he comes uptide on the prowl for food. Since you are standing higher, it is easier to see bonefish from a skiff, but conversely it is also easier for them to see you and for this reason it is essential to get a cast off all the more quickly. Once a bonefish sees that foreign body known as a fisherman looming up in front of him, all deals are off. He may not bolt, but he will certainly make a big circle around you without showing the slightest interest in your well- but too late-presented fly.

The fish are more easily seen if you have the sun at your back so its rays pick out the darker shadow of the fish against the light bottom. And Polaroid glasses are almost a necessity, allowing you to see through the water and pick up moving fish far more quickly than with the naked eye.

There are three different ways in which bonefish may be spotted. In extremely shallow water their tails will appear above the surface, waving in the air as they feed, nose down in the mud or coral rocks. This is called "tailing" and sometimes they are in such thin water, 5 inches to a foot deep, that their backs will be completely out and you can almost see the entire fish as he wiggles across the flat. When bonefish are found in such water they are such wary, scary creatures that it takes the stealth and quiet of an Indian to get within range. They will spook at the line in the air or the motion of the caster's arm. The slightest noise will make them flush like quail. It takes more than average accuracy and skill to place the fly in just the right spot, lightly, so not to scare them. It takes a special retrieve to make them hit. And once all this has been achieved and you have a bonefish on, he treats you to a wild, headlong dash for the deep unparalleled in fishing, sometimes covering as much as 600 feet in a wild dash that leaves you hanging on the ropes.

Again, they may be feeding in water so deep that even when

Joe Brooks

249

Bonefish are sought by fly fishermen on the flats surrounding tropical isles. This is in the Bahamas, but our own Florida Keys offer good fishing at times for these elusive fish.

they stand on their heads their tails do not reach the surface, but as they blow into crab holes or nudge the sandy bottom after some tasty tidbit, they put up puffs of mud, a milky cloud that the bonefisherman soon learns to identify as "mudding" fish. In this situation they are not nearly as spooky as in the shallows and often it is possible to take several fish from such a school before they become suspicious and panic.

Yet again, bonefish may be seen swimming just under the surface, in great schools, pairs, triplets, or singly, sometimes lazing along, and at other times approaching like miniature torpedoes. In the latter case, it is particularly important to get the fly in front of them quickly, dropping it far enough ahead of the first fish so that it can be retrieved ahead of the school, always moving faster than the fish so that it will not be beside or behind them, lifeless, to be mistaken for some bit of drifting flotsam. If the fly is given the proper retrieve you can almost depend on a hit from each school that comes by.

Absolute quiet is essential when casting for bonefish. A school that is 100 feet away will bolt for the blue if the poling pole is dragged across a piece of coral rock. Drop a pin in the bottom of the skiff and fish you didn't even know were there will spook all around you. Flub a cast, then snatch the line noisily from the water to repeat, and the fish will be gone. Occasionally, on remote shores where there has been very little fishing, you may be lucky enough to encounter a few bonefish that are "tame" and will stay for a second cast. But it only takes a few encounters with anglers for them to become wise and wild, so it pays to start with the premise that all bonefish are always scared.

Flies for bonefish are tied on hooks from No. 6 for very shallow water to No. 2 for water from 1½ to 2½ feet deep, and a No. 1/0 for water over that depth. Best patterns are a 2-inch bonefish bucktail with red hackle and single wing of white deer hair; my own favorite, pink shrimp: and the Frankee-Belle, a combination streamer-bucktail. The fly should be retrieved in slow, foot-long jerks and if a fish follows, but seems reluctant to take, the retrieve can be broken up, slowed, stopped momentarily, then speeded up. Sometimes a quick, 6-inch jerk will settle the doubts in the mind of a reluctant follower and cause him to hit that thing that seems about to escape.

Tarpon, the Silver King of our southern waters, is another fish that might have been designed just for fly fishermen. They like flies better than any other lure and perhaps better even than bait. They seldom turn down a well-placed feathery fooler whether it be an underwater number or a surface bug.

You can take tarpon from canals, in bays and channels, over

the flats, and along the drop-offs. And regardless of where you find them you can be sure of a fight that will be an all-out, slam-bang, no-quarters-asked affair. One of the great sights in fishing is a tarpon in the air, mouth wide open, whole silver-clad body atwist, as he reaches for the sun or the moon, as the case may be.

Tarpon were among the first salt-water fish to be taken on flies when migrating anglers discovered Florida. They went for them with the same tackle they had used up north for large-mouthed black bass, plug larger editions of the same flies. Practically the same tackle is used today, the only variation being a stronger hook and a fairly consistent fly pattern—the breather-

Baby tarpon like this little fellow often provide fast action for fly-rod anglers. They are found in canals, rivers, and creeks.

PINK
SHRIMP

MULTI-WING STREAMER

HONEY BLONDE BUCKTAIL

POPPER

Favorite salt-water flies

type fly, also called the multiwing streamer. These flies have three or four saddle hackles tied on each side of the hook shank, placed so that the feathers flare outward. When the angler pulls on his line, retrieving in slow, foot-long strips, the feathers close

253

in on the hook. When he stops the strip, they flare out again. A series of such strips brings the fly along opening and closing in a breathing motion that gives them their descriptive name. And that lifelike breathing is what appeals to the tarpon as he pops his scales trying for the fly.

Other great tarpon flies are the all-yellow No. 3/0 honey blond and the all-white 3/0 platinum blond. These flies have two bucktail wings tied on top of the hook, one just back of the eye and the other at the bend of the hook. As with the breathers, a foot-long strip will make the bucktail close in on the hook and when the retrieve is stopped it will open again. Tarpon from 50 to 100 pounds will powder these flies. Rocky Weinstein of Everglades, Florida, also ties an all-blue streamer that really make tarpon drool, using a No. 1/0 hook for the smaller fish and a 3/0 for the larger.

The tarpon is just as enthusiastic about a fly rod popper in certain circumstances as he is about big flies, and again the action is important. The popper is dropped on the water and given a smart pop by pulling back with the rod tip, then is left still on the surface for perhaps half a minute, then given another pop, another half-minute rest, another pop and another rest, then popped all the way in. Often a tarpon will follow such a retrieve, interested but not quite willing to hit. Each time he turns away, another of those little pops will bring him 'round and eventually he can't resist it any longer.

Frequently when a tarpon loops up and takes, his mouth is wide open and too quick a strike will pull the popper away before he can clamp down on it so the strike should be delayed a bit, to give him time to turn and start down. However, baby tarpon, those weighing up to 20 pounds, are extremely fast on the hit and you have to strike at the flash of silver as they come up or they will take momentarily, eject the popper, and be gone. It is especially good fun fishing for these babies in roadside canals or in the narrow channels among the Keys. Among many such waterways in Florida the angler can stand on the road and cast across the canal, dropping the fly as close to the mangroves as possible, allowing it to sink a bit if it's an underwater fly, or rest if it's a popper, then bring it back. Repeated casts to the same spot will often bring out reluctant fish and the noise of the fly slapping down hard on the surface may also attract a lurking school whose curiosity gets the better of them. Once they have seen the fly, they will have a go at it.

Fly-rod men soon learn to drop the rod tip when a tarpon jumps, because tarpon are heavy, their scales are rough, and all together they are well equipped to slice or shatter a leader tippet when they fall on one, or fray through it with their rough mouths.

Often a hooked tarpon in a canal will fling itself high in the air and come a cropper in the mangroves. It's quite a thrill to see your hooked fish fly up in the trees, hang first from one limb, then another, and so drop into the water, leaving the broken, hookless leader hanging in the branches. Again, a wild-leaping tarpon may jump on shore, and then the angler makes haste to get the hook out and return the gallant fighter to the water. Tarpon are for sport, as are bonefish, they are not good to eat, and they should be returned unharmed to the water unless you want to keep one for a mount or perhaps an extra big one for entry in a tournament.

Those extra big ones, while hardly classifiable as "fly rod fish," provide one of the great challenges of the salt. To go out in a skiff on one of the "lakes" in the midst of the bonefish flats in Florida Bay and see a school of 70- to 100-pound giant tarpon making a daisy chain across the shallows, to cast a big breather fly or a flashy popper in front of them and see one of those monsters, as long as your skiff, come up, take, and when you strike, head for the sky, fall back in with a splash that displaces the whole bay, and then head for the horizon, stripping your reel as he goes—this is one of those moments that makes even bone-fishing seem tame. And though your chances of landing that horse of a fish are one in a hundred, you get in there and fight, till at last he leaps again, far out, throws the hook or cuts the leader, and leaves you with one of the greatest memories of all time.

The snook is another southern fish found in most canals and rivers and along the shores of bays and islands, in waters ideal for the fly fisherman. Sometimes old rogue snook cruise the ca-

255

nals just under the surface, putting up a wake that is easily spotted. Then anglers cast just ahead of the swimmer and if there is no hit they run ahead again and cast again, and it is a common sight to see half a dozen anglers running full pelt along the canal bank, casting, retrieving, running, casting, retrieving, all desperately trying for the big leviathan. Snook up to 28 pounds have been taken by such anglers in canals in south Florida.

They also have a habit of nosing into brackish and even fresh water and are often found where fresh-water rivers pour into the salt, savoring a little of both. In such places, for instance around the mouths of Lostmans and Shark River in the Everglades section of Florida, fly casters often find good fishing for snook around the many oyster bars at the river mouths.

In many ways the snook is a lot like an exaggerated large-mouthed black bass. He hits a popper in much the same way, only he's a hundred times more bombastic and he fights with a hundred times the gusto. He's bigger, too, long, lean, and mean, with a very black lateral line down his side to identify him, and a knifelike cutting edge on his gill covers or cheeks that can play havoc with leader or fingers.

The snook is inclined to feed best at dusk or dawn, preferring to lurk in the shade of the mangroves during the heat of the day. But even then he will sometimes come out to a well-placed streamer fly, again a breather type, 4 to 5 inches long, red and yellow or red and white, and occasionally all blue. Hooks for these run from 1/0 to as high as 3/0, the latter making a good all-round snook fly because the weight of the hook gets the fly down when the snook are resting deep.

Along the shores of islands, the fly fisherman seeks his snook in much the same way he would fish for fresh-water bass, casting close along the shore, into the shadows laid by logs or bushes, close to stumps, and working the fly or popper carefully all the way back to the skiff, for Mr. Snook may follow it home.

In canals, snook will often herd a school of minnows against the bank and strike into them with open mouth, inhaling a dozen at a time. This kind of feeding is easily spotted by the loud, slashing slurp the fish makes with each new foraging attack. This is one time when "match the hatch" applies in salt water. A small

A rambunctious snook slugs it out with a fly rodder in Florida's Tamiami Trail Canal. Surprisingly big snook are often found in these narrow waters.

fly tied to imitate the little minnow will get better results than will the big breather flies. The choice fly is a 1½-inch white bucktail on a No. 1/0 hook. It is cast across the canal to the spot where the fish is feeding, allowed to sink, and then is brought back in slow pulls, and if he's around, the snook will snatch at

257

that minnow and you have him on. Which is not necessarily the same as landing him, but at least you have a chance.

A welcome addition to the fly fisher's list in more northern waters is the striped bass, or "rock fish" as they are called in Virginia and the Carolinas. Throughout their habitat, from Cape Cod to northern Florida, and on the West Coast from California to Oregon, this rambunctious breed are ready hitters of flies and fly-rod poppers. You can usually find them in the shallows of the bays, as you walk the banks of salty guts in the marshes, or push along in a skiff, casting to undercut banks and sand bars. That's where you get the larger ones, running up to 10 or even 15 pounds, as they nose into holes or probe the grasses for crabs and shrimp.

The way a striper swirls under a popper, refuses, then comes back and swirls again, moving the water up in a big bulge, and finally takes with a *whoomph*, is enough to give you a heart attack and makes this one of the favorite ways of going for the species. But they also hit big streamers and bucktails with abandon, showing a preference for big juicy ones as much as 5 inches long, tied full, like the platinum blond and the breather flies mentioned for tarpon and snook. They like these retrieved in slow, foot-long strips, increasing in speed as the fly nears the boat. Often a fish will hit just as you raise the fly from the water.

School stripers can often be spotted out in the bays, slashing and splashing after baitfish with the complete abandon of an abnormally healthy appetite. Experienced striper men always keep an eye cocked for diving, screaming gulls as they gather over such a school to share in the feed. Then the technique is to run out toward the school, get ahead of them, kill the motor so as not to scare the fish, then cast into the school when it is within range. Even with such care it is usually possible to take only a couple from each school before they become suspicious and sound. Then you wait until they come up again, once more run around them and ahead, cut the motor and cast. Stripers are scarier than most anglers seem to think, and at all times a quiet approach is more likely to get you fish.

When stripers are found in rivers, as for instance the Susquehanna and Potomac in Maryland, and the Mattaponi and others in Virginia, it pays to fish the river pools just as you would a salmon pool. Start the fly or popper at the head of the pool, casting across the current and working the fly back. Then extend each cast a couple of feet until you have covered the water for about 70 feet out plus the corresponding distance your fly has been swept down by the current. Then move halfway down the pool and repeat. In this way you are pretty sure that you are showing that fly to any striper that may be in the pool.

Of the other salty fish which may be taken consistently enough to be classified as fly-rod fish, the barracuda is one of the sportiest and most underrated. A 10-pound barracuda will run 150 yards, jump 20 feet across the surface. Like the bonefish, you usually see and cast directly to him, but unlike the bonefish you can sometimes tease a barracuda into a strike. They like the fastest retrieve you can possibly impart to that fly or popper and they may refuse it for half a dozen casts, then suddenly, red-eyed and mean as a mad Jersey bull, dash out and slash at it with lightning speed. This is particularly true if a loud-talking surface fooler is tossed out time and again and popped hard, 5 or 6 times. Eventually temper will get the best of that barracuda and he'll go for it. Of course, many times cudas will cut through the leader, because they hit at the head of the fly and their long snouts are armed with sharp, slotted teeth that can cut anything but wire. But the game is worth the risk, and after a few encounters with cuda on your fly rod you'll try for every one met.

Another great salty battler is the ladyfish, a leaping, gyrating bundle of energy often found around bridges when the tide is running out, or in channels where they wait for the outgoing tides to bring foodstuffs to them. Sometimes you can also find them by casting "blind" as your skiff drifts across a grassy flat.

Because they are mostly nocturnal feeders, ladyfish are not encountered as often as they should be, according to their number and wide disposition in southern waters. But when you do find them you'll remember them for their leaps, fantastic displays in mid-air, and the exceptional runs the larger fish make. Ladyfish like the conventional salt-water streamers and bucktails in red and white, retrieved in fast jerks, and they are particularly fond of poppers. A popper should be thrown uptide, popped once, then allowed to sit on the surface, drifting with the current. Ninety-five per cent of the strikes will come while the popper is thus lying still. But it's that first pop that gets the eye of the passing lady.

Spotted sea trout are also good fly-rod fish and when you find them on the grassy flats you can have a field day with No. 1/0 multiwing streamers or a popper. The popper should be played very slowly, hardly moving, with long rests between pops, while the streamer is also handled slowly at first, but with increasing speed as it nears the boat. In some areas, as for instance, Cocoa, Florida, the sea trout grow very large. Many 6-pounders are taken, and some of 8, 10, and even 12 pounds.

Channel bass or redfish also range the shallows within reach of the fly rodder. They will hit either popper or streamer. Since they are a little short-sighted, the fly must be dropped, or rather banged down, hard and close to get their attention so they know where to focus those blurry eyes. Though nothing like as sensational as bonefish, they sometimes feed in the same way, tailing up on the flats to provide an exciting target. In Florida the channel bass range from 2 to 25 pounds in weight and will run a good 100 yards when hooked and also have a disconcerting habit of nosing down in the bottom, trying to rub the hook out.

Sharing the flats and shallows of the southern salt are many sharks, several species of which offer good fly-rod targets. The bonnet shark and the blacktip both take a fly and make runs of as much as 200 yards, and the blacktip is also a flashy jumper. Almost any fly will attract them, even a popper, the main thing being to drop the fly right on their noses, because like the channel bass they are quite blind.

Offshore there are many fish which can be taken on flies. Now and again a charter boat will run into a school of bonito or tuna and a fly dropped in front of them will get a strike. The flashy and beautiful dolphin is a fly taker from away back. A 5-pounder will give an aerial display you'll never forget and a 20-pounder will keep you busy for an hour. They will hit bucktails, streamers, and popping bugs and the best part of this species is that they come in schools and you can guarantee yourself good fishing for quite a while by the simple expedient of hooking a fish on trolling gear and leaving it in the water. The others in the school will swim right along with it and when you cast a fly to them, they will take.

One outfit will do the whole salt-water fly fishing job, a 9- or 9½-foot, slow-action rod, a GAF fly line and a reel big enough to take the line plus 200 yards of 18-pound test nylon squidding line backing. I prefer the 9½-foot stick because you can get off a better back cast with the longer rod, you can play the fly better in shallow water, and you can raise the line higher when the fish is running, thus often avoiding getting caught on underwater obstacles and possibly ending up with a broken leader. The slow-action rod also has the advantage over fast action because it requires fewer false casts to get line out, an all important point when you are casting to an approaching fish. It also has the temperament to "wait" for the large, wind resistant streamers and bugs used in the salt. These flies take a considerable time to make their way out to the full extent of the back cast. With a fast rod, the forward action starts too soon and the fly caught still moving back on a loose line collapses somewhat on the forward throw.

The GAF line is also adapted to the salt-water atmosphere. With this line, if the caster remembers to bring his forward cast down hard and low he can shoot those big lures right out into a pretty fair wind.

For salt-water fly fishing the leader should be 10 or 12 feet long and tapered from a 30-pound test butt section down through 25-, 20-, 15-, and 12-pound test to the required tippet. For some species such as the suspicious bonefish, this tippet should be no heavier than 8-pound test and on flats where there are not many obstructions you can go as low as 6 and get more hits. In fact, with bonefish you will get twice as many hits on a 6-pound test tippet as you will on a 12.

There are a few other points about tackle that every fly fisherman should keep in mind when going to fish the salt. In the South, for instance, there are many tournaments, such as the Metropolitan Miami Fishing Tournament, and most of them allow only single-action fly reels, so it's wise to choose your reel accordingly, because someday you may want to enter an especially good catch. Also many tournaments now provide two classes of competition for fly men, one known as "light fly," which means the traditionally accepted outfit in which your tippet is the lightest part of your equipment, and another, called "heavy fly," in which a length of wire leader or a section of extra-heavy nylon is permitted. With these heavy tippets you can land tarpon as heavy as 100 pounds, because in the case of the tarpon it is the fraying through the leader that causes most lost fish, rather than leader breakage. The wire will also save you many flies when fishing for barracuda, bluefish, mackerel, or snook. However, unless you are definitely out for a tournament fish in the heavy classification, there's a lot more sport in the traditional tackle.

*Chapter Nineteen*

# CALIFORNIA YELLOWTAIL AND ALBACORE FISHING

*by* CLAUDE M. KREIDER

CLAUDE M. KREIDER of Long Beach, California, covers almost the entire Pacific Coast, dashing off to Mexico or up to Oregon and Washington in search of fresh- and salt-water fish. In recent years he has devoted much of his time to catching the gamey yellowtail and the albacore from the party boats on light tackle. He likes to make his own fishing tackle and to experiment with rod, reel, and line combinations. He writes for many outdoor magazines and has also written books such as *Steelhead* and another on making fishing rods. He is at present angling editor of *Western Outdoors,* a Southern California monthly magazine.

$A$SK any salt-water devotee along the California south coast to name our sportiest game fish, and the answer, most surely, will be "the yellowtail." A speedy and tough brawler, this great member of the far-flung *Jack* family, he is also canny and ultra-smart, always a challenge to the experienced angler, often frustrating for the new hand.

Certainly, in this reporter's opinion, the sporty "yellow" rates as leader of the "big three" including the albacore and school bluefin tuna, sought by countless sportsmen on the charter and party boats plying from the Long Beach–Los Angeles area down the coast to San Diego and into Mexican waters.

Highly predatory, through most of the season demanding a live, fast-swimming sardine or anchovy bait, often extremely boat-shy and usually already well fed after raiding the natural bait schools, this beautiful battler presents problems. His keen eyesight can detect a tiny No. 2 hook, a telltale swivel, or small sinker. Thus, we fish him with hook tied directly to clear or mist-colored monofilament as light as 12- or 15-pound test.

But the necessary light tackle adds zest to the sport, and there's just no fishing thrill to compare with that savage strike, the sizzling of line through the guides, and the vibrating arc of the long, supple rod as that wild bronco tears out to sea. Far out in the blue wavelets your fish will stop to chug and "bulldog." You gingerly set the drag a bit tighter, hoping to recover precious line. Then, he's off again.

A long series of careful pumpings will follow, broken now by shorter, deep-down charges before your fish will really tire and be in to the gaff. A half hour for a 20- or 25-pounder on light monofilament is about par for the course.

The use of live bait, carried in quantity in a big tank of circulating water, is the secret for successful fishing: the ideal combination, ample anchovies for chum and lively sardines of about 6-inch size for bait.

The great schools of yellows usually appear in spring first in San Diego waters, coming north with the warming currents from their breeding grounds along a thousand miles of the Baja California peninsula. At first, hungry and "uneducated," they may prove "easy," but soon will have learned all about the fishing craft scouting the waters up the coast and across the channel to famed Catalina and more distant San Clemente Islands.

The past two seasons, with warm year-round water temperatures on the coast, a certain number of yellowtail seem to have remained. And the appearance of many small ones may indicate they have actually spawned in local waters.

Standard tackle for many anglers, and my own choice, is a whippy glass rod of 9½ feet with flexible tip section for easy casting of a light bait; a star-drag reel holding at least 250 yards of line (12- to 20-pound test) and a supply of short-shank "Eagle Claw" hooks in sizes No. 1 to 6. The latter are really of freshwater "trout size."

The mere proper hooking of the sardine is important. Through the bony part of the nose lets him swim without harm. But first, it is essential to choose an offering from the tank that *will* dash away in lively fashion. And the cast should be high—and far out— reel in free spool, of course, the little fish not "spatting" the water, but simply dropping in, unharmed by shock.

Claude M. Kreider

Long whippy rods will send a small bait far out, and their constant arc helps whip the big fish.

With a school of yellows boiling up far astern for the chum, it is the best caster who first "hooks up," can shout out his ringing, "fish on!" And for extremely boat-shy yellowtail, hanging far out beyond the best possible cast with the conventional revolving spool reel, I've found the large salt-water spinning reel ideal; it is capable of a long cast with even a little 1-ounce anchovy.

Normally, a sinker is unnecessary, generally a handicap, as it slows the bait's swimming speed. Yet at times, when the fish are hanging deep, a half-ounce of lead, clamped a few feet above the bait, helps take it down to the fish level. Then, if no takers on a "free-swimming" bait, a short, jerky retrieve will sometimes spur up the predatory instinct—and you've a fierce yellowtail going places fast. Then, over a rocky bottom or kelp bed, and you hope to apply sufficient pressure to keep that sounding demon above the hazards, still without breaking him off.

Thus, to know the potential of each rod–line combination, I've found it wise to run tests first in my workshop, end of line through rod guides and to a spring scales, rod flexed to under the line-breaking point, a reading taken; then a similar test without scales to know the "feel" (noting rod arc) that is still safe.

It is these "little things," apparently minor as viewed by the tyro, that put fish in the sack. And invariably, when you hear that dismal pop of a break-off aboard your boat, it will be due to a reel drag too tightly set by the excited new hand.

Always we learn new tricks from the veteran skippers, who come to almost "think like a fish." There's the occasion when we know the school is deep, and when a sinker will not do. Then we've found that a hook inserted just under the sardine's pectoral fin, and the little fish not cast, but just dropped overside, will cause him to swim straight down; and often right into the wide mouth of a hungry yellow. This "blind" fishing can be a lot of fun, too. While it lacks the excitement of watching a school of surface raiders sweeping in to the chum, there's the element of the unknown, for down deep can be the wise old "mossbacks," battle-scarred veterans of 30—even 40 pounds—who have festooned many a weary angler's broken gear over the bottom kelp.

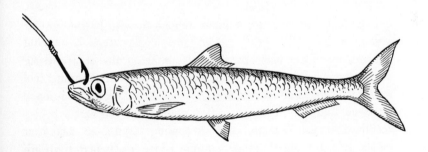

Hooking sardine through nose for yellowtail

Live bait is all-important in yellowtail and albacore fishing. It is seined by bait-haulers at night, then transferred to party and charter boats in the harbor.

And occasionally—we never know when—an epic battle can be imminent.

Then, there are ways of simply tantalizing the sporty jacks into striking artificial lures. The scene, perhaps, the calm, blue waters off the Coronado Islands, out of San Diego. Two score boats out that day, all distributing chum, plus the bait schools, will have the fish "fed up," and just loafing down deep. This can be the time for "jig slinging," a game I love for its fast, frenzied action. Up on the bow for a free cast that will not endanger other anglers, a 3-ounce jig of chrome or white, or variously painted metal, is sent as far out as a fairly powerful rod can cast

it.

Permitted to sink a moment to what we hope is the "fish level," the lure is retrieved like mad; and a specially high-geared reel is almost essential. That flashing, erratic action can awake the yellows from their noonday siesta—and the resulting strike is simply dynamite. Nothing less than 25-pound test monofilament for this game, else tribulation. Each season the moody fish seem to want a different pattern of jig, and all others will be useless.

Then, the old-time skippers swear "it's the action that counts," which I believe. A dozen lures of the same make and pattern, and just one will take fish. The balance, or special attractive wobble in that one lure will make it priceless, and its eventual loss a real tragedy.

Come autumn, and the squid sometimes appear in great numbers—great food for the hungry yellow, easy to secure. Then he wants nothing else. We hope for a supply of freshly seined members of this strange jet-propelled clan, but can do even with frozen ones, for the yellowtail just becomes "squid happy." Fished with No. 1, even 1/0 hook, permitted to sink, then retrieved up fast, and here's sport approximating that with the flashing jigs.

Always, we hope for the real giants of yellows, not of the current schools, but "loners" living deep along the island cliffs. Then, we save a few pound-size mackerel, perhaps taken in the harbor around the bait receivers, and fish this bait deep on husky tackle. Then, once in a blue moon lady luck smiles, and we come ashore with a 35- to 45-pound monster which can justify a little bragging.

Each season a few such big fellows come to "the faithful," and those of 50 pounds are not unknown. Then, if you want to specialize on the grandpas of the clan, there are specially equipped boats taking limited parties for a week or so down to Mexico's great Guadalupe Island, some thirty hours journey to the south. Up-welling currents here off that rocky, submerged mountain chain, and in them a wealth of baitfish which attract the predators. A yellowtail of 35 pounds is common there, and monsters of 80 pounds have come to rugged anglers.

Here in these fertile waters can be almost "anything," and that unseen monster which strips your reel of heavy line *can* be a yellow of record class, but more likely is a 150-pound yellowfin tuna. The record yellowtail came from the Gulf of California, weight 105 pounds; and there are still larger to be caught, I feel confident.

By contrast with the island and coast-hugging yellowtail, the migrating albacore wanders over the entire Pacific, his range so wide, breeding habits and rate of growth so little known, even to the enquiring marine biologists, he is well-called "the fish of mystery." Often designated the long-fin tuna because of their long pectoral fins, and distinctly of the tuna family, these blue and purple migrants with burnished skins, are game fish to reckon with when they visit coastal waters.

A big albacore comes in over the bow after a fierce battle. Many are lost when excited anglers fear a stripped reel, set the drag too tightly.

Some summers the albacore do not show at all—at least within reach of sport fishing boats—although the commercials may find the huge schools far at sea. They are intolerant of water warmer than about 66°; thus last season, with warm waters inshore, the great migration swung far out. But out in "the blue" 100 miles offshore, great milling schools of literally thousands of fish enticed us there in overnight voyages in the larger, well-equipped craft.

And I know no greater angling thrill than, after a night's sleep on the gently-rocking 85-foot *Falcon*, out of Long Beach Pierpoint Landing (my favorite albacore boat last summer), to awaken with the fading stars, hurry on deck, and watch for the first splash astern to indicate a longfin has taken the trolled feather jig.

A sure way of locating the surging schools, this 6-knot trolling.

A 20-pound yellowtail comes over the rail at North Coronado Island, out of San Diego.

It covers a lot of water, will raise the fish most surely when you do find them. And then, with luck, huge excitement. There's just "something" about this albacore quest to cause you to forget breakfast—even that first heartening cup of coffee.

Thus, a typical July morning, after the first tremendous schools have been reported to us by short wave from the commercial trollers, Bill Nott, our fish-wise host from the Landing, yelled, hauled in the handline with a surging longfin thrashing on the Japanese feather jig. Jim, our bait tender, ready at his big tank, ladled out anchovies in the wake.

Ready, with long rod, I gill-hooked a little 'chovy, sent it out into the first angry boil. A terrific strike, and my first "alby" of the season was going places—fast. That initial run is so powerful, you simply hang on, drag set at moderate pressure, and wait. At 200 yards the fish stopped, to dive and chug; another savage run, and I applied a bit of pressure. And it was 20 minutes later before that 30-pound bundle of dynamite was in to the gaff.

And our dozen other yelling enthusiasts were all "hooked up" before my fish was decked. At my elbow, Bill Strachen, our marvelous chef. "Just as well fish too," chuckled Bill, "these guys have forgotten my ham and eggs, hot cakes and biscuits. They're going to waste—and who cares?" Bill at that moment had a charging demon of a fish of his own to worry about.

Now those fish were wild, taking a bait right on the surface without a second glance as to telltale hook or heavy line—although most of us used monofilament of 20-pound test. How different from the usual schools of educated yellowtail. And we held the school for two hours, with several of our most diligent experts sacking up their legal limits of ten fish.

Then, perhaps well-fed with chum, the blue torpedoes became quite "choosy," and I resorted to my favorite long, supple spin rod with big salt-water winch and 15-pound test line. They were lying well out, but a long cast with a darting anchovy, and a free-swimming bait still had its customers. I watched for the next "boil," ready to put a bait right there—just like dry fly fishing for trout. And thirty minutes registered on my watch before the next wild one—of 35 pounds—was ready for the gaff.

Perhaps the real charm of albacore fishing is in the mystery of it all. From whence did they come—where do they go? Fish have been tagged by the Department of Fish and Game biologists off Catalina Island, one recovered off Japan 197 days later, having logged 5700 miles had he traveled straight-line! This is an average of almost thirty miles per day, not counting necessary forays for feeding on that long journey.

Other tagged albacore have been taken off the Midway Island, indicating perhaps that their "great circle" route of the Pacific may sometimes be circumscribed to a greater or lesser extent. And always, when they do appear in our waters, the initial schools will come within a week or two of July 1, without fail. And some seasons their stay off Southern California ports will be brief, with one great school replacing another in rapid succession. Then, as if by signal, all are gone, to be reported by commercial craft off San Francisco's Golden Gate, the mouth of the Columbia River, and off the Oregon and Washington coasts as far north as the Strait of Juan de Fuca.

Locally, we find the longfins' moods change from day to day. The weaving jigs will pick up a few strays, and the schools apparently scorn us. Again, we sight them—a welter of churning splashes far across the heaving swells, as they raid the bait schools —and only a fast boat will be able to head them off. Then, with the jigs cunningly swung ahead of the leaders, we're in business, with heavy chumming holding the fish until all anglers are fighting those flashing torpedoes.

And not always will "just any" jig bring in the initial customers. One day it must be of all-white feathers, with chrome head and a big glass eye. Next time, red and white will be the proper lure —and another day there must be blue in that weaving attractor. And I've come to always put out a brand new jig—hoping for the right color combination—as disarranged feathers seem to be refused in nearly every instance. The albacore's huge eye is, indeed, all-seeing.

We have learned, too, that the fish may swim at various levels. Some days on the calm waters, not a splash to be seen, nor a single taker of our surface-trolled jigs. Then, we stop and drift, put out a live bait with a 2-ounce sinker, let it down a hundred feet or more—and wait.

This is as slow and tiresome as catfishing in a farm pond, until a deep school of fish is located! Then, perhaps a dozen hookups at once—your alby is one to follow the leader—and the sport is breath-taking. And always grand sport on light tackle, the albacore, for there's hundreds of fathoms of blue water below, no danger when he sounds. On light tackle, such as the salt-water spin gear, and perhaps 15-pound test line, you may thrill to that vibrating, deeply arched rod as long as you like, its constant pressure finally whipping this marvelous adversary.

All solid meat, the longfin, to be put in the deepfreeze at home for later baking, garnished with tomato sauce; or smoked with orange or corn cobs to golden tan, and served with an *hors d'oeuvre* lunch, with a mug of foaming brew to supplement the whole. And the housewife, with her pressure cooker, may can the delicious meat to equal, or surpass, the commercial tuna sold in millions of cans each year.

A perpetual challenge, this great game fish, coming from "nowhere," disappearing into the blue, and those golden days of midsummer, far out on the heaving Pacific, never to be forgotten. Then, with the mysterious travelers gone for a year, there's still the yellowtail coming up the coast, to occupy us. And they, kings of all the *JACK* family, may, and often do, stay on until winter.

## Chapter Twenty

# CATCHING SWORDFISH AND GIANT TUNA

## by CAPTAIN FRANK T. MOSS

CAPTAIN FRANK T. MOSS came to Montauk, New York, in 1938, after five years of cruising the oceans of the world with the U. S. Merchant Marine. World War II saw him in service with the U. S. Navy and when it ended he returned to Montauk in 1946. He acquired a boat, the *KUNO*, and a reputation for returning to the dock with fine catches of striped bass, tuna, swordfish, and other salt-water species. Until recently Frank helped his customers catch these fish from his second charter boat, the *KUNO II*, and in his spare time wrote about fishing and boating. Frank now devotes all his time to writing. His work has appeared in many national magazines.

U NTIL the summer of 1958, the broadbill swordfish was probably the least understood of our great game fish. Some writers called him the most ferocious and powerful fish in any ocean. Others, just to be contrary, swore he was an old boot on the end of a line.

Between the time William Boschen caught the first swordfish with rod and reel off Catalina Island in 1913, and the end of the summer of 1957, fewer than 600 broadbill had been taken by anglers throughout the world. Those who caught them consistently were a close-mouthed crew, chary of sharing their tricky secrets.

Then, in the summer of 1958, a growing competitive urge to master these frustrating fish, fostered by sportsmen and boat owners on eastern Long Island, sparked a break-through in commonly understood baiting techniques. As a result, more than 400 swordfish were caught by anglers in the next three summers within the area bounded by Long Island and Cape Cod.

The swordfisherman's troubles begin with trying to find a fish. You don't just go out in the ocean and start fishing. You have to locate a swordfish visually before you can present the bait. Fortunately, good swordfishing areas exist not more than thirty miles from shore all along the coastal sweep of ocean extending eastward from Shinnecock Inlet on Long Island, past Montauk and Block Island to Cape Cod.

The first migratory invasion of swordfish into coastal waters begins in May and builds up to a climax early in July. Successive waves of fish keep anglers busy well into September.

Traditionally, swordfish are described as being located when lookouts spot their high, black, recurving dorsal and tail fins on the surface. In reality at least half of all broadbill taken commercially and many caught by anglers are found cruising a few feet under the surface. Spotting underwater fish requires a mast or elevated lookout tower. An underwater swordfish appears as an elongated chocolate-purple blob, quite distinct in the lighter blue or blue-green of the water in which he swims.

After a swordfish has been located, a baiting technique is followed that must be described in some detail to be understood. Exotic baits like flying fish, ballyhoo, and southern mullet are effective on broadbill, but perhaps the most abundant and popular bait is fresh, native squid, prepared in this manner:

Take a fresh squid about a foot long and run a 15-foot leader up through the envelope and out through a tiny slit in the pointed tail. The hook can be a 10/0 or 12/0 Sobey, Martu, or Sea Demon model, chosen to match the size of the bait. Bury the hook in the body of the squid with the point and barb projecting through the flesh for quick penetration. Sew the hook and leader into place and sew the squid head to the body with a loop of thread. If two hooks are used, place one in the body of the squid and the other in the head.

Swordfish rarely rise to a trolled bait in the manner of marlin. The bait is normally placed in the water only after a swordfish has been located and the baiting pass started. The boat is maneuvered at a speed of about 5 knots so as to pass in front of the swordfish at a distance of 60 to 90 feet. As the boat comes abreast of the fish, the bait is dropped from the cockpit into the water and about 60 feet of line paid out. The bait is towed in front of the fish, not skipping, but slightly underwater.

Captain Frank T. Moss

A fresh rigged native squid makes a top bait for swordfish. Here the hook is an 11/0 Sea Demon model and the leader 15 feet of No. 12 stainless steel wire. (*Dave Edwardes*)

A swordfish has a big eye and good vision. Little escapes his notice in the water. Lookouts watch the fish closely as the bait approaches and the instant the fish is seen to turn and start for the bait an "assisted drop-back" is started. This enables the fish to pick up a motionless bait, greatly increasing the chances of a successful strike. It is accomplished this way:

The angler sits in the fighting chair with the reel in the free-spool position. He holds his gloved left hand lightly on the spool to prevent a backlash. The mate or an assistant hauls line down from the tip of the rod into the water as the boat moves slowly away from the fish, working against the pressure of the angler's hand on the spool.

Stripping of the line into the water continues until it is evident that the fish has picked up the bait, or until the nerves of the

Fighting a giant tuna or a swordfish often results in a long, grueling battle with little or no rest for the angler.

crew can't stand the waiting any longer. Then, when it seems time to strike the fish, the angler engages the gears and star drag and the boat operator guns the boat ahead for a short spurt so the angler can strike the hook home against a tight line.

If the fish has been hooked, he is fought in the manner of any big, active fish. If he isn't hooked, don't give up in disgust. Circle back quickly and prepare a fresh bait. You may get a second crack at him.

Swordfish seem to like fresh squids that retain the ink and oil of the live animal. Don't wash squid baits after rigging them. Pack them in individual Saran plastic bags to keep the flesh of the bait from contact with the ice in the bait box. File the points of hooks needle-sharp. Make sure you have at least four rigged baits ready to use and more squid in the box that can be rigged at sea.

The leader can be either cable-laid stainless material in the 180- to 250-pound class, or solid wire in sizes from No. 10 to No. 13. Don't place a big swivel on the end of the leader. Make a small, strong wire loop instead and put a stout stainless steel snap swivel on the end of the fishing line to permit quick changing of baits.

A representative outfit for Atlantic swordfish is a 12/0 reel loaded with 130-pound test linen or synthetic line, mounted on a 24-ounce Fiberglas tip. Many experts won't bait a broadbill with line of more than 80 pounds breaking strain, while others use 50-pound IGFA tournament tackle. A person seeking his first swordfish, however, can be excused for preferring heavier equipment.

Auxiliary equipment includes a good fighting harness, a fighting chair with adjustable foot rest, a flying gaff, tail rope, and gin pole for lifting big fish into the boat. The boat should have a flying bridge, and a mast or tower is a great help in spotting underwater fish.

Success in swordfishing depends on individual skill and also on competent teamwork between the guests and the crew. While searching for fish, many skippers have their anglers run a rotation system of short watches on the swordfish rod. This equalizes the chances of baiting a fish.

Swordfish do not travel in compact schools like tuna, but they do move in great, loose groups. Where one is sighted there are often more. One real secret of successful swordfishing is to exercise restraint when tempted to steam away from a known, productive area, especially when nothing much has happened for quite a while. Such a spot is the well-known Butterfish Hole, nine miles south-southeast of Montauk Light.

Along the western side of the hole there is an underwater bank that is easy to spot with an electronic sounding machine. During the summer this bank swarms with schools of whiting, red hake, and butterfish. Knowledgeable swordfish congregate here to stuff and wax fat. At intervals during the day bunches of these sword-

Joseph R. Morton came all the way from North Carolina to catch this 324-pound swordfish on Capt. Frank Moss's boat. Recent advances in fishing techniques have greatly increased the number of swordfish taken by sportsmen using rod and reel. (*Canadian Gov. Travel Bureau*)

fish rise to the surface to sun themselves, and, it is said, to burp. As many as twenty swordfish have been baited, hooked, harpooned, and variously molested in as many minutes within a three-mile circle when the fish have decided to show.

The biggest swordfish ever taken by rod and reel was a 1182-pound monster caught off the Chilean coast in 1953 by the famed sportsman, Lou Marron. Atlantic swordfish are smaller, averaging about 300 pounds. Only a few fish under 100 pounds or over 500 have been taken by anglers. However, the accessibility of northeastern broadbill to centers of population in the New York–New England area has made them increasingly popular with a rapidly growing fraternity of ocean game fishermen.

Sportsmen have discovered in the swordfish a robust, contrary, hard-fighting adversary whose capture is one of the great challenges of the deep. When a fisherman takes a broadbill swordfish with rod and reel it is no ordinary fishing event. It signifies a unique personal and collective victory in what has been described as the most difficult and frustrating type of big game fishing in the world.

It is often difficult to explain to nonfishing observers the fascination the giant bluefin tuna holds for some salt-water sportsmen.

"Who in the world would want to sweat for hours over such a huge lump of fish meat?" is the rather disdainful question often voiced.

The answer is: only a fisherman who knows the big bluefin for what he really is—the fastest, most powerful fish in any ocean.

The attraction these fish hold for some anglers is compounded by the fact that a skilled fisherman, fishing from a well-handled boat, can often whip one of these streamlined bundles of power not in hours, but in mere minutes. This trick requires jujitsu seldom described in print.

Imagine a torpedo the size of a full-grown tuna—about 9 feet long and weighing 500 to 1000 pounds. It's easy to see that pushing such a shape through the water at speeds of 40 to 50 miles per hour requires the consumption of fuel and oxygen at a fantastic rate.

In order to perfect his streamlining and protect his delicate gills, a tuna has to clamp his mouth tightly shut when putting on a burst of high speed. This means the oxygen consumed by his muscles during the sprint must be "borrowed" from his blood and his body tissues the way a human runner "borrows" oxygen from his tissues during a dash, replacing it later by heavy panting.

Now if you were to sneak up behind a human sprinter as he finishes a 100-yard dash and give him a heavy jolt in the rear end with an electric shocking device, he probably would uncork another fast sprint. But this cannot go on forever. Sooner or later you will drive the runner to the point of complete collapse. He'll fall in a dead faint and his automatic, labored breathing will gradually restore the "borrowed" oxygen and he will recover, provided his heart has suffered no damage.

However, if you goad a hooked tuna to the same point of collapse and then stop him dead in the water, he will die. This is because the tuna cannot lie still in the water, gulping or "breathing" water in the manner of a goldfish in a bowl. From the time he is hatched until he dies he must swim forever through the water to maintain the flow of life-giving water over his gills. Stop him dead in the water and hold him there and he'll soon suffocate. When such a fish sleeps is his problem, not ours.

This explains how a clever angler can perform a seeming miracle of strength and skill when he takes a tuna weighing hundreds of pounds in only a few minutes fishing time. He drives the fish to the point of collapse in those few minutes, and then stops him dead in the water, suffocating him after the fish has become too groggy to know what is happening.

Lest this explanation be guilty of oversimplification, it should be pointed out that fishing this way requires the angler to be in top physical shape, the tackle to be of the finest, and the boat to be fast and well handled. Also, the fish himself has something to say about what happens after the hook has been set.

It is a mistake to think of a fish as being "smart." A fish cannot contemplate the angler the way the fisherman can study and analyze the fish. However, some big tuna seem able to comprehend the angler's intention to drive him to the point of oxygen starvation and will resist to the uttermost all efforts to bring the fish to the point of collapse. Even the most experienced tuna anglers dread battles with these occasional intransigent fish.

Tuna of this particular stripe explain in part day-long struggles between anglers and fish. The other part of the explanation is more mundane. Fighting a fish this big and active is exhausting, exciting labor. All too often a soft, inexperienced angler runs out of gas before the fish's will and power have been broken. When this happens the unhappy victim prays that a pulled hook or broken line will end his agony legitimately before he is forced to surrender his rod to a fresh angler.

Giant tuna are fished by two different techniques, chumming and bait trolling. In the North, at places like the famous Mud Hole off New York Harbor, where tuna fishing on the East Coast first gained much of its popularity, chumming is the most effective way to attract and hook big tuna.

The boat is anchored or drifts with the tide and a thin soup of ground menhaden mixed with sea water is ladled overboard to form a tasty, but not very nourishing, slick in the water. To this is added a slow doling out of chunks of cut menhaden or other baitfish. Baited hooks—usually not more than two, are drifted back among the scattered, slowly sinking chunks of cut chum.

Effective baits are the tail cut of a menhaden, a tail half of mackerel or whiting, or a small, whole butterfish. Live baits of whiting or mackerel are extremely effective. Whiting can be caught by bait fishing on the bottom while chumming. Mackerel frequently appear in the slick under the boat where they will take small jigs or bait. Hook live baits firmly, but not too deeply, through the meat of the back.

A hook of 8/0 to 10/0 size in the Sobey model is good for live-bait fishing. Larger hooks up to 13/0 size work well with cut bait. The best leaders are made up from tinned piano wire of No. 15 size, although stainless and cable-laid leaders will take fish. The length should not exceed 15 feet. Leaders of excessive length give no real advantage.

When chumming, place the fishing rods in the holders of the fighting chair and face the chair toward the drift of the lines. Fish one line close to the boat by hand. Cork the other out to a

Big, round, and streamlined, the bluefin tuna packs a lot of power in its muscular body. These were caught at Wedgeport, Nova Scotia. (*Canadian Gov. Travel Bureau*)

distance of 100 to 200 feet from the boat, placing a split-cork floater 30 to 50 feet up from the bait. This increases the spread of the baits while reducing the chances of getting a double strike.

Hooking giant tuna while chumming often requires real trickery. Sometimes the fish can be seen milling in the water behind the boat, picking up chunks of chum. When this happens, it often pays to take the baited hooks completely out of the water and slowly feed the fish one chunk of bait at a time. Then, in time with the feeding of previous chunks, a chunk with a hook in it is presented and allowed to drop slowly back with the tide at exactly the same rate of speed as a free-drifting chunk.

If a fish takes the bait, strike him instantly with both hands, yanking on the line as a handline. As soon as the hook is set, let go of the line lest you sustain line burns on your hands as he takes off on his first run. The rod in its rod holder in the chair can then be grabbed up by the angler who gets into the chair, buckles the harness straps into the reel rings, and finally, when all set, tightens up the reel drag to fighting tension.

When fishing this way, the drag tension should be slacked off to very light while the rod is in the holder, awaiting a strike. Don't try to strike the fish with the rod itself. Use both hands on the line. However, if an angler is in the chair and a fish runs off with a bait and it's impossible to grab the line to strike home the hook, this can be accomplished by quickly tightening the drag, striking against a tight line with the rod, then slackening the drag to a lighter, fighting tension.

On some charter boats only one rod is fished and the line, while chumming, is tended by the captain or mate, who strikes the fish for the angler, who sits in the fighting chair, all set for action. Under tournament conditions, or when anglers are fishing tuna without professional help, they must strike their own fish and fight the fish from strike to gaffing without external aid.

Caution is advised, since people have been cut or burned by speeding tuna lines, or variously injured when overtaxed rods or rod butts have broken during the first hectic moments after getting a strike. Anglers or boat owners who are fishing giant tuna for the first time are strongly advised to hire a good professional tuna guide, or secure the assistance of experienced amateur tuna fishermen, before attempting the taking of these powerful, unpredictable fish.

Bait trolling for big tuna is exciting sport, especially in clear, shallow water such as is found off Cat Cay in the Bahamas. Here, in May and early June, schools of migrating bluefins cross the flats of the western edge of Great Bahama Bank and are pursued by anglers in fast boats. It is necessary to speed ahead of a school to get the baits in proper baiting position.

In the Bahamas the best trolling baits are small bonefish and small Spanish mackerel. In northern waters, at places like Shark Ledge off Block Island, Nebraska Shoal near Point Judith, Cape Cod Bay, Bailey Island off the coast of Maine, and Soldier's Rip near Wedgeport, Nova Scotia, the best trolling baits are mackerel, whole fresh squid, herring, whiting, and black eels in about that order. Hooks and leaders for trolling are the same as those required for chumming.

Big tuna usually hook themselves when taking a trolled bait. Here, too, it is advisable to set the reel drag to a light value while trolling, searching for fish. The instant a strike is had and the line comes tight, tremendous pressure is exerted on the equipment as the speeding line pulls against the inertia of the spool of line. Also, if the drag is too tight, the angler may experience great difficulty in getting into the fighting chair and getting the harness buckled into the reel properly.

Tackle for big tuna must be of the very finest quality. It was once popular to use reels as large as 20/0 in size. Improved boat handling tactics and more skillful angling has made the most popular giant tuna rig a good 12/0 game fish reel loaded with 130-pound test line, mounted on a Fiberglas rod of 24- to 30-ounces rated tip weight. Many experts fish giant tuna with IGFA tackle in the 80- and 50-pound classes.

The rod should have roller guides and a roller tip-top to reduce line friction under heavy pressure. As in swordfishing, a good harness enables the angler to take the weight of the rod and the fish directly with his back, leaving his hands free. The right hand controls the drag and turns the reel handle. The left hand, protected by a glove, acts as a level-winder to guide line onto the spool or auxiliary brake when variable pressure is needed on the line.

Big tuna appear in northern waters in late June or early July. Fishable concentrations build up in July and August and frequently are present until late October. These fish are great travelers, however, and the tuna hunter must be prepared to travel far on short notice to take advantage of the appearance of fish at new or previously unproductive areas.

The best time to fish the popular southern Rhode Island and Block Island grounds is from mid-August to October, although slam-bang action has been had at Shark Ledge as early as the first week in July. Tuna in Cape Cod Bay, the Gulf of Maine, and Nova Scotia follow the same general seasonal pattern with the biggest concentrations of fish in the late summer and early fall.

The present world's record bluefin is a 977-pound monster caught in 1950 by Commander Duncan McLean Hodgson at St. Ann Bay, Nova Scotia. There have been many instances of tuna over 1000 pounds taken in pound nets or by harpoon. Tuna fishing contests are popular among the initiated and range from the exclusive Cat Cay shindig and the equally upper-crusty International Tuna Tournament held at Wedgeport, to the brawling, plebeian, U. S. Atlantic Tuna Tournament, which annually brings nearly 150 boats and 400 anglers to try their luck in the waters near Point Judith and Block Island.

Experts consider it only a matter of time before some muscular and lucky soul brings in a tuna that will top the half-ton mark. There's an insistent fascination about the thought of all that power and self-will wrapped up in one smooth, streamlined, black-bronze-and-silver skin, and the ability of a man to master it with a thin rod of glass fibers and resin in his hand and a quarter mile of fragile line.